41

AN AUTOBIOGRAPHY

JD BUFFINGTON

ANUCI PRESS

First paperback edition May 2024

Anuci Press edition May 2024
www.anuci-press.com

Book design by J.D. Buffington

ISBN 979-8-9896198-8-7 (paperback)

This book is dedicated to many people, like my brother Jeremy, his daughter Justice, and to our Mulroney family. To my dad, David, and the Buffington family. It is dedicated to teachers of both public and private schools who wrapped their arms around me, even those who only knew me for one year. The Hein and Peña families for being my extended family in some of my darkest times. My wife and daughter, Amber and Autumn, who listened and provided support as I worked through research and new revelations. But it is dedicated most of all to the memory of my mother, Irene, this is her story as well. Good times, bad times—she helped shape me, and in turn, continues to shape the world through her influence.

PART ONE
WITH

CHAPTER 1

1979-1983 – PLACES UNKNOWN, EAST COAST TO THE MIDWEST

There is a memory that I have held onto for as long as I can remember. Specifically, purposefully, with the knowledge it was valuable, to be preserved and never left forgotten. Even as a toddler, youth, into adolescence—I would recall it, to maintain it, to touch base with my deepest past. But every time it replays, the scanlines change the scene, the repetitive nature corroding the source material, the coats of gloss to keep it shimmering making it brittle. The very first thing I remember: a monster.

Trying to remember the beginning of my life, it's a lurching start. A halting, stuttering vignette of memories with no anchors in time. Scraps of film fluttering to create a lead: a nightmare; a museum of excitement becoming a den of dread; a *terrible* man; brief snippets of time ranging from pleasant to bizarre.

There are the intrinsic truths, the things I am aware of as my identity, I am Justin Mulroney, my birthday is September 5th, 1979, and that I was born in Mountain Home, Arkansas. I live with my mom, we are each other's only family, though people came in and out of our different places, or us into theirs. There is no place I know as *home*, I moved often.

I know the old memories are twisted. We're not typically wired to hold onto great amounts of detail for our entire lives. I've felt different ways about them through the years, shaping them, changing their light. They are details of a tumultuous childhood that I constantly think about. Traumas that flap along the walls of my mind, draping behavior and coloring impressions that have always been there to recall. Maybe that's the beginning of my anxiety: holding onto this disparate catalogue of mostly fear.

The monster.

It starts with red eyes. I know I'm in a crib, there are vertical slats. Beyond, a beige expanse of carpet leading to the wall where a window is letting a pointy headed demon glare inside. A thing of smoke and menace with a dusky sky beyond. Glowing red eyes and heaving wings, pressing closer, until I've had enough and turn my head the other direction. Menace, malice, just outside and looking at me, and my only recourse is to look away.

I know *now* there was no demon, I saw a bush with its peaks of foliage and a car's brake lights through it. For a long time, I considered it my first nightmare, and that's why I've always held onto it. My earliest memory is of fear, yet I remain. I survived.

However, *fear* would be a constant companion. My mom took me to the Smithsonian Natural History Museum in Washington D.C. when we were living nearby in Maryland. Within the entrance was a Woolly Mammoth on display, and to the right was a hall filled with dinosaur displays. I waited outside the women's restroom waiting for my mom, staring at a Stegosaurus from across the way. My imagination began to convince me the bones could move. Not animatronics or puppetry, that the monsters would come to life.

I *had* been excited to see them. Kids and dinosaurs, right? I held my mom's hand as we walked toward the museum during a sunny day talking about what we would see. Once I saw those mighty skeletons, though, saw both death and real monsters? I began to cry and resist. I know nothing moved, but I believed the dinosaurs would attack, and I wasn't having it.

My mom tried to convince me it was fine in that way we remember 1980's mothers with uncooperative children: cursing and dragging me along frustrated with my behavior. She bitterly relented instead of allowing me to escalate further. We didn't leave, though—or perhaps it was a different visit—I recall the production model of the Enterprise from the original Star Trek series. It wasn't an entirely wasted trip.

The most frightening memory remains vividly detailed: we, as in myself sitting on the floor watching television. My mother sat on a couch behind me with a man, quite specifically of no relation I can sense—I have no concept of his relationship with my mother, but I knew he wasn't a father-figure. We are zoning out on a sunny day. Sunlight dancing, somewhere with a tree outside.

I'm between one and three-years-old, transitioning from diapers to underwear, which I have soiled in this scenario.

The man reacts with unintelligible nonsense and yanks me from the floor and drags me to the bathroom where he strips my lower half and holds my dirty drawers to my face.

He then says, clearly, "Do you want to eat *this*?"

Sunlight continued to dance elsewhere.

I'm horrified. I'm ashamed. I'm disgusted, both with him and this —but with myself, too. I'm bawling, of course, and I think I'm trying to cover my face with my free hand. The toilet flushing was scaring me. Was he going to flush *me* down the toilet? Would he *kill* me that way?

For all that my tiny brain was going through, I never wondered in that moment "where is my mom?"

I hope she was there, yelling at him—fuck, even at *me*—*be there*. But it was me, this man, threatening to force feed me the shit in my underwear, and a flushing toilet.

My mom was somewhere beyond the background.

CHAPTER 2

1983-1989 – A HOUSE IN TULSA, OKLAHOMA

The story must *begin*. My "run of memory." There is a point in time I feel I have a firm grasp on most everything that has happened since.

We're living in Tulsa, Oklahoma, 1983.

It's the black Firebird with a gold emblem on the hood. It's cold outside. I clamber into the passenger seat unaided, quietly proud of my growing independence. I see Stephen King's Different Seasons between the seats. It's the recent release of the paperback with the four angry elemental representations of the seasons.

"What's that?" I asked.

"It's a book I'm reading." My mom answered.

Irene Frances Mulroney. Twenty-two. Born May 12th, 1961 in the Bronx, New York. Single mother. My only guardian in the world, my only family, my only friend. I want to describe my mom as a blend of Lucille Ball and Norma Jeane Mortenson (specifically before she was Marilyn Monroe). I mean this in both how she appeared, and the content of her character. She was ready for anything and usually excited to take it on. She also desired romance while wanting the means and independence to go wherever she felt the breeze was leading her. "Complex" is too simple to explain her.

The limited things I knew about her at the time were that she had been part of the Army Reserve, that she could be called away at an instant. A hanging, idle threat that she could disappear. I knew that I had an older brother, and I knew that she was young to have two sons. Her first, Jeremy, at fourteen, and me when she was eighteen, with a man who had abused her while pregnant with me. She was from New York and that's where a lot of her family lived, but, for reasons I can only speculate were a lateral move away from Arkansas to another state that was affordable to survive in, we had landed in Oklahoma.

The engine starts, but it'll still be cold for a while yet. It might only start getting warm inside the car by the time we reach the daycare center. I'm excited because this place lets us watch He-Man and the Masters of the Universe, my new favorite cartoon. It's late 1983, I'm four years old.

"Can I read it?" I ask, intrigued by the intense depictions of the seasons.

"No, it's a *scary* book." She laughs, trying to sound spooky. "It'll give you *nightmares*."

Well, that was threat enough for *me*. Nightmares were the worst invocation to discourage me from something mature. Death, violence, the supernatural, sex—all those things will "warp you and give you nightmares. Cover your eyes when those things pop-up in—" *anything* made in the 1970's and '80's. Fear in the real world was pervasive, but avoidable, but God-forbid anything inspires a nightmare. Those came furiously, without warning. There was no mom, no guardian, only naked terror roaring at an exposed nerve. Nightmares were worse than spankings.

I wondered what He-Man would be up to?

I looked back down to the book. *I wonder what each season is*?

Could thinking about a scary story give me nightmares? How could something made-up be that affecting? Why would my mom *want* to read something that could give nightmares?

He-Man!

Angry seasons!

The book hung around a while. I would steal glances at the pages, not fully comprehending the words or their intended meaning. I don't think it was her favorite book, or even her favorite King book, but it was a rattling behind the door that didn't make me immediately retreat. This was a monster I could control the speed and volume of, the mental image as wild as my imagination was willing to show me. Literature. *Horror*. To be scared for *fun*.

To connect with her across time.

She would buy me a copy many years later, with a different cover. I devoured Rita Hayworth and the Shawshank Redemption, uncomfortably identified with Apt Pupil as I was reading it as a teen, and felt transported to an outdoor adventure of self-discovery with the Body. I never read the Breathing Method. I held it as a buried treasure I knew the location of.

Time inches forward here, still stuttering, but *this* is the main attraction, this is where the movie begins. It's a few apartments and the two of us. They may not all be Tulsa, it's a jumble of terrifying, weird, fun, and mundane flashes. Playing with a calculator, thinking that I was teaching myself math.

The morning my mother and a guy argued as I ate cereal and she being angry. She slammed her fist into the wall and shattered the plaster. I didn't care about the guy in that moment, but I *was* afraid of my mother right then.

Recalling this memory later in life to my mom, she explained that they were planning on moving the three of us to Germany with him as he was going to be stationed there, serving in some branch of the military. He decided to break up with my mom only a few weeks before we were going to leave. It broke her heart *and* left her in the lurch, she was understandably livid. But my mom expressed herself through violence in that moment.

There was a night—I'm not too sure of how, but I'm an adult now and I can put pieces together—my mother walked in on me in the living room watching basic-cable porn. "Don't watch that, it'll give you nightmares!"

Had she left the TV on when she went to bed? Did she hear the overly passionate moans that had already lured me out of bed? Did she have a date? Because I also remember examining stranger's faces laying in my mom's bed.

Yes. I was *that* creepy child.

Not that any of these are tied together. They coalesced around one night when we were going to move again—in with a new boyfriend.

CHAPTER 3

Cobalt air, snow falling like static on the memory, and the dirty yellow of old incandescent bulbs in unclean sconces colored the night. My idea of "helping" move was grabbing my own things one at a time and sliding them along the grooves in the bed of his blue F-150. A jar of jellybeans with a crafty cloth lid I had made in daycare standing out.

Wherever we were going, it seemed to make my mom happy. I was excited and scared. In this time of transition, a new spate of nightmares and nightmare-fuel would fill my nights.

David Buffington started at a Broken Arrow newspaper when he was a teenager and has been a printer his entire working life. I admire that about him. He has an actual skill and *career*, and it's something that has allowed him to keep up with technology as it changes around him. He's never been slow to pick up on new tech and science. More than being accepted and desired by a father-figure, he saved my life. He would come to be the stability I needed.

My mom applied for an open position at the print shop he worked at and there was an immediate attraction. He's the most important person my mother introduced into my life.

Moving in with him, I stayed in a room on the back of a house he was living in with a roommate. It was lower than the rest of the house, something you had to step down into. A sitting room that had a couch I slept on and a TV I could watch when I wanted to. I watched 1972's *Ben* on that little TV and had nightmares about rats.

What's strange about those early memories with David is that he's ephemeral until a little bit later. I *know* he was there, but it wasn't until we moved out of that house that I remember *him*, and more importantly, *us*.

Now, moving into our first house together was a milestone. I knew apartments, there were strangers now and then, but, the three of us? In a house of our own? Something we could call a home? This felt dreamy. Even at four years old, I recognized a security and stability in the prospect.

At four years old, I had moved an incalculable number of times and now into a new family dynamic. Permanence was a tenuous prospect.

Before I had new furniture, as my old bed disappears from memory, probably sold when we first moved in with David, I slept on the couch in the living room and the exposure I felt gave me nightmares. A repeating night terror of an angry eyed stranger staring down at me from the windows in the door. The windows at the top of the six-foot frame. Someone even taller than *that* looking down on me through those windows.

I would eventually get furniture in *my* room, but the night terrors did not cease. I believed the house was haunted, often thinking I was hearing someone in the kitchen repeatedly, *aggressively*, opening and closing cabinet doors. I was never brave enough to rouse myself and peek around the corner in the hallway that could see into the kitchen. I *didn't* want to see whatever it was.

There were nightmares within nightmares. I would sometimes come to my parents' bed after waking up in the middle of the night. One time, however, David told me to look in the mirror, where I looked at myself holding my own head against my hip. Behind me was an enormous skeletal hand wrapping its fingers around me. Except they were not bone, but a red-colored wood.

A transition in housing and family dynamic is stressful, to be sure. But what was David a fan of that my mother was, too? Horror. He collected Stephen King, as well. They both loved scary movies at a time when horror cinema was booming. I was now living with horror fans when I was terrified of being terrified. Yay?

We were a theater-going family. It would be this mutual love of genre cinema and fiction that kept this stuff on the shelves and screens of our house. They also loved music and MTV was on all the time. I was *seriously* a scaredy-cat. Michael Jackson's Thriller video would get played in full later in the evenings and I would casually try to excuse myself any time it came on. David and my mom tried to *force* me to watch it, "it's just on the TV, they're not real, they're not going to hurt you, look, they're *dancing*!"

It is a good video, but that makeup is *too* damn good.

They married shortly after moving in. September 21st, 1984. I was five and she was twenty-three. The photos in their wedding album show an empty living and dining room. They were building a life together, and I was a part of it. I did not know it at the time, but this was my mother's *fourth* marriage.

As one of my aunts put it, "I never met boyfriends, but husbands."

The romantic chasing the perfect arrangement. This one, however, stuck for a little while, and it created the bedrock for my life.

I would start a new daycare at Sidney Lanier Elementary School, not a "pre-school," I went from the daycare program to kindergarten. For a while it was daycare activities, games, readings, movies, naps, and snacks. I learned of bullies who targeted my name, *Mulroney*. For a while I was *Justin Macaroni*—despite Mulroney being Irish.

How do I, a five-year-old, elucidate to a fellow five-year-old that he's incredibly offensive? I don't. I fought back with words of defense, but jocular—or ignored them—I never got into physical fights. I didn't often maintain nemeses, preferring to either play along or shrink out of their notice.

I thought my own mother was calling me names when she out of the blue started calling me "J.D." I was shocked.

"That is not my name, why are you calling me that?"

"Those are your *initials*." She explained. "The first letters of your first and middle name."

"Middle name?" I asked, unaware of the concept or that I had one.

"Your middle name is Dwayne. So, your initials are J.D. That could be your *name*, too."

"My name is *Justin!*" I was starting to get upset.

I learned I had a middle name and, *oh,* I regretted ever sharing it with anyone.

"Dwayne," how mine is spelled, and how my mother pronounced it, and how I feel my name in my heart, is pronounced the way it's spelled, as in: those two weird consonant sounds smooshed together. Not pronounced Duane, or Dewayne, but like *Twain,* with a D. I would tell people my name, and they would attempt to correct me, "Oh, (insert preferred pronunciation because their brain can't comprehend the sound I made)?"

Shortly after their marriage, David would adopt me. I don't remember calling him anything other than "Dad." Somewhere in that swirl of moving, and landing at a school, I gained family. Someone else, other than my mom, *wanted* me in their life.

There was an office with dark walls, and a man asking if I was okay with being adopted. I was. I became Justin Dwayne Buffington.

Becoming a Buffington saved me from some name calling at school for a couple of years, but I learned some people would absolutely refuse to read a name correctly, even though it was their job. Telemarketers in the 1980's absolutely butchered my new name. My three-syllable, simple sounds combination of a name. It might be ten letters long, but it's easy to say. Telemarketers, though? "Bluffington? Boofington? Fubbington? Buffson?"

I vowed early on to take care to read someone's name and do my level best to reasonably pronounce it. This would extend to names from other nationalities and foreign languages in general. I have found people appreciate someone who knows how (or at least makes an effort) to say their name without mocking their accent. I have a terrible time *remembering* people's names, though, which is embarrassing, but I want to say names correctly after so much idle disrespect with my names.

Irene and David would be married for a few years. I went from daycare to kindergarten, first, second, third, and some of the fourth grade, 1984 to 1989, at the same school and we lived in the same house.

We had dogs and cats. Mandy, a black and white Lab-mix who gave birth to a litter of puppies. We kept one of her puppies, a classic looking Yellow Lab, and named him Buffy. Mandy, however, eventually went missing. We had Mr. Smith, an orange striped male cat, and Patches, a female tortie. I had neighborhood friends and school friends. I had sleepovers, slept over, playdates; the *normal* childhood experience—for the most part. It took some shifting and getting used to.

Our family would not grow, not beyond those pets. My mom ended up having a hysterectomy due to a prolapsed uterus. I don't know specifically how that affected her psychologically. She never struck me as wanting more children. She had had two entirely too young, and where she would say things through the years that sounded as though she would change her past, maybe wanting a daughter, she never seemed keen on having *another* child. She never indicated to me in all the time I knew her that the hysterectomy affected how she felt as a woman, but I can't deny that it *must* have affected her in some way since it happened to her so young.

I may have spent my known existence as an only child, but I integrated with other families as well. I developed some close friends, two Jason's, one at school, one in my neighborhood. They were completely different from each other, totally different vibes. Jason from school would be my longer-lived friend.

Jason from my neighborhood was a year or two older and the peer pressure-y type. We mostly rode our bikes together through the neighborhood. He threatened me with a knife once when I stayed the night. We didn't stay friends long after that.

With Jason at school, we played Star Wars at recess. Return of the Jedi made a return to theaters, and I wanted to see it badly.

Well, in truth, I had wanted to see the Care Bears Movie, and we were planning on taking *me* to a movie, not a horror for once, then a trailer for Jedi hit the TV and I was overcome.

Slack-jawed, I asked, "Can we see that?"

My dad lit up, "Well, we're already going to see the Care Bears; you can only pick one movie."

I didn't even think about it. "I want to see that."

I'm sure he was more excited by that option, anyway. We got the newspaper together and looked up the listings for when it was playing and where. I may not have been there for the true opening weekend, and my mom assured me she took me to Empire Strikes Back in the theater, though I wasn't even a year old—does it matter if she did? I enjoyed the opportunity to see one of the *original* Original Trilogy in the theater and it was a blast. I was hooked on Star Wars for life.

On the playground, we would climb the monkey bars, and someone would stand on the ground in the middle and would be the Sarlacc pit and try to pull down whoever was crossing. We did that a lot, played out our favorite scenes from movies and TV. Ghostbusters, Dukes of Hazzard, Aliens (which I watched through splayed fingers to hide if it got too scary). Masterminding ways to play games or make believe was a healthy way to channel my imagination.

Making things up, though, is a wheel that doesn't stop turning in my head. It led to a problem with lying, with making shit up. Bullshitting was an art form I seemed born with.

I took spankings in the 1980's from my mom, my dad, teachers, principals—if I lied to someone in the '80's, I was probably getting swatted for it. I was spanked often.

My dad recalls early on when my mom would deal out corporal punishment, the sounds he heard emanating from those exchanges left *him* uncomfortable.

In the beginning, early on, it probably was excessive. It was an unrestrained frustration from a young person whose own brain was still developing as they were trying to raise a child, struggling with issues none of us were aware of. My dad, a new parent by leaps, *took* the reins of punishment. At least it was more structured?

I don't begrudge my dad his punishments. I was uniquely difficult. Always *this* side of truly awful, hovering on becoming problematic. I've even recognized it as I've been doing it at times, through the years, as a kid, knowing I would be caught and punished—but what if it works this time? The storyteller in me was born out of subterfuge, fear, and anxiety.

I do not condone that kind of punishment. I don't personally consider that I was abused in those moments of punishment. It was the nature of my youth, I came up at the end of an era. If by some technical definition, today or in the future, it *was* abuse, then I forgive it.

I know a world before wireless and widespread internet. Yet I gravitated to the quickly evolving nature of science, technology, and society, including their effects on psychology. I have always tried to be a sponge for what makes us tick. I know how I grew up affects me but getting spanked became routine. I coached a kid on dealing with spankings when we were in trouble together.

First grade maybe? This was an organized crime. I was among three kids who were going to get a spanking from the teacher. The principal was going to oversee. This was meant to terrify each of us, we had to hear each other's punishments. This wasn't in front of the class, however. We went to an overflow classroom.

Early morning, light coming in through the windows and dust motes creating a film-grain to real life. Stacked desks, barely enough room to stand, and the three of us were sitting in an alcove where students could hang their coats. I think we were getting three swats each. The first kid yelped and that set my younger companion to tearing up.

"Don't worry." I told him. I wasn't afraid, I could *share* my lack of fear. "Does your dad spank you?"

He nodded, tears beginning to flow, but not yet bawling.

"It won't be as bad as that." I promised him. "They just want to scare us; they don't hit very hard. You already know it's coming, and you know you'll be okay. Think about recess coming up!"

He nodded hopefully. I was next. I was also louder than I thought (a persistent problem), and I got in trouble for telling other kids that the spankings weren't that bad. I never felt bad about it.

My dad figured it out first, that I had become accustomed to the punishment and was willing to continue my antics. Groundings continued...*forever*. I'm not entirely sure what I'm revealing about myself in my youth here. I was routinely spanked for years, probably until I was seven or eight, and at some point, I didn't fear the spankings. I lied. I was going to continue lying, because *sometimes* I got away with it. Spankings didn't dissuade me. While I didn't know the term "psychological warfare," when I realized that's what was being waged,

I think I stopped caring about being caught, and maybe tried to fight back in my misbehavior.

The pathological lying would continue. I would begin to channel that energy, slowly crafting my story-telling abilities. I mention in the introduction to my first collection, *PUNCH/PANTS*, making up a story on the spot in kindergarten about Jesus, knowing next to nothing about the figure other than what pop-culture shows: the nativity or the crucifixion. *Why*? Because my audience was rapt and I had a teacher who let me go on.

I did not grow up under any religion. I knew it existed. I knew people went to church on the weekend. I did not. I believed in God. Santa and the elves. Tooth fairy. The Easter Bunny. Things that snuck into your house if you behaved and left gifts. I believed in everything! I had no structure. My conceptions of all religions were fed to me through the lens of what was presented in pop culture and the media.

When I told a story of Christ convincing the Romans to let him down from the cross because he was thirsty and then running around in color coded flower patches, I think my teacher was probably as rapt as the kids were with this teetering on blasphemous nonsense.

Another byproduct of a constantly churning imagination, I had an invisible friend who assisted me in lying and betrayal, a complicated individual whom I called Buster. I don't know how common growing up with an imaginary friend is, but I'm sure those of you who did probably have fond memories of these ghosts we make up. Someone you could pretend to be to respond to your own thoughts, to not feel weird talking out loud to ourselves.

Did yours have backstories? Families of their own? Where they came from and that they weren't always there because of that family of their own?

You might be wondering, "Did you have an *actual* ghost-friend?"

I did not. Buster was an *alien*. He came from a yellow and green planet that existed in twilight. He was about my age, but far more intelligent, and piloted his own spaceship to visit with me. He would be there sometimes and others he wouldn't. There were times he was gone a long while, and that was because he had an uncle who was upset he spent time on Earth with me. His uncle was mean and abusive, and kind of different to Buster's "type" of alien, however, Buster could *become* that type of alien if he didn't stay kind.

I made this all up over years. I drew pictures of us, of the ship, of the abusive uncle who was monstrous compared to docile Buster. They were both humanoid, however, Star Trek-different—as in, *not much*. I know I'm writing this in the age of Star Trek Discovery which I love and the aliens and themes are not as antiquated and simple as they were in The Original Series. I still love TOS, too. I think Buster was based on Spock. I think I wanted to *be* Spock.

I can recognize this extended family, the abuse, and rules of existence were also efforts to process something in my own life.

My most vivid memory of Buster is also because it's probably the last time I thought of him, and realized I *was* him. I was using my dad's Xacto blade to cut some craft I was working on and sliced my own finger. I was by myself. Maybe seven. Both my parents worked, and I was walking or biking myself home as early as the first grade.

I said a thought aloud, "Buster says to put a balloon on it."

I might have thought it was absurd, but the end of an uninflated balloon served as a tourniquet to staunch the bleeding *and* the pain. I left it on for several minutes, maybe half an hour, and when I took it off my finger was pruney, but no longer bleeding. There was a discolored gash that I was able to wash and then correctly put a bandage around.

I still blamed breaking a lot of stuff on him. He didn't know his own strength. Earth's gravity was different. I was a klutz who couldn't be honest and apologize. Buster, this thing I had made up, looked out for me.

Sometimes honesty was instead what *got* me punished. My mom had come home on her lunch one day and had herself accidentally broken a vase, cleaned it up, but didn't let anyone know. I got home and didn't notice anything amiss. My dad got home and saw the broken pieces in the trash and asked if I broke it. I was innocent in this *one* case, but I was such a habitual liar, why *would* he believe me? I wasn't establishing trust, or was I unwittingly eroding it—both? When my mom got home and he told the tale, she explained in turn what had *actually* happened. My dad did apologize, but I cried wolf more often than not.

I'm positive the problem with lying being engrained, early on, is some sort of preservation tactic. I have worried about how others perceive me, and I weigh the worth of my thoughts against others' opinions, yet I have lied, cheated, and stolen. I have a criminal-element —do I want to be *caught*? For what?

CHAPTER 4

Despite my chronic troublemaking, this period in my life was adventurous. Family vacations seemed to be annual. We would load up the truck and head to the lake to fish on the weekends, or vacations to Colorado, New Mexico, multiple Buffington-family holidays in Texas. I had new uncles and an aunt and a grandma and cousins, all happy to accept me from early on and for the rest of my life.

There was one vacation with only my mom to New York to meet her family. *Our* family. There's weird imprinting and weird connections between my families.

Flying in the 1980's, '85 or '86, wasn't complicated. It was no different than getting on a bus. There was next to no security, anyone could come right up to the boarding ramp with you, and people smoked *everywhere*. Ashtrays were built into the armrests of waiting areas, into the arms of the plane seats.

There *was* a period as the plane was being pressurized that you *weren't* allowed to smoke and there would be a little light that said you could either smoke or not at that moment. Whatever kind of plane we flew, it was wide enough for three rows of seats and, yes, I was a child, it was roomier than today's flights. A big plane, sure, but I've flown as a child, adolescent, and as an adult pre- and post-9/11. Planes weren't always sardine cans. We flew fewer people more times and fucked up the environment, *that's all*.

The in-flight entertainment was some six-month old movie that was neither in theaters or available to take home on VHS yet. It was projected on the wall that separated coach from first class. You could purchase headphones from a flight attendant; we did not. I think my mom had a book and I was left to watch a silent movie or steal glances through the window I was unfortunately not sitting next to. I don't remember what movie it was, but I do recall a video *before* it of our model of plane flying through the sky, from above and behind, another plane shooting the footage. I thought it was *live*, being beamed directly to us from a jet following us.

I was *not* meeting these people for the first time, however *I* was meeting them for the first time. Now that my memory was becoming more solid and not sporadic flashes, I sadly did not recognize any of these people, but they recognized me. Something *within* me remembered at least, I would feel especially at ease with one aunt, though the connection wouldn't be revealed for quite some time.

My mother had several siblings, my grandfather having more children beyond his marriage to my maternal grandmother. Save my mom, my Grandpa had most of his kids around him. These were mostly young adults, not far in age from my mom. There was a "prime" set of siblings, those aunts and uncles who came from my mother's same set of parents. She had a good relationship with most everyone in her family it would seem, but the grandmother I was meeting was a step-grandmother and my blood-relation grandmother was a mystery for a long time.

Jeez, even trying to establish who was there starts showing you the cracks of weirdness that branches our family.

Nearly all my Grandpa Fred's kids had gravitated around him and settled in New York and New Jersey. He was an apartment building superintendent and development opportunist. He took me to a building he was considering fixing up. Part of the floor was caved in near the center of one room and dropped into a lower level. I found a lot of coins. The image of a decrepit NYC building in the 1980's. His buildings were fine, this was someplace that had succumbed to disrepair.

We sight-saw. Driving through one of the tunnels was nerve-wracking for my tiny brain. We went to Battery Park and boarded a ferry to see the Statue of Liberty. I was with my mom, maybe an aunt, and my grandpa and step-grandma. There's a photo of at least my mom, me, and my grandpa with the NYC skyline, Twin Towers in view, behind us as we're on the boat to or from Liberty Island.

On Liberty Island there was one of those wooden standees that you put your face through to be whatever, a Lady Liberty here. My mom wanted a photo of me in it, but for some reason I decided I did *not* and threw a fit. My mom threatened me with a spanking which only made me fall into a tantrum as displeasure turned into dread. Why spank me because I don't want to do this photo thing? She didn't beat me there in front of a crowd, I don't think she ever followed through on her threat at all, but, I didn't want to put my face in the hole, I don't know why.

At some junky gift shop, I got a stereotypical robot toy. Black plastic, flashing lights, motorized arms and legs; a clockwork forward-walking block of a thing. I think I loved it because it looked absurdly generic. But, it was in the one bag that got delayed. Sometimes your baggage gets thrown onto the wrong plane, or wouldn't make it to the baggage terminal for some reason. I was quite upset about this, I wanted my robot!

Waiting for a child—for a child who wants something back they already had—is hell. I had better toys! This black robot, from *New York City*? I had to have it back.

It came eventually. That, along with some plastic wings I got from a pilot, I showed off at school once I was able and told everyone about my trip to New York, about meeting family and seeing the Statue of Liberty. Somehow, having family in New York, no matter their station —that they lived there—felt as if I was related to royalty.

I met my paternal family only once, briefly, and I barely remember it at all because it was seemingly only in a doorway—and generally *strange*. My mom and dad drove us over to Arkansas around Christmastime, and I met my brother Jeremy for the first time. His (technically *my*) grandparents supervised the meeting and gave me a gift. A Tonka truck I think.

What's strange? They're Jehovah's Witnesses. I didn't know much about religion at all, but one thing I knew from my mother's own experience with this family was that JW's do not celebrate or exchange gifts for holidays or birthdays. I was the only one getting a gift and everything felt lined with tension.

Even though this was the first time I was meeting my brother, the first time our mom had seen Jeremy in—I don't know how long—I could sense the awkwardness. My mother was facing her abusers to see her other son. They were acting out of character upon meeting me. There were awkward attempts at small talk, but I wasn't paying attention to any of it. I wondered if someone in *particular* lurked in the house, and I was terrified of meeting him.

I knew I had a biological father. I have always referred to him as that. He is not my dad. He is not a capital-F father to me; he is someone I share genetic-code with. My mom referred to him as that, setting the boundary early on. He was abusive, he and his family *stole* Jeremy from us, and had threatened to take *me* away from her as well. She led me to believe there was a lawsuit involved and she offered Jeremy up if she could keep me. A sacrifice I always felt guilty for, ashamed of, and angry with my mom about.

Part of that trip was my mom and dad seeing if there was any way my mother could regain custody of Jeremy. My dad was willing to help, to adopt him as well, to bring our family *together*, to make it *whole*.

It didn't happen. I didn't know why. I wouldn't for many years, but I think it hurt my mom in new ways, and tore open old wounds.

Mom and I would visit Jeremy again, for a few days next, to let us spend time together. We got a hotel room. He taught me how to make farting noises with the back of my knee and hand, similar to using your armpit. We swam in an indoor pool and annoyed the grown-ups in the hot tub. We saw a movie in the theater, maybe the Lost Boys. I think my mom bought Jeremy some new shoes and a Pogo Ball, super popular at the time.

A feeling began in my guts that has made me feel alien among the closest of company. I didn't share features with Jeremy and I didn't think I shared any with my mom. I was also seven, going through those growth spurts toward adolescence that make every kid look strange. I took it to heart, I felt personally out of place.

I was adopted, the only maternal family I had was—well, my *mom* —but I didn't seem to take after any of the Mulroney's. Meeting my *brother*, built differently than me, blonde haired (at the time), yet vaguely reminiscent of my mom, I didn't seem to match my paternal side, either. I wondered if I *was* an alien. Or switched at birth. Or someone else's entirely than my biological father.

Of course, I would settle into my looks, and now my brother and I are quite similar looking. The doubt I conjured would contribute to "othering" myself. I convinced myself I didn't belong—anywhere. I look back on photos and know they're me, but there are some in those years where I do wonder what the fuck my face was doing to me. I wonder if the changes weren't too rapid at the time, to my mind, that I didn't recognize *myself*.

I am related to both of my biological families. There were no mix ups. No other men. The lingering questions of where I belonged, unfortunately, shaped inner beliefs.

Some of that would come from half-heard and misremembered conversations and arguments between grown-ups. The phrase "blood is thicker than water" was something I heard that came to represent strain between my dad's mother and my mother. I took it, through the years, to mean my dad's mother didn't fully accept *me* because I was adopted.

I'm not sure that was ever the case, or if my own mom put the thought in my head. I know she got along with *some* of the Buffington's, and I would continue to see them at holidays and family gatherings for years to come. They are my family, I am accepted; for a lot of years, though, too many years, I didn't *feel* the acceptance. Not from family, not friends, not the people in my life that tried to reach me.

That's a feeling that crawls under your skin and sets a lot of hooks. The tiniest twinge in the "wrong" direction reminds you that *everything* hurts.

That self-imposed exile made me yearn for connection with

someone *else*. I was a romantic early on, too early. I believed that I would grow-up with, marry, and have children with my first girlfriend from kindergarten. That I could make my own family and we wouldn't be misplaced if we had *each other*. "Love," however, was a four-letter word, a *swear*—a reprehensible word children shouldn't say to someone who isn't related to them. I "like-liked" my "girlfriend."

Or—*girlfriends*. All three of them. At the same time. They were friends with each other and knew and were all cool with being my girl-friends together. Little kids, eh? One of them, though, I would pursue from kindergarten through the third grade—then for one day in the eighth grade, but we'll get there.

I *like-liked* her.

There was a love letter I gave to her where I drew us on a date at a movie holding hands. The scene I depicted on screen was from an actual movie, but not something I had seen recently. What I had drawn was the end credits sequence of David Lynch's Dune with the actor in portrait with their name to the side. I had seen Dune in the theater with my parents. It was a type of terrifying that was fascinating, and I would eventually become a huge Dune fan. Somehow, it was my ideal date movie for a fellow youth.

I never did get to take her to a movie. Instead, we played video games together at her house, especially the first Legend of Zelda. We would play in her yard. She lived in the same neighborhood as the school, and I knew a neighborhood route I could bike from my house. Her parents probably suspected that I adored her more than she real-ized or than she did me. I thought I was feeling something special, different from other friends, and I wanted to share that with her forever.

I get that from my mom. She wanted things both to last forever and to have a new adventure at the ready. Those conflict.

CHAPTER 5

My mom worked numerous jobs, moving from one to the next, at wildly different places and skill-levels. Eventually she worked in customer service at a car rental company. There she would be incorporated in a national marketing campaign where she appeared in a large staff photo that was used to show the company's human side. They were employee-owned and when you spoke to a representative, they were also a shareholder. There were some variations on it, large group, small group, "action" shot ("working" as customer service, but around a car); they appeared on billboards, and in newspapers and magazines around the country.

It was her first taste of modeling, which she tried her hand at for a bit, getting professional headshots done. I liked seeing those photos around the house, how done up my mom was, how the photos themselves looked of such higher quality than anything I had held from a polaroid or school photo.

It didn't take off. Or, it didn't take off fast enough for her. A lark, a blip in her career aspirations.

I don't know why she did it, but there were a few times, probably when she was between jobs, that she would "clean" house. This meant giving or throwing away things she no longer needed. Or thought that

I no longer needed. I had a large collection of stuffed animals. Of He-Man and Star Wars action figures. Randomly, I would come home to find a collection missing. Not all my toys, but a set, since I roughly kept them organized. I didn't always feel ownership of my space and property. The early betrayals of trust and being "stolen" from would put me at odds with my mom, I would move on in the moments, unable to get my things back, but tiny grudges piled up.

My dad knew I enjoyed my action figures and often got me GI Joe and Teenage Mutant Ninja Turtles. I was paid an allowance that I blew on toys and candy. I was a victim of the heavy commercialism of 1980's children's programming. TMNT replaced He-Man for obsessions, GI Joe and Transformers were constantly wish listed for holidays and birthdays. Frankly, 1987 was a cool year for kids. Captain Power was on the air, and I had one of the jets you could shoot at the TV with. I had an NES. I didn't want for terribly much, honestly. But coming home to find something of yours missing hurts at any age.

It would be the job hopping that landed my mom at an aeronautics engineering company that built flight training simulators, mostly for commercial aircraft. It would be here that my mother engaged in an affair. I wouldn't know about the affair as it was going on, my mother kept it a secret from me and my dad didn't talk about it until it was over. When they got divorced, I was sold that my mom was unhappy, she wanted to move on, and they were splitting up.

My dad was willing to forgive the affair if she would quit that job and they could work on things together. My dad wasn't rich, but we were secure, he offered *stability*. That wasn't what my mom wanted. She wanted something more and I was never certain I understood her at all. I get sometimes things don't work, you fall out of love, but those *weren't* reasons she ever gave. It was always about what she *wanted*. Yet, she never convinced me of *what* she wanted.

Four years as a family. Four years *of* family. That's what I got. I was four when I got it, and eight when it was over. That was a *lifetime* for me. I had gone through a lot in those years. I had gone through a lot more in the first half, though; but I only remembered those snippets at the time. Two four-year periods. Seasons to my life.

CHAPTER 6

1989 – TWO APARTMENTS, TULSA, OKLAHOMA

I do not recall either of my parents crying over their split. In the moment, it happened as if it were planned, as if divorce and moving on were steps in life. They were frustrated with each other. There was arguing. I took *part* in their arguments. The lighter ones, my mom in the bedroom, my dad in the dining room, me running back and forth to trade whatever childish insult they felt okay saying through my mouth.

I maintained my relationship with my dad, we had only moved about two miles away, I was still going to the same school for the moment. I would finish the third grade and begin the fourth grade at Lanier, biking either to our new apartment or my dad's house after school.

Calling my childhood home my "dad's house" stuck. My dad didn't move from that house for nearly thirty years! When my dad promised my mom stability if she would stay, he meant it. That stability was a pillar I would lean on; that house, *my dad's house*, would be my home again—eventually—but that feeling of never belonging, of ostracizing myself on behalf of other people's thoughts that I imagined for them, became a trait. Once I was uprooted, there was no more home at all.

As you're passing down Oklahoma Highway 51 you can see that house from the highway. I said "Hey, I think I saw your house," when I was old enough to be paying attention to such things out the passenger window.

"It's *your* house, too." He said.

He wanted me to know it was my home, no matter what, no matter who I lived with, because I was his son and that was *our* home.

I would, however, spend most of the next few years with my mom, visiting my dad alternating weekends and different holidays.

When our move was complete, there was an odd familiarity to the situation. It may have been half-my-life-ago, but I had been here before. There was a comfort at first: the coziness of the living space, the time with my mom. We shared a lot of long evenings either listening to music or watching shows or movies—for a little while.

She was no longer working at the company she met her other man at. Now she was working for our local CBS affiliate, KTUL, Channel 6. How she landed what job she did there, I haven't a clue, but she seemed to have all her fingers in multiple pies. She was familiar with anchors, writers, editors, videographers, the production crew... Maybe she was a secretary and simply that friendly. That's a blind spot with my mom.

I'll admit it. There is a lot of my life that are memories that feel inescapable, yet much of it I *choose* to remember. Yet, I didn't appreciate my mom in the moment enough to know what she did. My dad was a printer. One thing. After the rental car company, my mom was something else every eight months. I grew tired of keeping up. Some jobs would stand out, she worked in TV multiple times, but mostly, she never let work define her. Maybe that's not such a terrible way to think of it.

I also spent a *lot* of time alone in that apartment, latchkey-kid that I was. My mom would go *out*, renting me a video game to placate me. I also listened to music by myself often. My mother's tapes and records, the radio, I have danced and sang to my personal delight for as long as I can remember. Eventually there was a dog, Buddy, a Rat-Terrier, that I loved. We played. He destroyed things. I cleaned up. Rinse and repeat.

One evening I came home to find Buddy convulsing on the floor, my mom's purse toppled and a blister pack of presumably over the counter medication—but I honestly have no clue what she had in her purse—mostly chewed up and scattered across the floor. This was an era before cell phones. This was my mom's *big* purse; she didn't always take it with her. I called her at work.

"I bet he got into my allergy medicine, I'm sure he'll be fine." My mom was dismissive of how concerned I was for my dog.

She wouldn't be home for a long while, it was deep into the evening before she arrived. I stressed over Buddy. I tried to pet him and calm his convulsions. His whole body was quivering, he could do nothing but lay and shake. His eyes looked at me terrified. I know I did little to calm him. I pet him all the same. He did come out of it, but that night showed me helplessness.

We walked him in the evenings, but in the morning, living in an apartment complex, we would leash him to the banister of the outside steps. Small dog, long leash, it probably wasn't the best treatment of an animal, but I tried to keep my dog relatively safe and offer a *little* freedom of movement for ten or fifteen minutes while I brushed my teeth.

My mom, however, became lax in this discipline she herself had established. She would let Buddy out without leashing him, come inside, not even watch him, and call for him before we would leave for the morning.

All it took was once. He did not come back.

I was outside calling his name hard enough I was becoming hoarse. My mom nonchalantly said it was time to go. I disagreed, we had an emergency, our dog was missing!

"He'll be fine. He'll probably be sitting here when you get home from school. But we have to go, we're already late."

I didn't trust her. I didn't believe her. "You did this!" I cried. "This is your fault!"

She was not moved. Buddy was gone without a trace.

That apartment was the downstairs of a two-story building, identical to the surrounding buildings. The apartments weren't bad, there was a lot of outdoor area, and a tree in each courtyard between buildings. I played outside as much as inside. I made acquaintances with neighbors, including a woman suffering the early stages of Alzheimer's who mostly talked about her cat, Tex.

Sometimes seeing her struggle to continue a thought she was in the middle of, or repeating sentiments verbatim day after day, I felt *her* helplessness. She had a nurse and family that routinely checked up on her. I guess she was okay enough to live on her own with that monitoring. The sympathetic horror I felt for her, of the mind becoming unmoored, the loneliness even if you're surrounded by trusted loved ones?

Fears are born.

CHAPTER 7

Tim Burton's *Batman* was a huge success, everyone was seeing it more than once. The movie stands out for me because there was a film renaissance that could happen for *me*. The Superman movies had gone campy, though to a kid, it was still a superhero on screen. This was dark, disturbing, thrilling—a betrayal of the comic character, sure, but an amazingly good time.

It inspired my Halloween costume for 1989, the Joker. It was a wet October that year. I had a pair of purple shorts that I was going to wear with a green shirt and my dad was going to do my makeup. I watched it rain through the school windows, worried Halloween was ruined.

It wasn't. It was a Tuesday night, I trick or treated in my dad's neighborhood.

My mom entertained my newfound interest in comics. Randomly, she would purchase comics for me at a gas station or the grocery store. Sometimes collectible trading cards including for the Batman movie, Garbage Pail Kids, Star Wars, Dinosaurs Attack. A lot of it inspired a love of drawing my own comics.

I started listening to the radio a lot more at this time, especially late at night. I preferred those call-in shows requesting romantic ballads with some smoky-voiced DJ telling the lonely hearts there's someone out there for them.

Why did I need to be in love at ten? Was I emulating my mom? Jealous? Truly lonely? I accidentally typed "looney." That might be true, too.

That girl that I like-liked and I weren't a thing anymore, but there was a Halloween event at the school where I tried to tell her, I *wanted* to tell her, to *say*, that I "loved" her. I needed to. I wasn't even sure it was true. I needed to be in love with someone. I made things awkward, and I think she probably got that I was trying too hard for something clearly out of reach.

I had that feeling a lot of kids who go through changing family dynamics probably go through, that my mom was not paying as much attention to me as she had when we had been alone. I think that was the familiar comfort I had enjoyed when we first moved into these apartments, that I had my mom to myself, that it was only us and we were all the emotional support and affection we needed in the world. Then there was M and his kids. Her attention was becoming split. I understand as an adult that that new infatuation would have been alluring and fun for her, but I was beginning to change emotionally, becoming emotionally dependent, and dependent on someone who betrayed trusts.

There was something unsettling about my mother's other man— boyfriend? She hadn't stopped seeing him, even though she had moved on from the job that introduced them. She didn't bring him around or have me along on dates. Not for a little while anyway.

When I met M, it was late at night, after I had already gone to bed. I think I got up to use the restroom. I saw the TV on, providing the only light in the living room. I leaned out and there sat a man on my couch watching our TV. She *was* having him over; only after my bedtime? Or was this the first time?

He sat up, surprised to see me, and tried to smile. He introduced himself.

I didn't trust him. Something struck me wrong about this guy. I was suspicious of his face, mannerisms, and as I would begin to learn about him, I learned loathing. I did not see what my mom saw in him. I was powerless against getting drawn further into their relationship.

M was a married father of four, his sons whom I will refer to as One, Two, Three, and Four, by oldest to youngest, ranged in age from not much younger than my mom to not much younger than me. I worried about my mom taking on the responsibilities of a full family not her own with the rollercoaster of discipline and exampling I alone had been provided.

After I met M, things accelerated, and he was over often, and that Christmas he brought Four over and gave us both radio-controlled Ferrari's that we played with in one of the emptier parking lots.

We *kind of* bonded. Early on there was a mutual distaste for our parent's relationship. M was now going through a divorce because of my mom. He was apparently leaving an alcoholic, and it wasn't that their parents were getting divorced, his sons understood their mother was sick and the relationship wasn't healthy, but neither was jumping from one extreme to another. We were kids and got that. Both of our RC-cars crapped out before the end of the day. They looked cool, but were cheap.

M's job at the simulator manufacturer sent him on international trips, and he would come back bearing gifts. Usually, international candy at a time that was much rarer to come by. It may have been after that Christmas he was gone for a few weeks and my mom and I moved upstairs and across the hall. The apartments were nearly identical, only the kitchens a little different from each other.

I would get a bunk bed for when I had one of my friends over, or if Four came with M to stay the night. I slept up top regardless—my bed, my room, my rules—despite the effort to climb down. The novelty of danger.

I met Three almost the same way I had met M. I noticed the TV still on late and slipped out to investigate. We had a sleeper sofa, and there he was. I walked up and offered my hand, introducing myself.

M's kids took after him. They were tall, faces and eyes similar to his. Meanwhile, I still worried about where I belonged. He was a couple of years older. I was getting these new relationships thrust upon me, but I was being forced on them, too.

They would express frustration with their dad. He was too old for my mom, the age comparison they made was that my mom could have been a flower girl at his wedding to their mom. He was after some younger tail; my mom was keen on chasing luxury. Though they weren't exactly respectful of their dad and his new relationship, he was *their* dad. The battle lines were lain no matter how much or how long or at what times we ever got along.

We got another dog while living upstairs, a black Lab-mix, I named her Keisha. We had her for a few months, long enough for me to fall in love with her. My mom didn't want to deal with her growing appetite and gave Keisha away quite by surprise one night to some stranger I had never met before. She got rid of the dog. I clung to Keisha, crying, devastated. The woman taking the leash assured me I could come visit her.

Of course, when I asked the next weekend, and after that, if we could go visit Keisha, I was denied. Another dog gone.

CHAPTER 8

There's a vein to this story I haven't been discussing because it was an issue *every* day. My mom loved to cook. She was a fantastic cook! While I loved her red wine spaghetti, I don't particularly care for—anything.

I'm more than picky, a lot of things will make me nauseous if I force myself to eat them. Psychosomatic, I'm sure, but I suspect I'm a "high taster." Some things are too intense. Other flavors report as inedible to my brain. A lot of vegetables register as "not *food.*" My nose and tongue inform me I am chewing on random leaves with no digestible content, that I should spit this out.

I'm embarrassed about my pickiness and tastes. I eat what I will, of my fill, and I am done. I do not enjoy eating socially. I do not enjoy dinner parties. Eating isn't my kind of entertainment. When people ask if "that's all" I'm having, I feel pressured to engage in something I actively detest. I avoid it.

There's that awful old memory, "Do you want to eat this?"

My mom attempted an Irish dish, at least that's what she claimed, of spinach wrapped baby potatoes. The potatoes and spinach both from the can. I could tell from the smell I wasn't going to eat it and I informed her. That wasn't acceptable, I would stay at the table until I finished my dinner.

I said, "Well, I guess I live here now."

She got upset and turned the light off on me and watched TV behind me in the living room. I sat at the table, my back to her, and didn't touch my plate. I will probably reach starvation levels before I eat some things, and this was one. I didn't cry, maybe sighed a few times, but didn't complain. The dining room table and this awful smelling plate were my home, now.

She eventually got up, took my plate from in front of me, and told me to go to bed. I was happy to oblige.

Eventually, people get used to my limited palette, even my parents. Despite frustrated outbursts, she understood I was picky at a fundamental level. She would tell me eventually she worried about my pickiness and disinterest in being fed when I was an infant, taking me to a doctor. I was a healthy weight, developing normally—I would eat when I was hungry. That's been true my whole life.

Becoming lactose intolerant suddenly in my thirties further limited my diet. I have to special order everything, everywhere. Still more anxiety to pile up on eating in a group setting. I can't help feeling judged by restaurant staff, family, friends; even though I know I should not care.

Here, though, I *was* being judged. And I reacted. My behavior changed. I was growing bolder and ruder, arguing constantly. M's kids weren't exactly great influences. I was cussing by the fourth grade. My mom gave and denied me two dogs, and seemingly, chose to give more of herself to a bad example of a man and his kids. Those bad tendencies I carried within me became amplified.

I got sent to day camp at the downtown YMCA to occupy my time during the summer between third and fourth grades, even at one point getting sent to a weeklong sleepaway camp. I'm sure my mom wanted to help me socialize outside of school, to not be alone all day, but I grew bitter, thinking I was being discarded. She wanted to provide me with experiences, I took offense.

I felt I was being pushed away. Not that I didn't pull some positivity from those experiences, but I always felt she was offloading me any time she set me up for these things. Everything was seen through a lens of she would rather have more time with M than with me.

Summer camp, even though I only went for a week, was jam-packed with activities. Archery (I sucked and sliced my finger with the feather), swimming lessons in a pool (this was fun), watersports on the lake (I couldn't hack), horseback riding (I nearly fell off at a full speed run), crafts (I wasn't skilled with friendship bracelets, but tie-dying was fun), there was something to do each day or all day and a loose schedule to take in a little bit of everything.

There were some kids staying on longer stints who got care packages. Snacks, comics, trading cards, small gifts. One kid got a baseball that had an accelerometer in it to determine how fast your pitch was. We took turns pelting it against the cabin to see who could throw the fastest. I don't remember any numbers, but we weren't burning holes through the wall.

Since I was only there for a week, I didn't get anything at mail call. My mom would have had to have sent something the day I left for it to arrive in time before I would come back. I understood, but I still hoped to get something. To get that modicum of excitement hearing your name and receiving something addressed to you with love.

Instead, when I got home from the trip, my mom gave me a gift in the car. A broken Transformer knock-off she had bought at a yard sale —that day. I didn't hate it, but there was a painful disappointment. Why should I get upset over a toy?

Was this her love? Used. Familiar, yet unrecognizable. Things were shifted clunkily between us, like this faux Transformer. Our focuses were realigned. Some thought went into it, though it read as an afterthought.

This black and orange, faceless, missing one arm, dollar-store transforming toy went from robot to jet—mostly, considering the missing arm didn't lock the one side in. I revered it in a disdainful way. I remember playing with it as though it was expendable. Used, already broken, this was who took the hits from the heroes when I played. This was what I thought my mom thought of me. This is what she thought would make me happy after being gone for a week.

CHAPTER 9

One night I was bathing before bed. When I stepped out of the bathroom, I saw the TV on in the living room, and figured my mom and M were watching something. I needed a comb and knew one was sitting on my mom's dresser. My typical routine was to go and comb out my hair in her mirror. I thought *nothing* of opening her bedroom door and stepping in, hand already reaching for where I knew the comb was.

Except—the bed was occupied by M lying on top of my mom, both fully undressed. In the split second I saw them, M jumped off my mom and behind the bed, leaving her *completely* exposed and she slithered off the edge of the bed.

They were shocked, I was shocked. I knew what was up, and I might have apologized out loud before shutting the door and retreating to my room. In those one or two seconds it transpired, the thing I took from that moment, in that moment, was that M was a coward and had jumped behind my mom. He could have—should have?—shielded her, but he left her flat on her back.

After he was gone for the evening, unable to deal with the embarrassment, my mom and I sat on the edge of her bed and I pleaded with her, for the umpteenth time, to stop this.

"Why can't you be happy for me?" she asked.

It was an angry question.

"*I'm* not happy." I said.

"Do you want to go live with your dad?" She was venomous, she had loaded the answer for me and there was an incorrect option. "Because I will *let* you."

She was daring me to abandon her, to steal myself away from her and further ruin her happiness I was trying to deny her right now. I felt hurt. Because the "let" was sincere. She was also declaring that if I *did* decide to leave, she would abandon me as well.

I thought about it. She sat a little too big in the moment, looming. I *did* want to live with my dad. *Could* I take the opportunity? Could I go *home*?

"No." I said defensively, reflexively.

"M and I are getting married and I wish you could be happy for me."

There was a pause that I did not fill up.

"You can go to bed."

I felt weak. I felt a failure had occurred. I wasn't sure whose.

CHAPTER 10

1990 – A HOUSE IN BROKEN ARROW, OKLAHOMA

They did get married, in a ceremony at Woodward Park in Tulsa. Four and I were ring bearers and had to stand alongside Three next to M in the ceremony. There was a reception at one of my mom's friend's houses, where I'm pretty sure that woman's husband let me drink the spiked punch. After the party we drove straight to South Padre Island in Texas for their honeymoon. I liked the place, but wished I wasn't there with them.

Our first house together was a two-story house a block into the neighborhood. Mostly box shaped, living room led into a large kitchen/dining area, to the left of that, behind the stairs, two bedrooms, mine on the front, M and my mom's on the back, and a restroom between their bedroom and the kitchen. The upstairs had a restroom at the top of the stairs, and bedrooms over mine and the living room, Four and Three's respectively. They had vaulted ceilings and where walls had been constructed, it was within the remaining angle they had "closets" and basically attic storage area.

We had a backyard with a privacy fence. A friend of Four's lived behind us, and we would jump the fence to hang out at each other's houses.

I saw the fall of the Berlin Wall on the news in that house. In that neighborhood, I would see Metal Gear for the first time at some random kid's house. I think I got dragged into a stranger's house by an acquaintance and stood around with more random kids and watched someone play Metal Gear. That, and Four buying some Namor comics at a garage sale that I think I read more than he did are idle, yet pivotal memories. Someone in that neighborhood had a go-cart. There was a dog you could track by the drool it trailed along the way their human had walked them.

We had dogs. First came Jordan, a medium sized Collie mix who was supposedly Three's own dog. Three wanted to name him Mars after the Spike Lee Air Jordan commercials character. For some reason, none of us cared for Mars. We forced him into compromising with Jordan. Then came the American Kennel Club registered Cairn Terrier my mother spent a ridiculous amount of money on because she was supposedly related to Toto from the 1939 Wizard of Oz film. Her name was Kansas City Pepper Pie, though we called her Pepper. She resembled Toto, as most dark Cairn's do, mostly grey but struck through with black and a few silver and blonde streaks.

It was probably the most any of us ever got along, even though the tension between *everyone* rarely abated. I tried to run away one night from this place. My mom took the side of my stepbrothers in a family argument of some sort, it wasn't the what of it, it was the alienation. I felt singled-out and ostracized in what was supposed to be my *home*. I decided I would extricate myself.

I packed a bindle! Red, paisley bandana with a PB&J and a can of soda, one of my Ninja Turtles (Michelangelo). I was going to run away and go back to my dad's. I did indeed sneak out. I made it to the main street, then I wasn't sure of which way to *go*. I knew a general direction in space, but not the streets to take. I turned back, knowing I would only get lost and maybe seen by somebody—who knew what kind of trouble *that* could lead to? I made it quietly back into the house. No one, as far as I knew, was any wiser of my brief sojourn.

The hurt was deep. I was lonely yet surrounded. I know it led to demanding reaffirmations of whom she loved more, and all the unfair questions kids ask their parents.

Sitting in their bedroom one night, having one of those discussions alone with my mom, she called Four a "brown-noser," and we laughed together. My mom didn't get along with her stepchildren, but the stress of having to deal with three boys fairly close in age going through the same age-related changes all about the same time? It made that tension palpable.

Four confronted me about the conversation because he could over-hear it through the air vent. Have you ever had to explain why some-thing is an insult to the person the insult was levied at?

"Running away" wouldn't be the last time I would sneak out, though. By myself, with friends, my stepbrothers; it became the thing to get away with. That viscous friction made escape precious.

Even from early on, I wanted nothing to do with this family unit or complying with what was expected of me within it. I was supposed to start school at Arrow Springs Elementary, deeper into the neighbor-hood, but I felt robbed of a school holiday that Tulsa had scheduled, but Broken Arrow was in session for, I expected a day off, this was after a dramatic move and I was going to be the new kid and let me have my day off, dammit!

My fit worked. I left the TV in the living room on E!, which would run movie trailers for hours at a time. In a time when you couldn't easily watch movie trailers at will, especially for anything you might be excited about, having a channel that ran them in blocks, repeatedly, was thrilling for me. I would find a lot of escape in movies while living in that house.

I was only a few months into the fourth grade at Lanier before switching to a new school. Mrs. Wilson, my science teacher, stopped me on my last day, and told me that Broken Arrow schools were a little tougher than Tulsa schools. I think she knew I might struggle, be it my aptitude or attitude, I'm sure she had seen a few kids going through divorces and remarriages and what that did to them. I understood what she meant, though, she knew I was bright enough to get it. A fair warning from an adult looking out for me. I may have even appreci-ated it in the moment.

When I did finally start going to school, I was quickly deemed learning deficient in math. I was hurt, but unsurprised. Once division had entered the picture, I was losing the battle with math. It's a language and I do not speak it. The little bit of basic math I do, I still don't trust myself 100% of the time.

Being in learning deficiency classes wasn't bad. There were only a few other kids with a math teacher who had a free period and we got individualized attention. I never absorbed the how of it, resigning myself to a fate of barely passing grades in math for the rest of my education.

I would manage making new friends. A new "best friend" would develop in Broken Arrow as time and distance kept me from my old friends in Tulsa. I don't know what his parents did, but they did well, living in a house with an in-ground pool and a library of VHS movies. VHS was not cheap. A lot of entertainment we take for granted today was prohibitively expensive then. And all the plastic waste we were paying for! They had a lot of movies, grown-up movies, kids' movies —he had a sister—there was a Disney collection and I know those in *particular* weren't cheap.

Something I will never forget from being at his house, we were watching Stephen Segal's Hard to Kill, and the line "You can take that to the bank!" was uttered and his mom announced from the hallway, where she was oblivious to the movie, that she was going to the bank. We cried laughing.

We were easily entertained and laughed together often. Something I didn't get much at home, going to his house, staying nights on weekends, and even going to church with his family.

I learned the youth church had video games you could play before services began. I thought it was a fair enough trade. I played a *lot* of the Batman NES video game there. I was worried at one point I was concerned I would be expected to take the Eucharist when I saw some kids lining up. I was assured I wouldn't and to take it without being part of their church might somehow be offensive. I gleaned no spiritual growth from the couple times I went with them. I went to play games. More escape.

Sometimes my stepbrothers and I *would* get along. We would play video games, watch movies and shows, and listen to music together. We crank-called restaurants. I'm sure the staff knew the usual suspects thanks to the Simpsons and set the phone down for a minute, why not tie up the line to keep it silent for a little while? Other times my step-brothers and I were at each other's throats, nearly literally.

Four and I would get into it roughhousing too aggressively. One time he landed a blow with a head-butt, busting my lip. There was a lot of blood, flowing quickly. I rushed to the bathroom, knowing nothing else than to at least bleed somewhere that was easy to clean up? I cried at first. Four was visibly terrified, at the sight of the blood, knowing it was his fault, knowing he was going to get in trouble.

I began to laugh. At his plight, sadistically, but also in a calculated move. If he got into trouble for our fighting, I would no doubt get into trouble because of the fact there was fighting. I told him to calm down and how we could cover this up, we were playing, and this was an unfortunate accident, *no one* gets in trouble. I would rather forego retribution if receiving it meant I would get in trouble, too.

We weren't the only ones that fought. A popular phrase between us was "I'm leaving, *forever!*" in as dramatic fashion as a situation warranted, often followed by a slammed door. We were making fun of an argument M and my mom had, where she said that, loud enough for the gods, followed by "Justin, we're leaving."

She wouldn't leave me behind, not "forever."

These fights occurred often, I'm not sure how violent they were behind closed doors, but they were a loud couple. I don't even know what their fights were about. I had tuned out their anger. I imagine it was about her trying to live beyond their means. Or maybe his work hours or business trips he would have to take. Honestly what they fought about doesn't matter. It lingered. It was always in the air. I think they had "fun," but they didn't make each other *happy*.

CHAPTER 11

Sitting at the table in the kitchen/dining room, eating cereal, I felt a sharp pain from the back of my head.

"Ow!" I said, grabbing my head thinking I had been stung.

My mom was standing there staring incredulously at a hair she had plucked from my head.

"You had a gray hair!" She said, showing me. "You're too young for that!"

There was something to her tone that was accusatory, as if I had chosen to grow it.

I'm ten. I'm in the fourth grade in a new school with a learning disability. I'm in a family who gets along about as well as caged animals. I'm sure I have *no* clue what could possibly be stressing me out. The tone she used, though, this genetic slip was my fault. I was stressing her out, reminding her of her own mortality. She seemed to consistently misread the situation she knew I was in, that she was holding me in.

On the weekends I spent with my dad, we would get pizza and rent movies, or go see a new movie. When the weather was nice, we would go fishing at a couple different lakes near Tulsa. I enjoyed the activity, appreciating a silent morning or having conversations. Sometimes it became a test of strength and a game of manipulating move-ment and momentum, but I couldn't *land* the beasts. I was scared of sticking my hand into their jaw, and of getting the hook out. I don't know that I was afraid of them hurting me, but either hurting *myself*, or causing the *fish* too much trauma. Sometimes we fished to keep and cook them ourselves, sometimes we appreciated nice days together.

Once, I caught a huge Big Mouth Bass, within the first few minutes of even casting our lines. I was certain I had become snagged, my hook catching a stick or limb mired in the mud below. I had pulled the line taught and the point in the water wasn't moving. I handed my pole to my dad as he started to maneuver the boat toward the spot with the trolling motor. The release in tension on my line caused an unexpected reaction.

This massive, white-bellied monster launched out of the water, line whipping through the air from its mouth. It was one of those moments you wish you could snap a photo with your eyes.

My dad shouted, "You're not snagged, you've got a fish—reel it in!"

I resumed "fighting" it, I think it was four pounds of pure muscle in the water and I was a kid. I wasn't about to touch the damn thing, I brought the end of my pole over to my dad to do his thing for me. We both had fun with that experience.

I wanted to take it home for my mom to prepare. Instead of being impressed with my achievement and bounty, she was exasperated with my dad for not having it prepared to her satisfaction. Then she burned it. I don't think I knew what *petty* was at the time, but I knew I was seeing anger taken out on food and me for nothing other than being annoyed.

In that house, I felt the resentment growing between us. There would be plenty of times in each of the four houses we would live in together with the W family that she would treat me as the outsider, but *here*, I felt at a loss. Why was I putting up with this?

I thought I could protect her from this negative environment.

If I clung too tightly, if I was an anchor on her life, I'll admit I was trying to keep her grounded as if she would float away. In the W households I feared her and *for* her. Her drinking increased. She would say and do things that from now on were steps away from me that could never be regained.

There was a day I expressed an unspoken rage, by myself. Home alone, I dragged my box of GI Joe's into the kitchen, got a hammer, and proceeded to smash every one of my action figures. I can't tell you why I did it. I can't explain why I have held onto my reactions, not the inciting events. I often wonder what that means? It can't be healthy. I cleaned up my own mess and hid the plastic carnage in the garbage.

Maybe someone had said something at school about GI Joe being for little kids or something. I do not know why I needed to brutally destroy that collection. I did it and felt *nothing*.

I did find release in the movies, though, especially when Teenage Mutant Ninja Turtles: The Movie came out. I would ride my bike up to the theater outside of our neighborhood in a strip-mall, by myself, and watch it every weekend they held it on screen, sometimes multiple times in a weekend. I did that with other movies, too, I saw Ernest Goes to Jail more than once only to get out of the house. I would go day or night. That theater became a sanctuary.

Strangely, the same theater would pop back into my life in 2002 when a friend would run the projectors there and I got to see a private screening of Star Wars Episode II: Attack of the Clones. There would be times I would watch movies on my own again, waiting for my friend to get off work. I recall specifically sitting in a crowded theater watching the Mothman Prophecies. It's a small world and the past always seems present.

We didn't live there for long. I suspect my mom didn't much appreciate living quite literally in the same neighborhood as her new husband's ex-wife. Four and Three got to go another year in school with their friends while I got uprooted midway through a school year. The next move would set a pattern that wouldn't break for years, and no one was safe.

CHAPTER 12

1990-1991 – ANOTHER HOUSE IN TULSA, OKLAHOMA

Fifth grade would be going to the Union School District, at Boevers Elementary, another school buried deep within a neighborhood. Four and I managed to avoid being in classes together, thankfully. We made friends on our own and some of those friends of course crossed over. My clique of friends, however, got me hooked on Topp's Marvel Comics Trading Cards. A collection I retain to this day.

Living in Tulsa again, but at the other end of it from my dad, I was within bike riding distance of Eastland Mall. It's a different thing now entirely, a family fun center and office space, but its distinctive tarpaulin shuttlecock roof design remains. Here I would start blowing my allowance on TMNT figures *and* comics at the KB Toys on the upper level.

The lower level was the food court, movie theater, and arcade. I saw movies on my own here, too, but not quite as often. My dad knew I would want to see something kiddy or we diverged on what we wanted to see on a particular weekend. He would purchase us our own tickets, concessions, and we would meet back in the lobby. We would eat junk in the food court and play arcade games for an hour.

Eastland Mall was another one of those escapist releases, and I'm glad my mother at that time was urban. I had some safe spaces, albeit in commercial zones, and I can see how that shaped my sense of the world and values. I can be guilty of executing retail therapy. Entertaining myself this way kept me sane.

The house we lived in backed up to an empty church. Four and I would play around in the abandoned parking lot. There was an on-site residence which you could enter through a hole in the wall. I managed to step all the way onto a nail and stab my own foot through the sole of my shoe. Don't mess around with building clutter, kids.

We had a small backyard, we had our dogs, we had cats that mostly stayed outside, but we didn't spend a lot of time in that space.

I think I started gorging on junk food at this age. If there was a pizza night, it was a contest to see how many slices I could down. Ice cream, snack cakes, I enjoyed sweets and my stomach could handle junk. I got enough nutrients, I stayed alive and gained weight.

My mom and I would take walks, and it was in this neighborhood that I would start to complain about shin splints. I would ride my bike and adventure on my own, and often. I would be overweight for my size in my early teens, yet with a lot of stamina. The shooting pains in my legs were real, I got them walking any more than 10 minutes. This didn't happen at school, in gym or recess. Why only on these walks? I was frustrated with my body. I appreciated my walks with my mom, though I constantly complained.

I know I spent too much time in the bathroom in that house, though that was often chosen behavior, though perhaps subconscious at that. I would read Indian in the Cupboard and the novelizations of the TMNT and Batman movies *over* and *over*. I know I spent a lot of that reading time on the toilet. Whether I was shitting or not, I was not getting off the pot until I finished whatever chapter.

Going to a Union school was daunting. Everyone in Tulsa kind of envied and feared Union's better facilities and supplies and the advanced and accelerated learning that provided. I ended up in learning disability classes again. Now I knew what to expect of myself and my commitment to my own education. Was I lazy in science because it was complicated? Sure. Did I fuck off in English because I was bored? You betcha. Math? Not my tongue. Physical education? That—depended. Sometimes I was active, most of the time I was vehemently *not*. Something about team and social settings, I could not get into. Creative arts I excelled at—any chance to make something up and be graded for my imagination I looked forward to.

Education notwithstanding, I made friends here who also loved TMNT as much as I did. I had feared going to a more prestigious school meant they would somehow be more mature and find my interests childish by their standards. I was twelve and truly worried about my TMNT movie poster folder being seen as immature. I felt shame for my fandom, and I had no idea who anyone around me would even be.

Thankfully I was wrong. My new friends introduced me to the Marvel trading cards. One obsession slowly gave way to another.

I've been cataloguing memories about this house, unable to put it into order. But this house is where shit hit the fan. This is where I would lose confidence in my mother while also positioning myself as some sort of guardian for her. I would grow to detest M more intensely the longer I lived with him, but in this house, I would begin to feel actively disrespected by him.

It wasn't the W's alone, though my stepbrothers had strife with my mom that I couldn't come between. I was no angel. I was angry all the time, I hated my living situation and the "good" times barely made it worth keeping my sanity. My mom and I started leveraging expectations on each other about what the other was supposed to be doing. That family was psychological warfare. There were violent outbursts, but we all mostly seethed with disdain for each other while our parents thought they had *something* together.

There was a night M was away on business, and mom and I were watching TV when Three started playing music too loudly. My mom went to tell him to turn it down, and of course had to shout, which lead to a shouting *match*, and Three decided to kick my mom in the back when she turned to exit. It knocked her down, and I was paralyzed with fear from the sounds down the hall. There was angrier shouting, and Three and Four left the house, I think to go to their mother's or a friend, I don't recall, I know we were alone afterwards. I think I asked if we should call the cops? I think I begged again for her to leave all of this. She wouldn't. She wouldn't always be my ally even if I tried to be hers.

CHAPTER 13

Operation Desert Storm kicked off August 2nd, 1990—basically live on television. I thought it was another Vietnam, watching a war unfold on the news in real time. How often we compare new American battles to Vietnam. A litmus for worthy causes and issues we should be keeping our troops out of.

I looked at my mom with a little bit of fear *and* pride, "You were in the Reserve; could they call you?"

My mom smiled at the thought, maybe a thrilling fantasy born in that instant. "Maybe!"

Her term with the Reserve ended in 1987. She knew that. I, having only my textbook reference of Vietnam and movies I had seen, viewed the Reserve services as a sort of volunteering in place of a draft, unaware of the terms of commitment. Not completely joining, "but if you need me…"

I used to worry about such a situation arising. It seemed scary and wrong, calling random people from the public to go fight a war no one supports. I can't say why she wouldn't calm my fears if she knew. I grew clingier, she didn't immediately discourage me of it.

There was an abundance of patriotism pouring forth at that time. We did the yellow ribbons to wish our troops a speedy return. I drew a picture of a Ninja Turtle's hand with a yellow ribbon tied around one of the fingers.

As the war was declared, a whole flotilla of aircraft flew into Tulsa International to refuel as they dispersed across the United States to pick up troops and supplies. It was loud. It happened during recess at school.

We all agreed this must be what World War II was like.

I've been to airshows. I've seen a lot of planes in formation. To see a military operation in progress? Awesome—in the greater sense of the word, inspiring fear and respect.

It was a terrifying time. I developed a lot of existential fear here. I found escape in video games and books and buying Ninja Turtles and comic books. I buried my head in the sand and when things got their worst, I was ill prepared.

CHAPTER 14

An uncle came and visited us. I dared call him by the name when I last saw him and was quickly corrected that *that* was no longer his preferred name. His old name was a childish throwback and he went by his proper first name now. I was reminded of when I had been called "J.D.."

It was the first time I had seen a Mulroney in years, and he had come to us here in Oklahoma. He lives in OKC now. I know he moved around a bit. A trait of the clan that I have resisted, outside of regularly rearranging my furniture to change my spaces.

Somewhere, sometime, Irene started smoking pot. It's not that I associate my uncle's visit with her starting to smoke weed, but the compression of time places the memories near each other. Maybe they got high together, I don't remember it specifically.

One night, we were alone and she was high. I don't think I quite *got* that then. She had to have been. Maybe I need for her to have been. Maybe *I* was because of the smoke in the air? I was probably 11, M away somewhere, step brothers off with their mother or friends, the two of us sitting in the mostly dark living room with some music playing.

My mother and I gave each other back and shoulder rubs. I carried my stress in my shoulders even then and there was a sense of needing extra affection in front of these *other* family members. Pack animals displaying alliances. I would sit on the floor in front of her where she would work on my neck and shoulders. I would do the same for her from behind her chair. We would ask each other for these favors; primates picking at each other.

Whatever it was we were talking about, she asked for a back rub, but she wanted me to do her whole back, a full massage. I said, "ok, sure, whatever," but she stopped me.

"I mean like a *real* massage." She said wistfully. "I want a whole-body massage, and you're so good at it! I want you to do my neck, my back, my legs—my *butt*."

"Like, *naked*?" I asked. I was getting uncomfortable.

"It's okay, I'll keep a sheet on and lay on the floor."

I wanted to please her. I was also unpleasantly thrilled. I felt awkward. I *feel* awkward recalling it. I let her set up and came back into the living room when she called.

She was on her stomach, nude, with a sheet covering her legs and buttocks. Music was a little louder, Beatles I think. An incense burning. It was all quite romantic. That's a problem isn't it? It felt ways in concepts I didn't have yet. These individual presentations weren't out of the norm. I saw dark rooms filled with smoke and glowing embers. Rubbing my mom's back isn't unusual, I've touched her bare back when we've been out sunning. There's *always* music on. These events are converging. I tried to convince myself, anyway.

I may have used baby oil or lotion but massaging my mother didn't last long. Somehow, she relaxed herself straight to sleep. I noticed when she started snoring. Yeah, we didn't talk much once I got started. I tried jostling her, talking to her, *shoving* her—she was out cold. I was left, for all intents and purposes, alone in the house.

I covered her the rest of the way up, turned off the stereo, and put myself to bed.

The next morning, she would ask why I let her sleep on the floor. I told her I tried to convince her to get up. We laughed it off. It never came up and she didn't ask me for full body massages ever again. Maybe she got low and lonely, and I was simply the only person available to *touch* her. I'm sure I've got issues from this lone incident, like why didn't I refuse?

That's probably not a fair question. I don't share this often with people, I feel *dirty* about it, but also know that I was put into an awkward position at an awkward age by an awkward person at an awkward place in her life. There was a lot going on. Signs of her own depression? Lonely enough within her marriage she would seek that kind of attention from her own son? It's difficult to consider. I'm simultaneously furious and empathetic.

It would *not* however be the last time she smoked weed around me. There's a lot of looking back on memories of interesting conversations we had where I always felt she talked to me as a person, not a child. I'm not sure if she got high *to* talk to me or if I wandered in subconsciously attracted to the smell and those conversations happened. Mostly they were *normal*, talking about life, as viewed from a preteen. Sometimes begging to tear this family apart. I don't want to blame the behavior on weed. The weed might have been keeping her steady in an incessantly unsteady world. I no longer begrudge her chosen vices. Life is hard, and we have these naturally occurring substances that seem to make it a little easier to make it through the day.

I've got *my* vices now. I was afraid of mind-altering substances for a while. Not having control of myself, some*thing* else taking the driver's seat in my brain if I was inebriated in any way made early interactions unpleasant. Since then, I have said inappropriate or poorly worded sentiments under the influence. Haven't we all? Or have we? A few of us, maybe. I can sympathize despite the infractions, right?

It didn't always have to be inebriated that I appreciated my mother. There were the walks and talks, but we also had an upright piano in that house. My mom taught me Chopsticks and Heart & Soul. It was special sitting next to her and finding the rhythm in the music and executing songs harmoniously. We always sang together, but for a little while, we played music with each other.

I spent a lot of time in my room alone, though. There were the last vestiges of my old family. The desk with the Apple IIC. My old TV with the bad coaxial connection and my NES on the rickety TV cart. Pieces picked up along the way as well. Half of the bunkbed and the toy chest from the apartment life. In my room I found comfort in familiarity.

I got good at Tetris. I beat Bad Dudes and laughed at the George Bush lookalike who wanted to get a burger after I saved him from ninjas. I played Defender, Space Invaders, and a typing game on the old Apple IIC. I did a lot of homework and drawing at that desk, too.

Introduced to the Marvel trading cards at school, my dad was eager to show me the comics they were from. I began *collecting* comic books here, buying a lot from a grocery store up the street from our neighborhood. If *any* store had the trading cards? I would beg for cash to buy a pack, desperate to find a holographic card.

I still have a Batman retrospective book that collects facts, stories, covers, selected panels and pages from the entire franchise from 1939-1989. I received this and the TMNT graphic novel the first movie is mostly based on for Christmas. My mom did not mind or dissuade me from loving anything nerdy at all. I think she saw how much it inspired me to be creative and that was one thing she never stood in the way of.

CHAPTER 15

At school, I saw a kid break his collarbone in the gymnasium. How he flailed and screamed in pain? I locked up, knowing what he was feeling was something that I did *not* know. Here at eleven-years-old I was seeing someone break something for the first time and they flopped in agony while none of us could do anything. Terrifying.

I dared ask him when he came back to school, "What did it feel like?"

He looked at me as if I had offended him. "It *hurt!*"

"No, that's not what I meant…" I tried to explain, I was genuinely curious, *how did it feel?*

I had been in lots of different kinds of pain, but a broken bone was not one of them. I think I wanted to know what made him go wild on the floor. I didn't want to experience it myself, but a firsthand account might prepare me for the possible occasion.

At some point in our stay there, I don't recall the exact date, M took my mom with him on one of his business trips, this time to France, where he would take her to Paris. This was the romantic adventure my mother always wanted to chase. She wanted to be a world traveler—

who doesn't want to be able to hop a plane on a whim and be in a different country?

Here in the United States, taking a vacation to the next town over can be difficult to plan. A lot of us making average living wages can barely save up enough to cover house, medical, or automotive emergencies, I know all three have negatively impacted my finances throughout my life. M got sent on these international trips once or twice a year, and this time, my mom got to go, though I'm sure it wasn't on the company's dime.

This is one of those things that I know they took photos there, with my mother in front of recognizable landmarks—the typical touristy scenes. I don't have any of them and I bet they've all been destroyed. My mother went to Paris, though. She had her romantic adventure!

What did the boys and I do? I think Three—even though he was only a couple of years older than us, was "in charge"—but we fed ourselves, I think we were left some cash for pizza delivery. M and my mom were gone for a week, maybe? What we did wasn't as impressive to my memory as the idea that my mom got to go to Paris.

It might have been July that they went—it could have also been the New Year—my mom described the people of Paris firing bottle rockets and Roman candles during evening celebrations *at* each other and passersby. It sounded fun, scary, *and* annoying. I don't think they went into the catacombs. I may have been disappointed.

There was a new best friend, among the clique of friends that got me hooked on trading cards. His house was on the other side of a field that, at least then, separated the school from the next neighborhood. An undeveloped tract of land. His house wasn't the only one I would visit across that field.

I would ride my bike around the neighborhood for something to do. One day, some girls sitting on a porch hollered at me to come over to them. I might have rolled passed them a few times. They went to my school, no surprise. The blonde girl, who resembled a real-life Barbie, liked me.

Me? Being pursued? A jest! I would talk to her on the phone and at school and on neighborhood stoops for weeks afterwards. About nothing. We enjoyed each other's company. Well, that and I would sing along to the popular song Iesha by Another Bad Creation while singing her name in place of the title.

I also didn't know how to *spell* her name, only ever hearing her and friends say it. The one time I tried to write her a love letter, it ended up becoming a joke between her and that same friend who had helped initially call me over. Names and spelling, my weaknesses meeting.

I put an adjustable ring from the mall into a plastic, gem-cut ring box I used as a treasure chest for my action figures. I set out across the neighborhood and field, practicing what I would say. How I would try to make it official.

She refused the ring and me. That was that. I'd pushed too far. I wasn't terribly heartbroken; I understood my being entirely too serious for eleven-year-olds. I was disappointed I'd pressured her. Not that I would learn any lessons from that.

A few years later—which to children can be lifetimes given the changes our bodies go through—I think we saw each other at Eastland Mall, of all places. I was in a hurry when she made eye contact and waved at me. I smiled, caught between *who are you* and *ohh*. I'm sorry I didn't stop or wave back.

My mom got another Cairn Terrier, a blonde named Petey McPete, whom we called Pete. Pepper loved him as her own puppy, but my mom had intentions on breeding them. Life would get interrupted, though.

As the school year was ending, M was part of a massive corporate upheaval that was going to send several employees to Akron, Ohio for a summer project, and then he would be moving to the Tampa Bay, Florida area for work, the family in tow. *I* was in tow.

The dogs, Jordan, Pepper, and Pete would be going, but our cats mysteriously vanished before we got to packing. I have no clue what happened to them. Four and I searched for them throughout the neighborhood. Our cats weren't the only things vanishing quickly ahead of our move.

M and my mother started selling off bigger items they didn't want to have to store or move halfway across the country. Without warning, I came home from school to find my bedroom nearly empty. They had sold my bed, my desk, and my old Mac. I was given some foam egg crate and sheets to sleep on. This wasn't the first time something I thought of as my own was taken out from under me by surprise. Maybe she thought some of those things I had outgrown, but, this was my bed! I felt robbed. Someone had come into my private space and took my *bed*—and I knew who.

As I lay there that night, coping with the novelty of sleeping on the floor and the fact my guardians didn't give a shit about my sense of space and permanence, M barged into my room and went into my closet. He turned on the light and rummaged for something, I don't even know what. No knock, no "excuse me." This was his house, he'd go where he pleased, my peace be damned.

When I made mention of it the next morning, he didn't care. My mother didn't care. I was in the way.

Coupled with the past when my mother took and sold my toys with no warning, I developed a desire to buy and own my own things. I wanted things to be *mine*. I wanted the security of having my own life that I could control the entry and exit of *things*. Clearly this is unhealthy and selfish. Here I was, struggling with concepts of loss and betrayal...by my parents.

I wasn't alone in this treatment, though. They had sold at least some of Four's furniture, including his bed, the other half of my bunkbed. The piano was sold off. The Camaro. My dad had begged my mom to sell it to him if she was going to sell it at all because he wanted to give it to me. She got it early in their relationship and it had been her primary mode of transportation until then.

I learned about that sabotaged plan much later. Another time my future wasn't in the plan—there was never a plan. I was getting that, but I didn't want to accept it at the time. I have looked back and wished I would have stayed in Oklahoma with my dad. I know I am who I am because of the *entire* life I lived, but...

CHAPTER 16

1991 – SUMMER IN OHIO, NEW JERSEY, & NEW YORK

We drove to Akron shortly after school had let out. Straight, that's about a fourteen-hour drive. Today. Might have been longer in 1991. We stopped several times to keep ourselves limber. The drive wasn't for sight-seeing, we had a destination and a deadline, M was expected for his job.

One of our stops was to get coffee. My mom and I headed in, Four wanted a cup, too. We asked what he wanted in it. Only sugar, and he waited in the car. Mom and I got ours—I wasn't drinking coffee regularly yet, but I couldn't fully fall asleep in the car, so I tried forcing myself to stay awake instead. We brought a sugared-up coffee to Four, who complained it was too bitter.

This was one of those occasions where you remember hearing a turn of phrase for the first time. My mom said, "You want a little coffee with your sugar?"

Loopy, I found it too funny. I imagined a cup of sugar and a dropper barely squeezing one drop of coffee out.

The apartment complex we would come to reside in was nice. A large interior courtyard with a huge pool and clubhouse. Gym equipment, a sauna, showers, a billiard room, lounge area… My stepbrothers and I played around in there all through the summer. There was also a creek that ran behind the complex and some thickly over-grown scrubs and shrubs we dared pushed our way into.

We bent and broke saplings to make a fort out of the greenery. It was a place within nature for us to call our own. We did some bonding I suppose. I got poison ivy or oak or sumac, I don't know, my skin exploded.

I saw the Rocketeer and Terminator 2 there. We went to Cleveland. We visited an art museum and the zoo.

We kept our dogs at a boarding kennel that had some grass and trees to walk the dogs in. I don't think we visited them as much as we should have.

What I cherished about that summer was getting to spend a little time with the Mulroney's again, this time in New Jersey. My mom and I drove from Akron to Glendora. I stayed nights with aunts. Got to be a kid by myself, my stepbrothers weren't around the first trip we took, and I was much older than my aunts' children, though I still played with them.

We drove a scenic route through the Appalachian Mountains crossing the breadth of Pennsylvania. I know my mom and I talked. I know. What I appreciated about the drive across an entire state were the verdant mountains. A frozen sea of green waves rolling endlessly around us.

We stopped at a gas station that had Clearly Canadian in wild cherry which I didn't find often. Mom deigned to buy me a TMNT audiobook and comic to kill some time on the drive.

Probably a six-to-eight-hour drive at the time. I know we arrived at Grandpa Fred's place in the evening, but there was still some waning daylight.

"Hey, Fred!" my mom said cheekily.

My grandpa resembled a real-life Fred Flintstone. With his name being Fred, my grandpa is Fred Flintstone in my head.

"*Fred* is it now?" he laughed as they gave each other a hug.

I saw my dad's mom once or twice a year for a few days around Thanksgiving or a family reunion. My dad's brothers lived in Broken Arrow near Tulsa. I would see my cousins in the wild—small-town syndrome. M's parents were both passed on. My mom's parents were only in the picture in my infancy, however impactful those moments may have been. There was the trip in the mid-80's, but of my mom's family, I only ever knew my mom. My desire to connect with family when the "family" I lived with, I didn't fit in, made me kind of want to stay with them forever. I felt wanted and welcomed. My mom lit up around her own family. She seemed happier.

I can't say everything was perfect between her and the rest of her family. I wasn't in the room for every conversation. What ideological and political differences had formed over the years didn't erupt in front of me as I have seen at other family functions over the years. This seemed to be a genuinely happy reunion.

It was summer, I swam with aunts and uncles who were closer to *my* age than to my mother's. I knew my mother was young having me. Her dad was young having her. Our family's generations and ages aren't always disparate.

I stayed with an aunt, and we listened to Pink Floyd all night. That aunt I felt somehow *extra* comfortable with from before. I recognized it more this time around. It wasn't that we liked the same music, I felt somehow at ease with this woman, as relaxed with her as with my own mother. That effortless comfort would remain a mystery for a while yet.

Staying with another aunt, we listened to '80's pop all night. She did a karaoke tape of Toy Soldiers by Martika and I thought she was a legitimate popstar herself. This aunt and my brother share a birthday, and today, live close together and are as close as any of our family seems to be toward each other.

Spoilers. I'm glad for them.

She lived around the corner from a magazine store and I was allowed to walk over and buy Spider-Man and Wolverine comics.

My aunt and her husband would go cliff diving in upstate New York and take me. We visited extended family while up there. We visited a house near to a railroad where we tried to throw sticks onto the rails. I don't know why, maybe we wanted to accidentally kill ourselves with wooden shrapnel.

Then we went for a long drive into forested, rocky cliffs cut through by creeks and rivers. The waters were cold, but swimmable. A lot of these places were dug out from the waterfalls above, leading to seem-ingly bottomless pits of crystal-clear water. There were outcrops and cliffs of all sorts of heights. Five feet suddenly looks high when you're jumping into water so deep there is only darkness below. Ten feet? Twenty?

The "cousin" I had befriended was braver than me and took that higher jump, feet first, but, he didn't close his legs. We knew when he reached the surface of the water.

He screamed, "My balls!" much to our amusement.

I couldn't do it. I stuck to the kiddy stuff. I did, however, explore further upriver, seeing beautiful forestry, stones, fish, and salamanders.

Despite this being a trip with my mom, she was not present for a lot of the time I spent with family. I do not know where she was the nights we didn't stay together at Grandpa Fred's. She could have been having time she needed with her dad. She could have been hanging out with old friends. I'm not accusing her of anything, she deserved her own personal time. I was bonding with my family, yet my mom wasn't always acting the surrogate. I was hanging out with acquain-tances I happened to share DNA with. She trusted these people who I barely knew, whom she hadn't seen since our earlier trip and before that...and I was okay with it. I felt safe with them. I didn't feel safe at "home" with the W's. These music and movie-loving artistic types from New York and New Jersey? I got them, and they got me.

My mom *was* there, though. She loved seeing her sister's newest baby. We babysat another aunt's child for a bit, this child swapping thing between sisters wasn't only *me* couch surfing. This was big family energy.

We went to Atlantic City. I wanted to see Trump's failed casino, but we weren't in that area. We went to a mall on the boardwalk. There was a store that sold holographic decorations. These were those black surfaces that when you shifted them around in the light a green nearly three-dimensional image appeared to float within the surface. I got a skull sticker that I carefully transferred to different surfaces for years afterwards until it lost its adhesive and luster.

Eventually we returned to Ohio, though we would visit briefly again along with the W's. While we were gone, M took his sons to an amusement park. There was a change in the apartment we stayed in. At some point, M shaved his beard and as the three of us boys talked about our day, I realized it. My mom and M started to laugh. I judged my stepbrothers' poor observation skills.

Before the end of summer, the job M was on came to an end, and we set to moving to the Tampa Bay area in Florida, another cross-country drive with a lot of Nutrigrain cereal bars and CB radio chatter with truckers.

I discovered I suffer motion sickness if I do fall asleep in a moving vehicle. I had slipped off in the back seat, curled up in a fetal position, only to wake up with an overwhelming urge to puke. I threw up behind the driver's seat into the floorboard—and farted loud enough my stepbrothers immediately started cracking up, caught off guard by the terrible combination of sounds.

I appreciated the humor, almost laughing at my own flatulence, but also felt inexplicably terrible. I crawled out of the car and continued to vomit in the bushes outside of whatever restaurant or gas station we had stopped at. My mom was suddenly at my side checking on me and then cleaning up sick from the backseat of her car. I've basically *had* to see outside while in motion ever since.

CHAPTER 17

1991 – A HOUSE IN CLEARWATER, FLORIDA

Before we moved into our first house, we stayed at some long-term hotel accommodations in Tampa, near the water. Basically, a studio apartment, the kitchen and living room were separated by a bar that was the dining area. Nothing separated the king size bed from the living room. The only closed room was the restroom, next to the kitchen. I think we only stayed there for a week, maybe two. Three, Four, and I shared a room, and we would rotate who slept on the couch and who shared the bed. Mom and M had their own, separate quarters, not even adjoined to ours. I'm sure they appreciated the privacy after having five people living in a two-bedroom apartment, nice however it may have been.

This wasn't *beachfront* property, this was a lot of docks, rock, and concrete. I saw my first horseshoe crabs here—organic tanks with stingers. They look primordial. They give the impression it would hurt to touch them. A few times we spotted dolphins further out in the water.

We visited the house we would live in for the next year one evening. It was empty. Only overhead lights were available wherever they were. There was that hazy eeriness that declared this was a liminal space.

In our first house in Clearwater, Florida, I would develop entomo-phobia, I would do private *and* homeschooling. Obsess with Mega Man 3 (a deceptively touching story about a lost, unknown family in an 8-bit action game) and make cardboard box fortresses for my Ninja Turtles. Sort of got along with my stepbrothers…in as much as we didn't kill each other, only abused. We all loved Ren & Stimpy.

My stepbrothers and I explored the neighborhood and surrounding area at length. Some of our private school classmates lived nearby and we would all run around the little patches of wilderness scattered around the neighborhood.

Florida is perfect for bugs. Roaches and slugs the size of your hands. We developed a flea problem and scheduled an exterminator. I forgot my house key on that day, but I knew how to jimmy the back door. I recall a puddle.

Getting into the house, I could feel something on my leg. A light tickling. Where I *expected* to see a flea or some other bug (Florida), I was a new level of horrified by what I did see.

A writhing black velvet pulsated across my lower leg—hundreds of fleas, scrambling for sanctuary from their death bath.

It was a visceral freak out. The kind of physical gyrating someone could mistake for a convulsion. An interpretive dance of abject terror.

I had never been *fond* of bugs or creepy-crawlies, but this made every crawling sensation and anything that might attempt crawling on me a forever nightmare. I still have a skin-crawling aversion to those that dwell within the earth and hide in humid shadows.

This wasn't just the birth of my entomophobia. The experience made horror really start to click for me personally. I was reading more horror for pleasure. Watching horror movies and television. But I started to create horror. I wrote my first horror short story inspired by the event. I started drawing my own gruesome monsters.

There was a shopping center that had a movie theater and a comic book store. Alien 3, Lawnmower Man, Bram Stoker's Dracula, all posters I loitered to stare at. Between purchasing Wolverine and Spider-Man, I would read Alien vs Predator and Creepy compilations from Dark Horse in the store.

I visited a nearby public library regularly. I don't remember *every-*

thing I checked out, multiple books a week, but it was there I picked up Adulthood Rites by Octavia E Butler, and I was absolutely fascinated by the concept of the Oankali, the regulation of human reproduction by an alien race in the wake of our nearly destroying ourselves, and introduction of a mediator to the reproductive process, the Ooloi, a sort of in-between gender person. Alien and human, purely sexual, and compatible with males and females.

Butler gave me a sci-fi that was equal parts body horror and body positivity, it made me feel compassion for people's general *strangeness*. We're all a little soupy, aren't we? Xenogenesis, aka Lilith's Brood, was a trilogy I read out of order, then again in order, and, for some reason, I wanted to be an Ooloi. I was twelve.

M and my mom were friends with a couple we would visit who had a couple of kids of their own. A boy and a girl and a baby on the way, the girl was the oldest, though a year younger than me. I wish I could remember her name. We adored each other but were both too young to know what to do with that.

It wasn't long until the baby arrived, and we all teased the mom about how she almost never looked pregnant to begin with and quickly bounced back to her fit self. One of those genetic lottery winners. Three kids and smaller than me, though I was beginning to grow into my own skin. Grown women becoming smaller than me was weird, especially when growth spurts would hit between long absences from seeing my Buffington family.

I used to tease the oldest with that fictional word, *Ooloi*. How did I *mean* it? It was a creature that was neither male nor female, but could interact with both, oh, and has tentacles in their armpits. Was it a *slur*? Did I think it was funny to watch her squirm, usually giggling, as I said this silly word at her?

I appreciated these two more than my stepbrothers. I preferred the company of multiple friends' families to my own.

The boy loved the Ninja Turtles, too. He was that dangerous sort of impressionable. He said something that made me think he wanted to *find* the Turtles—in the sewers—in Tampa Bay. Knowing this was a "Santa" situation, I told him first and foremost, the Turtles live in New

York City, far away, and that sewers are dangerous and not to be explored.

There was a day I think I had unwittingly volunteered to babysit, because it was only me and these two at their house. The boy had one of those Tiger Electronic single screen handheld games from the 1980's & '90's. I heard it go off in his toy box and I searched for what was being noisy. I found the game and made a few moves on the screen, then it "died." I checked the power switch. Thinking the batteries must be dead, I opened the compartment—*no batteries*. I quietly placed the haunted device back into his toy box and never said a word.

Later, when everyone seemed to be back in the house, I decided to play a prank on the girl. I was gonna jump out of her closet to scare her. But she carried her baby sibling into her room with her and started up a one-way conversation.

"What do you think of Justin?"

Oh no! I'm fucked!

Do I gently step out and apologize right now?

"I like him."

What?

Well, I guess this is how trolls and closet monsters are born. I live here now. I can never escape without causing us both great embarrassment.

Serendipity struck and before she could go on, someone called for her attention. I was able to slink away undetected. I was smart or respectful enough, or—most probable—too cowardly to bring it up.

I *had* to hide. I knew this. I heard something I wasn't supposed to, I knew that, and I had to respect the boundaries of her perception, right? I didn't lord over her or suddenly come on stronger. She was younger than me, though we would gradually flirt a little harder, faking a kiss with our hands between our mouths in a motion-freezing game of lights out.

CHAPTER 18

Four and I had been enrolled in a private school a few miles from our house. The public school we were districted in was surrounded by a tall fence and apparently had drug dealers hang out nearby, the fences going up because they would come into the school. Fortunately, my mom and M agreed that probably wasn't the safest place to send us. Three's high school was acceptable, though.

Carrollwood Academy, at the time, was a converted house with weird additions bolted on to form classrooms. Then a trailer in the "backyard" that was wide enough to accommodate two classes. It wasn't large, twenty to thirty kids ranging from daycare to eighth grade.

However, I was a boy hitting puberty in Florida, all the angst and grief I felt was only amplified by my biology. I was already an angry kid, now I vacillated between wanting nothing to do with this family and having only them to confide in—and being hormonal in humidity?

Our phys-ed teacher tried giving us basic tennis lessons at the YMCA we used for "gym" class. I wasn't striking the ball hard enough; I couldn't make it over the net to serve *or* return. She called me to the net. "Imagine it's your stepbrother," she said.

Maybe unprofessional, but she knew what button to push. She

served, I knocked the ever-loving shit out of it and sent the ball sailing over the fence and into the creek behind the Y. She watched it sail over, amused, proud.

"I'm sorry!" I shouted.

"No!" she laughed. "You *can* hit it over the net," she said pointing in the direction high above the fence and started to make her real point.

I was wearing my emotions plainly on my face, *all the time*.

I did get my first girlfriend at school, though we only hung out. Another situation where the girl I crushed on had a younger brother that I bonded with. I spent as much time playing video games with him as I spent with her—not knowing what else to *do*.

I mean, I knew I wanted to eventually kiss. I knew that would lead to—other things. But, how? When was that appropriate? I never asked or initiated.

I wasn't mature enough to express that I wanted to feel loved. I wanted emotional and physical connection, compassion from someone else. I was barely a teenager, and I thought love was the missing element in my life.

This girlfriend was a *good* friend. Again, I was too much too quick for someone unsuspecting and unprepared. She broke up with me when I seemed to waffle on how seriously I wanted to be boyfriend/girlfriend or not. I wanted everything. I didn't know what everything was. I didn't want her to reject me for wanting and not knowing what I wanted. Fortunately, she had the foresight to break it off before I spiraled towards any mistakes.

We were in a tiny private school together; we couldn't escape each other. We remained friends the remainder of my time at the school. She was patient when I was starting to show signs of dependence and unrealistic expectations. She was more mature than me. Thankfully.

I don't even remember "breaking up," but it was before Halloween, because I wanted to spend more time with her at the party we were having at the school. I wasn't convincing. We didn't kiss. It wasn't the horror-romance a young author writing horror fiction and comic book stories would desire straight out of a Stephen King novel.

I guess I had a thing for expressing emotional desires at Halloween parties.

The private school would end up moving location sometime after the New Year and Four and I weren't allowed to follow.

Allowed.

My girlfriend's mother was also our teacher and a stakeholder in the school. She *fought* with my mother to let us continue our education with them, she even offered to waive the rest of the year's tuition, at least let us finish the school year. Our friends in the neighborhood were willing to pick us up and carpool to the new location.

My mom refused it all. I never knew the real reason why. Maybe she thought she could do a good enough job being a teacher.

Despite having a few of our school friends in the neighborhood, our social group shrank significantly with this decision. For as alone as I always felt, I was making personal connections with classmates and family friends in far flung Florida. I didn't recognize them at the time. I do now, though. I was looking for what I wanted in a healthy family.

CHAPTER 19

picked up a terrible habit I still struggle with while we went to the Y. There was an Olympic sized swimming pool, and I challenged myself to hold my breath from one end to the other. It would be something I would continue to practice when we would move into a house with a pool. The "exercises" I developed, completely on my own with no supervision, resulted in irregular breathing habits in my daily life. I concluded that I only needed to breathe when I felt compelled to breathe, the same as hunger or thirst.

I recognize I was also trying to shrink, to disappear in silence. I only created problems for myself and exhaustion beyond growing pains.

The fatigue came from more than physiology, though. One night after I had argued with M, I don't recall about what, it wasn't an unusual occurrence, my mom barged into my room with the hallway light on. She sat on the edge of my bed, not blocking the light, but neither lit for how she sat. A shadow.

The sound of my mother's voice, but no words.

"What?" I mustered. "I was almost asleep."

She said something to the effect of I need to try harder to get along. She said it incoherently, maybe inebriated, probably coaxed or bullied into it by M. I couldn't go to my dad's on the weekend anymore to decompress. Once we left Oklahoma, the tensions steadily climbed. I'm sure my mom got tired of hearing the both of us bitch about each other. I was struggling to pay attention.

I told her I didn't care, I wanted her to leave me alone, that I wanted to sleep.

This wasn't her. This wasn't parenting. I felt harassed. Why put up with it?

I was assigned the chore of mowing the lawn, but it was raining off and on. M made snide comments about how I had better get my chore done or I would be grounded or not get allowance or some other threat to a kid. I was tired of hearing it and went out to start mowing the lawn.

In the rain.

My mom came out to stop me. Not M. M was inside bitching about my mowing in the rain, that it could harm the motor, but wouldn't do anything about it himself. She was having to play go between. I explained he had been riding my ass despite it was clearly raining. I said fuck it. I might have even said that out loud. I was swearing more openly. She told me that I did *not* have to mow if it was raining.

M saw me as a resource first, however devalued compared to his own boys. If I didn't complete an assigned task, it was failure and punishment time, excuses be damned, even if they were valid. My mom never took it seriously because she was being harsh herself. I was being grounded or denied some privilege routinely. I was bad, sure, but I was being bad because I was mad at being singled out by everyone in the family. I was stuck in my own negative feedback loop.

My stepbrothers got into their own trouble. Three got into expensive hobbies and drained M's pocketbook. His hobbies were technically minded, though, he got into radio-controlled cars and other electronics. His interests were fostered, even if M complained about it in the process.

What was I into? Video games, art, drawing, and writing. I wanted to get into graphic arts. What if those deep pockets had gone into my art? No, the lawn had better be mowed before Monday morning.

Everyone complains about their chores. Loads of people have strict and overbearing parents. M and I had no love for each other. I think we mutually agreed the house would be better off without me in it. Except—I wasn't leaving without my mom. I think that's what rubbed me wrong all that time, feeling constantly at arm's length from a family, on guard, even from my mother.

We increased our brood of pets. My mom rescued a ginger kitten I named Jesse who would let me wear her around my neck as a scarf. Her eyes were barely open, kittens found without a mother near where my mom worked. I used a paper towel to nurse her and kept her alive. She would eventually develop a habit of picking up her dry food and eating out of her paw instead of burying her face.

Pepper gave birth to her first litter of puppies. Starting in Three's room, she gave birth to eleven pups, birthing them through the house trying to drag herself to her dog bed. Fortunately, we found them all. Cairn Terrier litters range from two to ten. We got the full load. Pete did his job.

With the litter mostly sold, we decided to keep one a little longer than the others who was the spitting image of Pete, whom we imaginatively named Pete, Jr. With the litter eventually sold, my mom then wanted to let go of Pepper and Pete, Sr. I never understood why. Jordan stuck around. Did my mom only want to try out breeding for a round?

I was upset about letting go of Pepper the most. She growled at the old couple who adopted her from us. I always hoped she got used to her new family and they showered her with love.

Pete was a problem dog. I missed him when he was gone, he was playful, but that dog destroyed nearly everything at three inches high. The summer in the kennel had messed him up. Maybe I sympathized with him for that.

That was the house Four and I got rollerblades as Christmas gifts. I would get decent at going forward on them. I never learned tricks or stunts or even how to go backwards, but they became my primary mode of transportation, preferring them to my bike. I could judge distance and effort, of course, but if I wanted to get out of the house and roam the neighborhood or go to the library, it was on my rollerblades.

Among the rare moments of peace, my mom continued to light candles and listen to music. Whatever was catching her fancy at the moment. This habit never left her repertoire as far as I know. Being with her, from birth to a teenager, we'd sit and chill to music. Sometimes we would dance, and there was a lot of singing along with, to, and at each other.

She was into country at this point, it was Garth Brooks in the CD player. I tolerated country music for her sake, and for that I have a soft spot for specific early '90's country music. This evening when the two of us had the living room to ourselves, we danced.

It was dusk, cobalt blue underscoring the orange and yellow flickering candlelight. Beams of setting sun pierced the back windows. I could stand in the same spot if you took me there. We didn't talk, or we talked a lot, these moments weren't few and far between, mind you, this one was particularly serene amid the storm.

I'm sure my stepbrothers were in their rooms. M was away, who knows where. For a moment at least, the room was ours and we were close.

We danced slow to the slow songs, we bopped around to the fast ones, and sang along with the singles. For all the shitty things we had already been through, this was *our* time together. Candles. Music. Dancing.

I was already growing taller than her, but I would try to lay my head on her chest, under her chin when we hugged or held each other. I began to stoop to achieve it. She said I used to do it when I was little and didn't feel good.

CHAPTER 20

When it came to our period of home-schooling, my mom had let me and Four pick out our own textbooks at a depository, with no structure on what to pick. She then expected us to teach ourselves from the books. She made no effort to be an instructor for either of us.

She wasn't a housewife, I think she was either working part-time or was between jobs when she decided she could handle homeschooling. She just did it by staying in her room or watching TV in the living room. The only educational thing she did for us was take us to a science museum, once.

I did, however, invest time toward educating myself. Even though the last few months of the sixth grade were basically fucking off at our leisure. I tried to keep up with the Spanish I had been learning. I tried to teach myself how math worked with only a textbook and answer guide, no one attempting to contextualize concepts for me.

At the end of the school year, we were expected to pass standardized state tests to move on to the next grade. My mom scheduled us with someone who lived what seemed "out of town."

While Four was taking his test, I hung out in the lady's backyard and was struck simultaneously with fear and awe when I saw a vulture sunning some twenty feet away from me. It didn't care about me. It stood there, wings out probably as wide as I was tall. I was taking my yearend exam at an unknown lady's house to go into the seventh grade. I had only half a year of a small business private school sixth grade education. I felt doomed.

We both passed.

The day of our finals there was something on the radio about John Cougar releasing his newest album under his real name John Mellencamp. I remember talking with my mom about pseudonyms, stagenames, and assumed names. I was not aware at the time that I too was living under an assumed identity. One that she had crafted for me. One that she withheld when conversations like this about family and names naturally occurred.

CHAPTER 21

1992 – SUMMER, OKLAHOMA & TEXAS

Summer break between sixth and seventh grade I went and spent time with my dad. These were my decompression periods when I was allowed to be alone. Being all by myself was a rare privilege. I enjoyed time alone when my dad was at work during the week as much as spending time *with* him.

We saw A League of Their Own in the theater. Highly entertaining, vaguely educational, and emotionally effective. I don't know, I felt verklempt by the end, the juxtaposition of history affecting me. We also saw Cool World, I think right before it was time for me to go back. I think we both regretted wasting time in the theater for *that*.

Local video store and Pizza Hut on Friday night. We watched schlock and classics. Horror and sci-fi were always what we rented. I would rent a video game, too, for the week.

Pizza and bad movies should be every dad's date night with their kid(s). I can't have lactose now, and we have streaming video on demand, but there has been plenty of shared junk food and bad entertainment with *my* daughter. There are, of course, more enriching bonding experiences to achieve, and fishing with my dad, being on the lake and enjoying nature was that for me.

Pizza and The People Under the Stairs, though? *C'mon!*

That summer we went on a trip to somewhere in the middle of Texas to attend a family reunion. I would see people I knew, but I would meet our much larger family, my dad's mom's family. There were people of all ages there, and I indeed saw my Buffington cousins and aunt and uncles I was used to seeing at Thanksgiving, but there were a lot more older people, as old as our parents, children of all ages who cliqued off as they do. At twelve there were only a few other kids my age, most were much younger, the children of "children" older than me by ten years, or legit teenagers too cool for the up and comers.

There was one girl, on my dad's mom's side, a great-uncle's son's daughter. Clear? We were similarly aged and feeling lonely amongst family, both of us a little more artsy and liberal even in our youth than the elder crowd. We ended up off by ourselves and exploring a derelict treehouse. We talked about I don't know what; TV, music, movies, and books we were into. The companionship we found in each other helped us both feel a little less alone while completely surrounded.

We would see each other at a couple of other family reunions. I got teased when it became expected to find us together. We may have hung out collectively for all of a day's worth of hours in our only time together, yet we found companionship. I appreciated her for it. I still do.

Playing a game of family baseball, I took centerfield thinking no one could hit anything that far. I was proven wrong by that cousin's father. He smacked one straight up the center and I had been squatting, passively watching the game from a distance. I saw it. Stood up. Shielded my eyes against the sun. Held up my glove, barely moving, and caught the ball. *Everyone* erupted in cheers and hysterics. I was cussed out, too, but it was the easiest I had ever stolen someone else's joy and enjoyed it myself; I probably deserved a cuss.

There were a lot of games. The older folks in the Buffington's and this extended family could be spritely and active. There were the circles of older folks exchanging tales you think about at family reunions. I think it might have been at this family reunion I heard the gruesome tale of one of our members working in a machine shop with his father when he was only a child, maybe in the 1950's, and his father suffered a decapitation. His son carried his head to his neighbor's house to ask for help.

It wasn't told as a ghost story, it was as matter of fact as I've put it here. Horrifying, but it happened. They discussed the fact that it happening to a child, let alone *anyone*, could affect you for the rest of your life. They were talking about mental trauma and PTSD even if they didn't use the terms. There wasn't any jibing or ridicule, but a sympathy, "*wow*, that could really fuck you up."

The Olympics may have been happening around the same time. When it got late and everyone was tired we would all split off for our individual accommodations. My dad and I shared a motel room. We would bathe and veg out for an hour, call it a night, and go hang out with family again the next morning. It was a few days, and I would experience reunions a few more times. I appreciated them, but the outsider syndrome from my home life with the W's affected me everywhere, even with people I had previously felt comfortable with.

I spoke with my mom throughout my visit with my dad. They had moved house, a two-story, and Four and I had the upstairs to ourselves. We had a pool. We'd be going to a nearby public school. I had lucked out and didn't have to help move. I had moved and traveled across the country numerous times in only a few years, I was already tired of it all.

CHAPTER 22

1992-1993 – A HOUSE IN PALM HARBOR, FLORIDA

Our house was on a corner, but we didn't have any extra real estate as a result. One side was on a steep incline that we didn't do anything with. Mowing the grass along it was a pain. The front yard was a couple of palm trees and some decorative plants; there wasn't a lot of grass to mow, yard chores weren't as terrible at this house. The pool became the two-person job that we hated doing every time we did it.

I don't know where to start with this house. It's a jumble of significant memories and all of them want to scream to the front and I'm not sure I have them in chronological order. I know there was a pivotal trip to my dad's house for Thanksgiving. Well—the trip back proving to be the more pivotal part. This is when I started expanding my tastes in comics, music, literature; started flexing my writing muscles. Started becoming *me*. It was a painful experience.

When Four and I went to Palm Harbor Middle School to register as new students, I was only a month from being thirteen. Four wasn't a lot younger than me, but he was taller, and I was barely tall enough to reach the high desk of the registrar. I asked her, "Which one of us do you think is older?"

She guessed Four was, and I rubbed it in his face. I might be smaller, but I was *older*. As if a few months made me that much more *mature*. That meant something to me, then, with him, at that age. *Any* advantage.

Age, the *appearance* of age, has ebbed and flowed with time. Sometimes I looked too old and tired, getting offered alcohol when I wasn't even a teen. Sometimes I looked much younger than my age, getting carded and accused of having a fake ID. High school friends say I haven't changed at all (I have).

I never had classes with Four. Of all the school years we had together, only the private and homeschool did we share the experience. I can almost see our parents asking those public schools to keep us separated from each other, to avoid being disruptive to each other or the class if personal drama boiled over. Going to class, especially at this school, was getting a break from home-life.

The house in Palm Harbor—this is where I loved *Florida*, but not my family. This is where M and I would nearly come to blows. This is when I started to question my mother's love for me. Enough had happened I was already angry with—that I wanted to escape—but I always wanted to protect my mom, too. I wanted us to escape together. This is when it began to dawn, I might need to escape *her*.

There was a lot of arguing between M and my mom going on. Loud. Angry. Slamming doors and threats to leave rose again, but they weren't humorous to me and my stepbrothers anymore. All of us were tired of the stress. I think three hormonal boys trying to figure themselves out against each other, under parents who didn't get along, either, didn't *not* usher in the demise of that family.

For all the arguing, I don't know what it was about. I tuned out a lot. Retreated. Went upstairs to my room. Went outside to ride my bike or skate. The arguing was bad enough we went to family counseling. This was my first encounter with a mental health professional, and they were getting five people who didn't care for each other but supposedly were a family. They had their work cut out for them and we didn't take their advice seriously. We made fun of some of it, a way to decompress from how uncomfortable it had gotten and for all of us to bond in at least something, even if in discomfort.

One of the exercises was the counselor wanted us to arrange the family by their perceived closeness to us and to each other. Put people at a distance in space we felt they were from each other emotionally. On my turn, when I sat at the head of the imaginary table—we were sitting among chairs and a couch—I put my mom on my left, close, within hand-grabbing distance. I placed M, next to her, on her other side, but in a separate chair (we could arrange the furniture to make points). I had Four sit on the end of the couch that was nearer to me, but not *close* to me. Three I placed at the far end of the couch, which by proximity to everyone else, was the farthest from anyone.

I think Three took his spot without even thinking about it, and frankly, probably even agreed with the placement. He was older than Four and I, he was in high school, he didn't want to hang out with his parents or younger brothers.

M barked that that wasn't true and, "You should place—"

The counselor stopped him. "This is Justin's point of view." They turned to me to offer me the opportunity to explain. "And why have you placed Three so far away?"

If you were to look at the arrangement of our house, it wasn't dissimilar to how I had arranged everyone. My older stepbrother had a room that was on the back of the house and out of view of the living area. He spent a lot of time in there. Without the right concepts, I couldn't tell the counselor back then, "he's going through a loner-phase," but they understood.

The counselor said, after how everyone had arranged the family, I had probably been the most honest. All of us could learn from how the others in our family see us. We weren't a unit. We were pieces to different puzzles trying to force-fit.

We did not take it seriously. Not the family as a "unit," anyway. We never went back. Not together. My mom *may* have, though.

This was something I didn't know for a long time, and in hindsight, the anger and the strife, the hurtful things, the disappointment, the frustration, may have all been signs of what was going on that I didn't know about. It makes feeling angry about those things feel wrong. At the same time, the choices being made in that light weren't themselves great, and it reengages the anger.

At some point, I do not know if it was this time, earlier or later, but at *some* point, my mom was diagnosed with bipolar disorder, and signs point towards this time in Florida. I wouldn't know until after she was gone. She never shared that with me. It was the early '90's. Speaking openly about our own mental health was only beginning. We made fun of therapy after we tried it.

CHAPTER 23

M suffered a grievous injury on a date night with my mom. He slipped on a wet floor outside of a restroom and broke his hip. He was already older. This was one of those injuries that could fuck you up for life. If I ever had a reprieve from the hatred I felt for him all those years, it was when he was in a hospital bed and struck with a spasm. Pain is not fun to watch. I felt scared *for* him. These random, agonizing waves of sensation that would lock his body up rigidly. He could do nothing but ride it out. I sympathized, I *empathized*.

Not that trying to offer kindness and patience earned any merit. He became worse when he came home.

After physical therapy, once he was mobile on his own again, he had a cane. He didn't brandish it as a new tool to threaten us with, but there was one of those Peanut's parent-voiced arguments erupting from their bedroom and I heard a violent *whack*, wood against wood.

Privacy be damned, I burst into their room, not entirely sure of what I would see or could do, but it stopped the fight cold. He had struck the end of their dresser, knocking a hole into it.

I think the look of shock, but also malice, that I poured over them, put a stop to *that* level of arguing. At least while anyone was within earshot, anyway.

But often, I wasn't at the house at all. I would ride my bike down to the shopping center that was only a few blocks outside of our neighborhood. Between buying toys at Wal-Mart, comics in a magazine store, and random snacks at the Albertson's grocery store, I also rode around the neighborhood to pass the time. There was a huge tract of land that was being worked to connect some major roads at a more convenient spot behind our neighborhood. We called it the Sandpit.

At the Sandpit, when we saw no one was working, we crawled around the giant mound of earth that had been piled up from or for their ground leveling. It was too soft and loose to do anything with our bikes on, but crawling on it and sitting up higher than normal to look over the neighborhood was fun...for a thirteen-year-old. My stepbrothers were in on it, too.

Instead of smoking, Three picked up *chewing* tobacco as a habit. We learned how to tamp a can of chaw by holding it between your thumb and middle finger and snapping your wrist to thump your index finger on the can. That became a nervous tick of mine for a little while.

I never got the appeal of tobacco, chewing or smoking. Sure, I understood flavor, but I didn't care for it. The times I had inhaled a cigarette, it did nothing but feel bad. I had yet to intentionally smoke marijuana (save for all that lingering secondhand smoke). Even though media up to the 1990's made smoking look cool, what with James Bond's suave lighting up and scenes like Sharon Stone's in Basic Instinct (I remember the cigarette and lighter), I never got into it. Today, yes, I smoke weed, but not tobacco cigarettes. They do nothing for me. Chewing was a *no* outright. Just...*gross*.

I had an adventure that lasted all night long that started at the Sandpit. A friend was spending the night and after midnight we snuck out of the house and headed for the big mound. We were sitting at the top, talking, when a car pulled in at the far end of the lot, a good distance, but we saw their lights. We scrambled down and into the overgrown weeds, ducking out of sight.

It was a cop car! We had the perfect vantage behind a little rise of earth. We were close enough that when they swept their light over the field looking for runners, the beam went over our spot without illuminating it. Another car pulled up. *Back-up*? Had someone called the cops on us? Was there surveillance on the site now? Sure, we were indeed trespassing on an empty construction site, but there wasn't anything dangerous or valuable, it was a big mound of dirt.

My friend and I army crawled our way toward the road the cops had come in from. We couldn't go back in the way we came, that was wide open. There were more trees near the road. By the time we had crawled probably fifty yards, *seven* cop cars had entered the site. It is quite possible we were in the wrong place at the wrong time and avoided something else going on entirely. There was never any shouting or anyone getting onto loud-speakers searching for trespassers. Maybe these bunch of cops also hung out at the empty site. Had we picked the wrong time to be there? That first cop no doubt saw us fleeing, goblins in the weeds, as they pulled in and looked around, but never *pursued*.

Our adventure had begun. We decided against going in the direction the cops all pulled in from. We would take a long walk around the neighborhood until I finally recognized my route to and from school. The Tampa Bay area, and Florida in general, has weird neighborhood structures, they're labyrinths with coils and dead ends and streets that change names because they turned forty-five degrees.

As darkness began to turn to silvery light, black sky giving way to purple and pink, we heard a cat yowling, mournful, scared. It took us a little while to find this adolescent cat up a tree, too scared to make its way back down, no doubt chased there by something. I was smaller and lighter than my friend, he boosted me up to the lowest branch we could reach, and I proceeded to climb and coo and call to the cat. It wanted down, it knew what was up, and didn't retreat from me, but wasn't taking any chances of falling, it clawed into me as I gathered it close to me to try and climb one handed back down. Down was easier, but bloodier. It didn't stick around for a pet, running as soon as I let it go, but free from its plight.

If dawn's early light had helped us in our rescue effort, it also meant it was time to book it back to the house before anyone was up. Luckily, we made it. We hadn't slept at all, spending six hours *perhaps* running from the cops, wandering the streets at night, and being good Samaritans in the end

The wandering out at night, the hooliganism, I *am* lucky I never got into trouble—physically, with the wrong people, with the law. I exhibited some dangerous behavior that could have led to a life of crime or misery. I think I did it all, especially in all that time with the W's, because I felt outcast, shunned, at times by my own mother. I'd rather be alone in the world than with this family. I felt lonely *anyway*, might as well *be* alone.

At the same time, I recognized that I was *being* a bad kid. I was on a path, and I would course-correct soon enough, but if *not* for life's intervention, if I had not been given a choice, if I had stayed the odd-man out of that family, I would have been a different person. Even if I had stayed one more year, I might have been irreversibly damaged. I think I was anyway.

CHAPTER 24

Throughout my life, I had been unintentionally sheltered from death. Having none of my maternal family *around*, my dad's father had passed when he was only five, his mom and siblings were all alive and well, and the misfortune of not maintaining long term friendships, I did not encounter anyone else's dying family members.

I had lost fish. Unfortunately, it is quite difficult to emotionally bond with aquatic life that were pennies on the dollar at the back of Wal-Mart.

When I rescued a baby rabbit from our dogs, I thought we could keep it safe and maybe even domesticate it.

Rather than suggesting we take it to a vet or animal rescue, my mom didn't object. We barely knew the first thing about rabbits: they ate grass in the yard. We put some grass as well as greens from the fridge and some water into a pet carrier to keep it. It wasn't obviously injured or bleeding, the dogs having only briefly encountered it when I broke them off. It let me pick it up, too terrified to retreat. Once in the carrier, it seemed to ease up and move on its own again.

I wanted to keep the carrier in my room, but I wasn't allowed. I'm not sure why *I* wasn't allowed a pet, Four had an aquarium with piranha, Jordan was Three's dog *and* he brought ferrets into the house. Jesse and a son of hers we kept and named Buddy (not so original with the pet names at the time), an all-white cat despite Jesse's ginger stripes, were both outside cats, ruining the eco-system, but also hunting vermin. They did stay inside overnight, though. I wanted a bunny, for myself... The carrier stayed in the living room, right outside our parent's bedroom door.

The rabbit lived through the first night, despite the constraints and stresses. It did not, however, survive the second. Its demise still haunts me. I believe it was scared to death.

When I got up in the morning and came downstairs, through the kitchen, into the living room, I saw Jesse staring inside the carrier. Jesse had done this numerous times, sat and stared at the rabbit. I reached in feeling a cold to the touch and quite stiff *thing* where I saw a bunny. I think the stress from terror finally did the poor thing in.

I recoiled. I empathized. I understood being in a cage and being stared at by someone or something that desperately wants to kill you. I had had *that* nightmare many times. My homelife didn't feel much different. To *die* from being scared? I became inconsolable and refused to go to school. It was April 19th, 1993.

I was on funeral detail in the morning, making a sarcophagus for my wild rabbit out of a shoebox and some gifts of food for the afterlife. I dug a hole in the little bit of backyard we had, not too terribly deep, but enough the dogs wouldn't disturb it. I buried the rabbit and said what I hoped were thoughtful words and apologized for my cat scaring it to death.

When I came back in, the news was on, my mom watching intently. I'm not sure why she had stayed home, too, it was only us watching the news that morning—and for the rest of the afternoon. The Branch Davidians at Mount Carmel Center ranch, several miles north of Waco, had been in a standoff with the FBI. President Clinton let Attorney General Janet Reno handle things how she saw fit.

People died. Horrifically. Vividly. Live on television. The fires erupting from the compound disturbed me knowing people were inside.

I thought the Branch Davidians were weird—dangerous, even. My mom compared them to Jehovah's Witnesses, disdainfully, thinking them both cults. I had vague notions of religious cults. I knew of religious persecution, of course, of people wanting to break away to form their own groups, it's part of America's birth story. To see a cult, on national television, getting airtime on national radio, being fought with by the United States government? It created confusion. When is military or police intervention *absolutely* necessary? Is it *ever* necessary to *that* degree? Our country's official willingness to resort to violence continues to bother me.

My rabbit died, maybe scared of a cat staring at it in a cage. People in Texas were dying, maybe scared of government agents in a complex that had become a cage. It sticks out.

I met Bill Clinton, actually. The previous summer as school had started, he was still campaigning before becoming president. My mom was part of local Democratic campaign efforts, going hard for Clinton. I got swept up in it as well. He was going to be at a rally in Tampa. I got to go to the campaign headquarters, I made a poster with the Energizer Bunny with something about the "Comeback Kid" because polls had shown Clinton falling behind early on. I was at the rally, I listened to him speak, I held up my poster, things wrapped up, and suddenly we were rushing to the airport.

Literally on the tarmac, next to his private jet that would take him to his next speaking engagement, I had a photo-op with then Governor Bill Clinton where he signed my poster, complimented it, shook my hand, and smiled nicely at the cameras with me. I then rushed over to meet Hillary who was—a little less cordial—but not outright rude. I cannot blame a woman in a rush irritated with dealing with her husband's hangers on. She still signed my poster. I still have it.

It's weird to think that Clinton's two terms—eight years—would encompass a major portion of my life's events. Eight years is a long time. I was thirteen at the start of it and twenty-one by the end. That's a significant life change. A *lot* would happen in those years, for us both, and we were at the beginning, standing next to a private jet with a bunch of people snapping photos.

CHAPTER 25

I made a good friend at school who shared a name with an X-Man *and* loved Marvel comics, too. I had a few other kids, one or two a class, I was friendly with. I kind of had a girlfriend, for a little while. I got kicked off the bus for being a bully. I would develop long standing musical tastes during this school year. I would get my first taste of telling my stories to an audience and being "published."

Middle school, especially packed in with a bunch of *other* hormonal, agitated kids, was dismally terrifying. Seventh grade, in Palm Harbor, though, I saw some of the most violent fights between boys I've seen in real life, in all my life.

Arriving at the top of some stairs, two boys were writhing on the floor, wailing fists in every direction trying to land anything. There was blood everywhere. Kids were yelling "fight!" A teacher managed to yell high enough over the din to bring things to a halt. This happened a couple times a week. Bullying and fighting was rampant. I was immune to neither and perpetrated some awfulness as well. I did however manage to escape public school, entirely, without being in a physical fight. Well—there were some attempts by other boys to fight me, but I always got out of it. I learned both how to vanish in plain sight and defuse and talk my way out of problems.

The worst bullying against me was from one kid in my math class and it severely intensified after I got glasses. I knew I needed glasses from my Spanish class. Assigned seating had me sitting in the back corner of that class while my teacher wrote all along the blackboard, things I needed to read. I couldn't. The bullying didn't start at school with glasses, though.

We had family meetings, a useful holdover from the therapy sessions. I was sitting in one of the armchairs, I think Four was sitting next to me in the other armchair, usually our parent's seats. Three was sitting on the loveseat and my mom and M were sitting on the couch. I had my moment to express myself in the meeting and announced that my sight was going bad. I needed glasses.

M, inexplicably—*angrily*—denied it. I was used to being accused of lying. I did it. This was absurd, though. Why would I lie about this? Why would I want glasses? At this time wearing glasses made you a nerd when that was an insult (said the kid with too many comic books to count and obsessed with cartoons and video games, but wearing glasses?).

I stopped him in his tracks. "*You* are not inside *my* head, M! You cannot see what I see, and I can't see shit! I can't read the blackboard at school."

My mom stopped me, but not out of anger. She believed me. She wore glasses, she knew I'd probably need them eventually. Here we were. She would take me that weekend. M wanted to argue that I didn't need glasses, that it was too expensive, that I was seeking attention... She stopped him, too. I don't know if they argued more about it later, but this meeting was over.

I did go to an optometrist.

My first eye-exam was an *experience*. It was startling to see how *bad* my vision was. When we landed on the right prescription for me, I wondered how long had I let my vision go without realizing it? Perceiving individual leaves on trees, at a distance, instead of a cloud of color, I was seeing something for the first time all over again. I was excited to be able to *see*, I was grateful.

When I got to school and the kids inevitably started calling me names, it made me loathe my impairment. I *knew* I wanted laser vision correction one day. Something else, however, took over—with time—glasses became a part of *my* identity. My face looks weird *without* glasses now. Also, the rate of my vision's deterioration took laser out of the equation. It is cheaper to get glasses every few years than it would be to have the surgery only to have my vision go bad again in ten years and still need glasses anyway. It took a while to get there. At first, there was that one kid in math class.

"Hey, geek!" he hissed. "Hey, nerd! Hey, hey! Hey, *dweeb*!"

I ignored him. It was the most annoying sort of intimidation. Not even insulting—stupid, stereotypical words to throw at someone because of a studious appearance, which apparently glasses completed. It was when he started hitting me with spitballs from three rows over that I lost it.

"Fucking stop!" I roared as I stood, interrupting the teacher, and shocking the entire class.

Yes, I was thirteen in the seventh grade. Cussing—in class, in front of an adult—was certainly frowned upon. My teacher believed me that something was wrong.

When asked, I pointed and explained "they" were calling me names and shooting spitballs at me. I didn't know their names. Did they even know mine? They were picking on me now because I had glasses. A single change. A "handicap." *Anything* to get one over on someone.

She walked over, finally settling on my antagonist. He would face repercussions, being sent to the principal's office. My teacher would also keep me after class, and I was afraid I would have to face some sort of punishment myself for swearing. Instead, she said she was proud of me for standing up for myself. There may have been a humorous jab about watching my mouth. I did not get into trouble.

Later, that kid would apologize in a way to angle at making friends. I think I made a long "Eh," at him.

I had a few more teachers who were supportive of me. That math teacher, my science and history teachers, art, and my first English teacher, who ended up taking a leave of absence part way through the year and we had a permanent substitute.

I guess that's *most* of my teachers for seventh grade. I felt connected to these people, they cared about me and my wellbeing. They supported and fostered my creativity. Before that first English teacher left for the year, she put together a collection of poetry from her students that I got into. My first publication! She also let me read my X-Men fanfiction I had written aloud to the class. Somehow, that went better than expected, no one made fun of me, instead I think I made a few more friends.

I shouldn't have been surprised. X-Men: The Animated Series was a smash. X-Men will always be culturally relevant and topical. It speaks to the world, and at that time, I was telling my own stories with those characters and other kids did not care that I was just another kid. We all were weird and felt like mutants.

It would be *that* teacher that I felt comfortable enough with to share something my mom had told me.

I was sitting on the floor, drawing my own comic characters. Smoke lingered in yellow lamp light. Another evening M was away, traveling or working late. I don't remember the entirety of the conversation, but it was the early '90's and birth control, sex education, and abortion were a big part of the zeitgeist. I asked her about abortion, her thoughts, its place in the world.

She believed it was the woman's decisions about what to do with her body. She sounded reasonable. Why did I then ask her if she had life to do over again, would she abort me? What possibly ran through her mind *that* her son would ask that? Did she run some lines before answering? Time stretched out as she weighed her response.

"Yes." She said, "I was too young."

I didn't know how to feel, or that I should feel anything. I found it to be another reasonable response. I knew she had us young, I imagine her response could have been the same for him, too. She was too young and having kids put her in a bind she had to escape. I *understood*.

I can't say for certain I took offense, I didn't think in the moment she didn't want *me*, but if she could *have planned* her life, she would have had both of us later. Understanding how time and the nature vs nurture argument and biology all work, I wouldn't exist without my set of circumstances. Neither would she. Subconsciously, it started eating at me. The doubt and feeling unwanted percolated through the rest of the night and into my next day at school.

I knew something was off about my own mental well-being. This was probably early, situational depression. I turned to my English teacher. I told her about the conversation, the meaty bit, but I didn't know what to do with the information or describe how I felt. I didn't know how I felt or how *to* feel.

I think my teacher was shocked and could read my twisted-up emotions on my face. She was soothing, caring, she may have even given me a hug.

"I'm sure she didn't mean she didn't want you." She said.

She reminded me of my old kindergarten teacher. Another older African American woman who saw my creative potential and supported it as much as she could for a few hours a week. She wasn't my first teacher I sought emotional grounding with—she wouldn't be the last—I appreciated that she saw a hurt kid and didn't brush me off.

The fanfiction I had written included one of my original characters. I had decided to give him the "no guns" rule.

I was telling my mom about it while she tanned as we hung out by the pool.

"Why did you decide that?" she asked me.

"I don't like guns, really…"

Mind, of course I had drawn many a character, including this one, with guns of all sizes. This was the time of Todd McFarlane and Rob Liefeld, excessive weapons were part of a character's costume anymore. I wanted this character to be gun-free, someone who valued life.

"You probably don't like guns because you were held at gunpoint once." She declared.

"What?"

How she explained it made little sense. "Your grandpa was drunk and holding you in his lap, and when I tried to take you from him, he held a gun to your head and said if he couldn't have you then no one could."

There were too many questions, but I asked first, "What did you do?"

"I grabbed you!"

"What?" I exclaimed again. "While he was holding me with a gun?"

She shrugged. "I just did."

Then I asked, "Grandpa..." and I pointed vaguely north, indicating my Grandpa Fred from New York. "Or my biological father's dad?"

"No, not them. Not *really* your grandpa." She conceded. "A 'boyfriend's' dad."

In my personal narrative at the time, I understood that there had been my biological father. A vague concept of a guy who taunted me with my own dirty drawers. The guy that my mom shattered the plaster on the wall arguing with (though I could not be certain those were different men). Then my dad, followed by M. Was it the guy before my dad? This random detail belied a history I was completely unaware of, but trying to dig into my mother's past was difficult.

Get her talking about happy memories and she could go on and laugh and it was wonderful to hear stories of sibling rivalry, which made me miss my aunts, even though I had only met them a few times —from my point of view. Ask something difficult, even if I felt I deserved truths, she could bend the conversation back toward what *she* wanted to talk about or shut down. I know from others that this was a part of her personality, she tried to bury anything uncomfortable.

She never offered a satisfactory answer. It would later be corroborated by an aunt, but I trusted my mom when she told me stories about my past, even if just cryptic snippets. Were they slips? Did she regret the honesty and close back up?

CHAPTER 26

Now, I don't know what they had going on there in Florida, but sometimes school assemblies had *nothing* to do with school events or education. One time they had a big cat handler show us some tigers at school. It could have been one of the players from Tiger King.

However, one was an egregious and predatory advertising campaign to get kids to go home and talk all about…sound systems.

They set up in our gym these huge black screens with laser lights and stage lighting and maybe the entire wall was fucking speakers, but they basically gave us a half hour concert of chart toppers of the day at crystal clear, eardrum bursting decibels. We were jamming and cheering, school be damned, can we rock out for the rest of time? Indeed, *yes*! There was only thirty minutes left in the school day, it'd take everyone about that long to disperse back to class and settle down anyway, they let us go early for the day straight out of the assembly.

This is the day I heard Nirvana's Lithium at epic volume in a crowd of twelve to fourteen-year-olds going apeshit when the guitars started screaming. I had been listening to a lot of early '90's rap and R&B, I still did and still do, but that song, the last song they chose to play, made something click. I felt those words, those vibes, the electricity in the air, I think it was when I realized music wasn't only for fun. It was a language of sound and poetry that could speak to your personal experience. It could be truly *moving* while *also* being fun. It was energizing beyond my comprehension.

I kinda had a girlfriend who also helped with music appreciation. Another situation where we only hung out at school and talked on the phone. She lent me heavy metal tapes and it was music that we talked about a lot of the time.

Maybe it was being amped. Maybe it was getting out early and every kid on the street going in the same direction. Maybe it was me being a stupid kid. I was riding my bike home, I saw a large group of kids taking up the sidewalk in front of me, I chose to cross the street. I looked over my left shoulder, and saw kids, open street, and a car sitting at a T-stop waiting to turn. That's what I *saw*.

The car either was already in motion or we both punched it at the same time, but not even halfway through the street, I felt a sudden and jarring shift in orientation. My glasses flew off my face and I saw white light.

Quantum Leap was one of my favorite shows of the time and seeing myself enveloped in brightness, I said to myself, maybe out loud, "Oh boy."

There is nothing when you're knocked out. There is no void, there are no dreams, and there is no time. Nothing exists in there and there is nothing to remember if you come back. There is however, for me, then, an awareness that time was missing when I came back.

My memory kicks back in with me standing up. I looked down into a car with old people inside. I thought I had been knocked to the street —no passage of time—they got out and feigned concern. This seemed too cavalier, this situation required more urgency and care. Where is my bike? Why does my arm hurt?

"We didn't see you there," the old man said. "Are you okay, son?"

No, I have been hit by a car! I am still in my backpack, with books in it, and I was on the ground—*oof*! *There's* my bike!

"I'm fine..." I mumbled.

I picked up my bike, in a daze, I wanted to get home. I maybe waved off some follow-up questions. Why didn't anyone stop me?

These adults hit me with their car! No matter who's at fault for this accident, make sure the kid is okay! Why didn't I stop myself? Why was I leaving the scene? Why didn't I rage in their faces? This was a neighborhood, why hadn't any kids gone and knocked on doors?

Kid gets knocked to the street by elderly couple in a car, no big whoop.

I'll jump ahead here for a moment before we see myself home. I learned from friends and witnesses that it was hard to tell who was at fault, it happened fast, and everyone was shocked. As it was told to me, I hit the ground and slid halfway under their car. They got out to check on me where I was out cold. They then proceeded to *pull me* from under the car (no regard for potential spinal injury) and get back into the car preparing to leave. Some kids thought I was out upwards of five minutes. Then I came to and rocketed to a standing position and interrupted their attempted flight. Despite avoiding a hit and run, I took the initiative to saunter off.

Sense and reason weren't present on that street. Everyone was in shock, no one called 911, we all dispersed.

I hobbled my way home, unable to effectively operate my left arm. I stumbled into the house and then into one of the armchairs in the living room where an hour or two must have passed because the next thing I knew, my mother was home and shocked to find me in the darkened living room.

"What are you doing in here in the dark?" she barked. Her tone was accusatory, I don't know why.

I distinctly croaked, "I got hit by a car."

She leaned over me and turned on the lamp. I winced. She scoffed in disgust, "You're bleeding all over the chair! Get up!"

"Oh?"

Only then did I notice the gash and scrapes across my elbow and forearm. She urged me up and away, turning her attention to the chair.

It was a long night, alone, in my room. I cleaned myself off, shook the shock, told the story as I knew it when everyone was home. Everyone assumed I was okay.

That's it!

No rush to the ER to check for fractures or trauma. No feigned concern for my well being. I was being let down by everyone. I felt scared and hurt. I complained about my arm, but I didn't ask to go to the hospital, and no one suggested or insisted on it.

The next morning my left arm was throbbing and it hurt to turn. I knew I wouldn't be able to ride my bike to school. I asked my mom for a ride to school.

"You're fine." She chided, not giving me the time.

Feeling defeated and resigned to my fate, I got ready and tried my best to wrangle my bicycle out of the garage. I didn't beg to stay home, I didn't demand my mother's assistance, I tried to soldier on.

I'm right-handed, it's amazing how little you realize you use your non-dominant hand until it's suddenly incapacitated. Or worse, actively painful to use.

Before I finally got going, my mother called out to me as I struggled with my bike from the garage. She relented and would give me a ride. Reluctantly, though she didn't say that part, she emanated it. I was grateful, but her silence was making me feel guilty I was putting my mother *out*.

In one day, I became a grunge rock fan and witnessed a calamity of errors all around me while no one helped. Things changed then. I felt let down by every facet of society and people in my life. My willing-ness to go along with it was a result of not knowing or expecting any better from people.

I think there was some walking to and from school for a little while. That permanent English substitute saw me walking one day and offered me a ride. Then proceeded to talk about how evolution didn't make sense and I couldn't wait to get out of the car.

When I did start riding my bike again, I was *bumped* by another driver who let off her brake as I was weaving between stationary traf-fic. We met eyes and she looked horrified and mouthed "sorry." I shook my head.

Looking back on my life and all the times I was simply let down and not even worthy of an afterthought, I think my mother being more concerned with blood on her chair than the welfare of her own son after being struck by a car, *then* initially refusing to help again the following morning, stands out as feeling unwanted. I was now convinced I was a burden. After four years with this family, only ever to chase and "protect" my mom, I still felt I was held at arm's length.

The song Lithium can take me back to that afternoon. I can be in the gym, sitting at the top row of the bleachers eye level with the top of the stack of speakers. How *warm* it was outside when we were let go a little early for the day. I know I looked over my shoulder before I crossed the street, yet I always end up feeling gravity change suddenly and a gap in awareness. I can feel the shock, and then the cascading shock and disappointment.

CHAPTER 27

The pivotal Thanksgiving trip. It contributes to all this feeling unwanted. There are a few reasons I don't care for Thanksgiving, a lot of it around my food anxiety, but for a few years, I routinely contracted the flu, always around Thanksgiving. Always a miserable time. That year was no exception. What was *especially* bad about it, though, was the trip home.

I got sick in Dallas, throwing up suddenly on the concourse. I couldn't stop to feel bad, only having a few minutes to make my connecting flight back to Florida. I threw up, twice, in the air. I was incredibly embarrassed, but also apathetic. I was sick from the holiday. *Again.*

Arriving in Florida, I was greeted at the gate by M. Only M. I felt worse.

I think he made idle greetings, how was my trip and all that.

"I got sick and have been throwing up. I feel awful."

We got my bags in the back of the truck and I crawled into the cab, where my backpack was on the floorboard.

"I'm gonna drop you off at school so you can at least get half a day in."

I had gotten back the same day school was back in session.

"I am *sick*, M." I reiterated. "Just take me home."

"You worthless little shit." He said, and then nothing else for the ride to the house.

Before the end of the school year, though, M and my mom got into it bad. My mom was ready to leave. For real this time.

"Justin, get a bag, we're leaving right now."

I mean, *at least* she knew to include me in her threats to leave. Getting the least out of this family seemed to be the most difficult.

It was raining, heavily. I asked where we were going to go. She didn't know, she was tired of all the fighting and *wanting* to leave all the time. I packed a few days clothes, a few trinkets to entertain myself, and I stole money from the communal change jar as a last fuck-you.

However, our escape was short-lived. M chased us down and when mom stopped at a gas station, he stood pathetically outside the driver's side window, getting soaked, and begging my mom to come back, they could work things out.

I didn't listen to any of it. I don't know what they argued about because I didn't care what they argued about. It was always background noise, inane, pointless. When it became *my* decision to make, I fucked up.

He tried to apologize to me, too, that we could work on *our* relationship, too. Empty words.

My mom looked at me, "What do you want to do?"

It wasn't a question, though. She wanted my permission to give him another chance. If I didn't, it might be the apartment all over again, *why couldn't I be happy for her*? I was outraged they were putting this on *me*. They both knew I was unhappy. The rain came down, his hangdog face and wet clothes lingered in the window, and my mom pleaded through her eyes for permission she didn't need from me. She wanted freedom from responsibility.

We *all* think about old decisions. Old things we've said or done and how we wish we could have those moments back. We wish we could live life over again from a certain moment, then we could fix everything. I wished I could have stayed with my dad instead of ever moving with the W's. It can't ever come true, because that benefit of hindsight is only gained by living our lives.

But if I could pick myself up out of time and move me back in with my dad, *without* the benefit of future knowledge—only tweak history a little to get me out of there and let life unfold—I would have told them to fuck off. I wanted to. I hated M and I was getting there with my mom. I wanted to say I wanted to go *home*, but that meant to my dad's. Instead, I meekly agreed to go back.

Getting myself out of there sooner would have saved time, because after I left that house for summer break, I would never go back to Florida. There are experiences I had living in Florida that shaped me, there are people I met that helped form me. From 1991 to 1993, I was under constant psychological warfare. The shenanigans I got up to were threatening to get me into serious trouble one day. If I could close this chapter sooner, I would.

I stayed through the end of the school year. The students knew about a new school that had completed construction and some kids would be going to the eighth grade at a different school from Palm Harbor Middle. Some of us didn't know if we would see each other the next school year. I think, subconsciously, I had a feeling my time was ending here anyway.

I called that kinda-girlfriend. We had broken up when I became interested in another girl. I should be completely honest: that kinda-girlfriend I had was awesome, and I mistreated her when I had eyes for another girl I had no chance with. I still spoke with my "ex," we still had mutual friends. We were too young to be doing anything yet. When school was out and I was preparing to go visit my dad for the summer, I called her up to ask if she wanted to hang out.

What I *wanted* to say, but lacked the eloquence or tact to express was, I wasn't sure I would see any of my friends again. Of them, I knew I was going to miss her the most. I was sorry I broke up with her. If she was willing, I wanted a kiss goodbye. I didn't think I was coming back.

I didn't say *anything* to that effect. Instead, I was obtusely direct, "I thought, maybe, we could—kiss?"

"You want to *make-out*?" she asked.

She sounded incredulous, offended. I had made a mistake—

She said something to the effect that she wasn't sure if she and this other kid were officially a thing. She wanted to call him and then give me a call back. I agreed to wait.

She didn't take long. I don't know if she was telling the truth or not, it was an effective way to tell me "No," regardless. She said she did indeed have a boyfriend now and we said cordial goodbyes at that point. I hope she did call that boy and asked him outright, "Are you my boyfriend?" Even better, "*Will* you be my boyfriend?" I hope she took control of her relationship status and who she would do what with from then on. I can't claim I emboldened or empowered her, but I hope she kept it anyway.

There was no elaborate goodbye to the W's. Probably, "see you in a couple months." I was gone. Leaving Florida was that easy and uneventful. I wouldn't know I had *escaped* for a while. This was the end of my time in a stepfamily. The damage was done, and the cracks were spreading, I was the first chip to drop off. The damage and cracks spread further than the family; they were in me, too. The schism between my mom and I became a fixture, too.

CHAPTER 28

1993-1995 – HOME AGAIN, TULSA, OKLAHOMA

Summer of 1993 for a lot of American kids marks the year of Jurassic Park. I had partially read the book when the movie hit theaters, buying a copy for my flight home. I knew about the movie coming up. I had seen the secret and edited set photos in the months of production where they built viral interest in how they were going to make their dinosaurs. I had also sat in the back of the grocery store outside our neighborhood in Palm Harbor and read the last chapter of the book sitting on the edge of the shelf.

Yeah, I was one of *those* people, I needed to know how something ended to determine if I wanted to go on the adventure. I'm better about consciously avoiding spoilers, these days, but knowing stuff in advance can sometimes recontextualize an experience. In this case, the movie and book don't end the same at all, characters are different, some live who don't and die who don't, entirely awesome scenes from the book aren't presented until Jurassic Park III (an underrated and better follow-up to the initial movie) eight years later. Movies and books became competing mediums through which to judge a concept or story.

For the record, the book is better in my opinion, and the Lost World book *much* better than its film adaptation, but I enjoy Jurassic Park and JPIII as films on their own.

I devoured several novels that summer. I had been reading some youth stuff here and there, required text at school, and my comic books, but getting into paperbacks kicked into high gear. We went to the bookstore more often than the movies or to even rent movies. My dad and I would get a few books and then trade them until we had completed that week's haul and go buy three or four more mass-market paperbacks.

I was visiting my dad for summer break, fully under the impression that in August I would be heading back to Palm Harbor and finishing middle school, the eighth grade there at Palm Harbor Middle School.

Then my mom showed up. In Tulsa.

Drove herself and some personal effects. She was taking a break from M, and she wanted some actual distance and time to herself, so she followed me. I was flummoxed and exhilarated. Could my mom finally be breaking free?

I would spend time with her as well, splitting time between my parents by the weekend again, however vice versa from previously.

This one afternoon my mom was dropping me off, it must have been late or the weekend, I don't remember the date, but she said: "I'm going to stay here."

This was as perplexing as admitting to stealing Ronald McDonald's handkerchief. I don't think I said anything, but my face did.

"I'm leaving M and I'm going to stay here. *You* have a choice: you can stay with your dad, or you can go back to Florida—if you want to."

What the fuck? Go back to Florida *without* her?

"I'll stay here."

I was disgusted with her offer. Why would she even suggest that I would *want* to return to that family if she wasn't there? I was only there *because* of her.

There's a level of betrayal I'm only recognizing as I write this. Some of that spoiler-material that recontextualizes as it advances.

In a day or two when my dad was trying to make final plans for my departure, I corrected him saying that I would not be going back to

Florida. I was going to stay with him and Mom was leaving M, too, moving here permanently. He was shaken. I knew after I told him, by his surprise, my mother hadn't planned this. She was gambling that she was "safely" dumping me on my dad.

I've wondered about the phrasing she posed my scenario as. She was moving out. I could stay with my dad or the W's, as if that was even a choice. Staying with her wasn't offered among the choices.

I was being dumped. My dad was being burdened—and he will say he was not, but let's all be pragmatic, "Surprise! You must now clothe and feed a kid and get him into school in a few weeks when you thought you were going back to the single life!" is not, *not* a burden.

Not to sympathize too much with a man I loathed, my mom was leaving M behind in a lurch given a two-income household quite by surprise. She was shaking up several lives on a whim.

My mom *broke* free. From all of it. She had a moment to herself, and it might be back in Oklahoma of all places, but she was now truly single, self-reliant, and independent. I wonder if my mom thought I was, too? What if on the off chance my dad couldn't afford it? She was breaking free from *me* as well. Would she have kept me?

That's an intrusive thought, isn't it? Why *should* I think that? My dad *was* there for me, he rose to the occasion and challenge. My mom left the marriage I had begged her to never enter. My brain at the time couldn't comprehend she might need that level of alone time. Why should I be selfish and accusatory—except that I was thirteen and she didn't check with anybody first...

It is immensely frustrating, in real time, to recognize a woman in crisis, but also a woman with responsibilities, but *also* a woman who was or was not managing a possible mental health disorder diagnosis —but I didn't know it at the time. That keeping things from me makes revisiting the memories and how I felt about them until I learned *behind the scenes* details that she would never share with me herself, it shades everything differently.

My mother was flawed, and this was a major example: her skirting of *huge* responsibilities. If I play "what if..." games—*what if* she had tried to maintain the status quo and we had gone back to Florida? *What if* she had kept custody of me while trying to figure herself out when she felt maybe she couldn't do it anymore? Was that any safer for me?

The truth is, these slights and betrayals, they were always forgiven. She was happy to be alive. Even after a detestable argument with hateful words exchanged in the heat of some sort of inebriation, things could be waved away in a day or two. A walk at a park and idle chit chat bandaged a lot of the little wounds.

Bandaged.

The next year was memorably nice with her. She opened more about her past. Or, she at least told me stories that took place in the past, giving me an image of her past. We were back to catching films and appreciating new music. We did a lot of nature walking out in the Mohawk Park region.

She stayed for a couple of years, and true to fashion, they were a *packed* couple of years. I was living with my dad now, and my mom, the person I had lived with nearly every day of my thirteen years, was the part-time parent.

The lifting of the veil began slowly. The revelations yet to come. The choices yet committed to. The longer I was away from my mom, the more I saw the problems with the life I had lived. The objective truth that the last few years had been abusive, that she bore responsibility. That even before then, she had shown signs of her own brands of abuse.

She was my mom and that was the past and things could work out going forward.

I wanted it to be true.

There I stood with my dad at the calendar, confused myself at his confusion and this betrayal of confidence on everyone's part by my mom. Disappointment. My dad was willing to step up, thank whatever it is that binds us. He would have me enrolled at Woodrow Wilson Middle School and show me a route I could bike since it wasn't far. He was ready and willing to continue housing me under his, *our* roof, even if my mom hadn't checked with him first. Even if I had personally failed to discuss it with him that same day, thinking things had been settled between the adults. It doesn't matter, he played the hand he was dealt.

He still worked at the same shop he had met my mom at. He wasn't living in the lap of luxury, but he was comfortable enough for himself. He was *happy* to take me on as a responsibility. Hell, instead of sacrificing his season tickets for the local hockey team, he committed to buy me a set, too. I love him ever more for that. At the times I needed someone, and my mom couldn't be that someone, my dad was.

I began to trust my dad more than I trusted my mom. The structure, as light as it was, the routine, that I did not find monotonous, created a foundation I felt safe on. This was my childhood home. *My* old bedroom. My furniture, my space, my familiar surroundings. I had now moved ten times in four years. From 1989—from home to the first apartment, the second apartment, Broken Arrow, Tulsa Union school district, two apartments in Akron, Ohio, then to Florida into an extended stay hotel in Tampa, Houses in Clearwater and Palm Harbor, then back to Tulsa in 1993. This was the landing platform I needed, but I think I'll always be a bit shaky.

I am not surprised that I crave stability. I am not surprised that I am not good at making or maintaining friendships.

I wasn't done being a dipshit by any means. I had a lot more misbehavior yet left in me. I calmed down over the next few years a little. I think I was stressed out and acted out a lot more in the stepfamily. Acting out for my share of the attention. Finding that the attention I received was often negative. Here, I was the sole-focus. I didn't vie for attention, not even from my mom! She had stayed!

CHAPTER 29

That combination of "please pay attention to me" that was essentially alleviated at home, and the fact I didn't know how to make friends or express interest in people, made for a clown at school. I had reconnected with old friends every time I came back to Tulsa. This time around, at this school, though, there was barely anyone familiar. Back through the grinder of trying to be social, and I knew I would do it *again* when I transitioned to high school. I became a fool, a jester responding to the situation, because if people were laughing—at me, with me, I didn't care—if they were *laughing* then they weren't being mean.

I still had that fear of getting into some random physical fight. I didn't want to run into a hormonal prick with a fist looking for a face. It almost happened, though. I knew *no one*, I sat at the edge of a cafeteria table and scarfed what I wanted from the tray and then headed outside for recess. This was the first day, still summer, still hot outside. I was standing against the wall outside the doors of the cafeteria, in the shade. I was people watching, when out of nowhere a boy came flying through the air, his foot aimed for my chest.

Physics and my poor-breathing habits saved me. I didn't have much air in my lungs, I was against the wall, I didn't get knocked down or the air knocked out of me, I got aggressively shoved by a foot. He, on the other hand, flopped to the ground with me staring down at him, unaffected. I didn't say anything. Neither did he. His friend, who had either dared him to do it or egged him on in a threat, laughed hysterically from ten feet away.

I think my lack of reaction, that I didn't even pull my hands from behind my butt against the wall, that I was staring at him confused, sobered him to the fact *he* was the fool now. He got up and went back to his friend, maybe calling me a "freak" to say *something*. That kid would go on to persistently try to make friends with me. I wasn't interested.

I did eventually recognize someone, but someone I hadn't seen since the fourth grade, and I got perhaps a little too excited. That girl that I *like-liked* was on the playground with her friends. I called her name and began to trot over, but she squealed and hid behind her friends. They giggled and watched in confusion as I tried to get close enough to say "hi," but she wasn't having it.

I gave up, realizing this wasn't what she wanted at all. I would only see her between classes, and it was always as strangers. I had made my impression and she remained unimpressed.

I recognized her mother at a school event and said "hi" to her. She recognized me and seemed charmed. I didn't lament that her daughter had avoided me, only wished her well.

I don't blame her for it one bit, but my confidence took a blow. I wouldn't have a girlfriend for years. Not that I didn't try. I was bad at trying. I think my elementary school crush knew it.

Friends materialized, though. I had my old best friend from elementary school that I still hung out with on the weekends. The friends I made, though... That streak of misbehavior still had an outlet. One old friend from Lanier was already smoking weed, and kids would meet up behind the church across the street from Wilson and get high. Or play games that make you starve your brain of oxygen to get "high." We—kids are dumb, okay?

One time I was smoking weed, intentionally, of my own accord, offered by my friends. They criticized my technique, I didn't care. We sat there for maybe half an hour and shot the shit, then I realized the time, my mom was expecting to pick me up at my house soon. I rushed on my bike and probably worked whatever little THC I had in my body right out, but I did still get nervous around my mom, that thrill of "will I get caught—does she know?" She probably did as I ate three pudding cups from her fridge.

Those were the kind of friends I made in the eighth grade. Hooligans. Being bad on our own. We never got into vandalism or theft. We hung out and looked at porn and played video games. Sometimes there was smoking, cigarettes or joints, stolen from parents or older siblings. I didn't smoke often. I had a paranoid experience and began to fear it, remembering everything with my mom. I didn't want to lose control of *me*.

I only had one brush with trouble at this school. My first period was a study-hall, meant to give us time during school to, well, *study*, but also do "homework." We all treated it as a free hour and would sit with our cliques and play games or talk. Prior to this event and well afterwards, that continued to be the case, but for some reason, one day, our supervisor—a teacher whose job it was to mind us for the forty-five minutes we were there—was on everyone's case about being quiet and doing something school-adjacent, read, study, homework, *something*. I had nothing to do, neither did a friend of mine, I think one of us made the other laugh and the teacher called *me* out for it.

I explained I didn't have any homework to complete, and we weren't bothering anyone around us, but he wasn't looking for a debate. I think he told me to either be quiet or find something to read.

"This is dumb as hell." I said.

Now we *are* in an argument. "*What* did you say?"

"This isn't even a *class*, I don't have anything to work on, I'm not bothering anyone else, what does it matter?"

He was tired of me. "You can go to the principal's office."

"This is fucking bullshit." I said, picking up my bookbag and heading for the door.

"Wait."

Now I had done it. I turned on him, he handed me a slip to give to the office staff. He didn't take enough time to write an explanation of what had transpired, it was a hall-pass, but I knew I was going to be in trouble for swearing and being a jerk.

The principal took a while to see me, probably conferring with my study-hall teacher before sitting down to talk with me. I was never scared. Bored and frustrated. Even if they were going to call my dad, what had I done? Talked in a not-class? That's how I felt about it, never considering, sometimes kids gotta do what the superior says to keep the peace. I was never particularly compliant. I still struggle with it.

"Mr. So-&-So said you were disruptive during study-hall and refused to comply with his requests."

I waited for the accusations of the swearing. They did not arise. I was confused, but I stayed tight-lipped.

"We agreed a week's in-house detention is an appropriate consequence for your actions and we hope you will use that time to reflect on your behavior with teachers and in front of your peers."

Allusions to being rebellious? *Vive la rébellion étudiante!*

I reported directly to the in-house detention room. It was on the backside of the cafeteria, hidden away, and stored a *lot* of folding chairs. There were a couple of tables and maybe five other boys in there and another supervisor basically baby-sitting, but he was way more chill. He taught two periods of P.E. outside of watching us.

How it worked: a student-aide would deliver our day's assignments from our teachers in the morning. The expectation we use our entire time in detention working on those class assignments and any homework assignments. We were expected to turn in those assignments the following morning. It was basically self-taught and self-paced. Personally, I would do my work as soon as it was delivered, getting an entire day's reading and assignments done in an hour and a half. The rest of the day, we would play paper games, hangman, football, whatever. Sometimes we would get into conversations with our supervisor that were refreshingly adult while still entirely childish. Someone would have a CD, tape, or we would play the radio. It was the best week of school I ever had.

My appreciation for music continued to grow and become something identifiable, I knew what I appreciated and wanted more of. Tool's Undertow had come out in April, but Sober and Prison Sex, with their horror-tinted videos and cryptic songs about indulgence, were thriving on MTV and local rock radio. Nine Inch Nails would release The Downward Spiral in early 1994. I was decidedly horny and introspective. A teenaged navel-gazing psychosexual philosopher.

In December of 1993, Nirvana's Unplugged in New York aired. I know there was at least one night my mom and I caught it together. We were in her apartment downtown, a studio, the apartment I based the one in *Red Clouds* on. A kitchen, a living area, a closet, and little more than a water closet *inside* the closet. We sat on her couch and watched her 13″ tube television under lit candles and probably some incense.

When the CD was released a year later, after Kurt's death, my mom took me to buy it. She said I could get whatever I wanted, but that's what I picked because *I* wanted it. She said, "I'm so glad you got that, I want to hear it, too." We listened to the whole thing together. She was a fan of most of the grunge music scene.

My dad was too. They didn't mind the music I chose blasting from the stereo when I took control. Grunge and a lot of that back-to-basics rock that proliferated in the early '90's was a great way for kids around my age to bond with folks our parents' ages. Grunge was reminiscent of early '70's rock, what was already being called Classic Rock in the '90's.

Now being as far from my new music as my parents were from theirs and I hear something that actually tickles my fancy after a decade of subjective trash? I get why people hold onto their art and only stick to what they know. I *try* to continue listening to, watching, and reading new things. What you appreciate comes back around eventually in neat ways.

I survived eighth grade unscathed and didn't maintain any of the friendship's I made. There were a couple of notable instances, however. My mom surprised me at school twice, once, to take me to a daytime baseball game, because—no reason. It was nice and I felt that my mom wanted to spend some time with me. The other time was to have some teeth extracted. I didn't know she had even scheduled it for me. I got picked up, I went to the dentist, and I had several stubborn baby teeth wrenched from my skull.

I still have them. In an envelope. There are significant bony prominences. I didn't *feel* the extraction, but I could feel the pressure at the base of my nose of them breaking the teeth loose.

I never got braces as a follow-up. I don't know how much they would have helped. My wisdom teeth would begin to grow in while I was in high school, and they started screwing up my teeth further anyway.

My mom still enjoyed the movie-going experience. I loved getting to see Schindler's List (1993) and The Crow (1994) with her. Those are both cherished experiences. One is a phenomenal war drama about the depths of humanity, its greatness *and* depravity. The other is a good action movie where the star unfortunately died during filming giving sequences within the film heightened emotional impact. They're both about trauma.

She opened off and on about her past and own trauma. There were more colorful retellings of what she had endured while pregnant with me, that my biological father beat her with a bullwhip and her younger sister jumped on his back to make him stop.

I would also learn stories of genealogy, family relations, and histories. Some fantastical, such as our family descended from the "real" Guinevere. That my great-great grandfather was Black. Or that on my biological paternal side there was Native American. She made me feel as if I was descended from a robust and ethnically diverse, *inclusive,* family.

A DNA test later in life would reveal I am European. To be blunt: white as fuck. A good bit Irish, the rest English and Germanic. At least the being Irish was accurate.

CHAPTER 30

Our family would "grow." During my freshman year of high school at Nathan Hale High School, my brother, Jeremy, reemerged. After mostly silence from my mom on my brother for years, she announced he would be moving in with her in a new apartment she had rented in east Tulsa. She was excited. I was excited.

Jeremy had had a hard life of his own, though. He endured physical abuse from his (our) father, subterfuge by his caretakers regarding my mom's attempts at maintaining contact with him, drug abuse and dealing. He was on a path to prison, and his dad reached out to my mom and asked if she could take him. After all these years of hatefully keeping him from us, when Jeremy became too troublesome for his family, they shipped him off to us. I'm sure he has his own feelings about that transition, but we were excited and hoped for the best.

For a little while, we got it, too! There was an excellent Halloween out at a haunted hayride where Jeremy punched a guy who tried to scare him with a chainless chainsaw. A Christmas full of new CDs for everyone and Mom getting weirded out by some production effects on Pearl Jam's Vitalogy.

She claimed to hear subliminal messages. Jeremy and I got excited, wanting to know what was hidden. *Nothing*. There's nothing there. My mom would let herself get weirded out if something unsettled her. She was showing signs of growing conspiratorial.

She never tried to convince me of anything along those lines. She would rather cook tales about our own relationship and family. She didn't dissuade me from looking into the mystical and fantastical. She wanted magic to be real, I wanted magic to be real, too, but I knew it was more a matter of psychology and kept a foot firmly on the ground.

Not growing up with any organized religion gave me the ability to look at anything with curiosity. If someone *believes* in something, then it is real to them.

The only exception being those Jehovah's Witnesses. I know that some of the religion's practices and how it affected my mom, personally, with her relationships both with her own mother and my biological father's family, her first son; all of it was ripped from her and it was the JW's fault.

I saw them as cultish and mean. Unforgiving, exclusionary, deceptive. When Jeremy moved in, he only validated our conceptions, he was angry with them, too. I know not everyone in a community or organization can be judged by a person or even a group within its rank's actions. The brand of Jehovah's Witness that family adhered to, the same that caused the rift between my mom and her own mother, was how I saw *cults*. Divisive, leveraging love with unkindness.

Through experience, I began to see a lot of that same cultish behavior everywhere. Even my mom started getting a little too into apocalyptic fever, which, I guess is ever present. The early '90's was a dawning realization that the year 2000 was only a few years away and getting closer.

Picking me up from school one day to give me a ride home, she told me about a dream she had. She was a survivor in a battlefield situation. Things on fire, dead bodies, distant sounds of fighting. She came upon a building and inside was a baby, the only other survivor around her, she knew the baby was *mine*, and that this baby was important to humanity.

She believed she was delivering a warning. She had scried the future and was telling me of something she knew was coming. I bought into it. I reminded her of the constellation of freckles on my left hand similar to Orion. She remembered something about seven stars in someone's hand from the Bible (Revelations, Jesus, and allegorical reference to the system of churches at the time). It's one thing being told you're special by your mom...

I was absorbing a lot, and living in the United States, it was mostly produced from a White, Christian narrative, but even then, I was always more interested in the *history* of the religions. My dad and I both enjoyed Mysteries of the Bible and anything about discoveries in archeology around the world.

While I became more rooted, though fascinated by the supernatural, my mom thought the world was ending soon. She once went on a tangent about how things might be ending if California should succumb to fires, earthquakes, or violence.

She said, "You know Los Angeles means 'the City of Lost Angels.'"

I stopped her. "Los Angeles literally means '*the* angels.' It *is* a city, but 'Los' is just Spanish for 'the,' not 'lost.'"

It made her rambling crumble. Not that it ended. There would be moments I would reality-check her and she talked less seriously about it—with me.

This is the fuzzy delineation of loving my mom and judging my mother. I realize a lot of kids go through recognizing differences they may have with their parents, I was also re-evaluating a backlog of life events.

When my mom landed a job at KJRH, the local NBC affiliate, a sense of normalcy seemed to settle-in. It was a stable job that she enjoyed. She did writing and editing work. I got to visit the station a few times. Enough to make an impression that some anchors would recognize me later in life in random encounters. She made sure I was in the studio when some players from our hockey team came by. They signed some memorabilia for me. She also met a man that made her happy.

D seemed to appeal to my mother's adventurous side, he was an avid cyclist and outdoorsman. My last camping trips were with this arrangement. My mom, my brother, a new guy we were all okay with —could *this* become "family?"

We went to Rocky Mountain National Park. It was a lot of walking around, a lot of conflicting body responses: strained under the elevation, heated from exertion, the chill of the air, yet, I wanted to push on, to stare at trees, rocks, and sky, but continue to see even more. Mountains are beautiful. The forests around them are much more majestic than the woods between towns in the Midwest.

When my mom wanted to be surrounded by mountains, I got it. It's the cold for me, though.

After coming back to Oklahoma from Florida, having gone through puberty in a subtropical climate, cold weather causes me pain. I can feel it grip my marrow. No matter how warm the layers, I still breathe the cold into my lungs, it becomes *inescapable*. I start becoming melancholy anywhere below 60°. But I will occasionally brave it for an experience I know I'll appreciate.

We would camp somewhere over in the panhandle of Oklahoma with a friend of mine along that time. It was part camping trip, part work trip. D was a videographer and photojournalist, and they were capturing the park for a program about Oklahoma destinations. We were in a few shots. One of us face planted trying to jump across a stream.

We did not get famous for our television appearance.

For some reason, yet another difference of desires, she split from D and began planning a trip to Alaska. To me, it was absurd. D was a good guy and they had been happy together. Why Alaska? *That* far away? Why was it when things seemed to be good, she tried to run away? This reminded me of her split from my dad.

I was excited for her excitement, but I also felt more abandonment. I felt abandonment on behalf of my brother.

Jeremy wasn't doing good. They got into some strife, he got back into drugs, and she kicked him out. My mom was clearing the nest, she was ready to take flight again.

If this scattering of roller coaster highs and lows seems rapid, it was from 1993 to 1995. I went from eighth grade to sophomore in high school and she had moved more times than I think I'm even aware in those two years. And when it seemed she settled down, that we had a new family dynamic, it wasn't enough. She was out.

I tried to do decent in school, finding passion in drawing and writing. My dad and I went to hockey games, read our books, watched movies, and life at home was calm. I enjoyed it immensely, but my consumption of media continued to be escapism. But, I could enjoy it with someone in my dad, who was often getting me into *more* stuff to geek out about. There was peace when I was with my dad.

However, in the lead-up to my mom's departure, when she was staying with a friend, there were some moments that helped to set me on my path as an author. She had become friends with a guy at KJRH who was printing his own small press genre fiction 'zine, Outer Darkness. He published a couple of my mom's poems, Cut Me Deep and Controlled Pink. Sadly, I do not currently have access to them.

I had written short stories, but I was then writing a novel about a human brain in a robot body turning into a terminator (I was fifteen, we all must take our baby-steps). This magazine, though? That I was now acquainted with the guy who published it? I should write short stories! I submitted drawings and shorts that he never accepted but was always gracious about. My first true submissions and rejections. But I wouldn't stop. I began writing fiction regularly with my mom's departure.

There was finally some closure on our time with the W's. We were looking at photo albums when I spotted a photo of me next to Four, who was smiling. I was aggressively not.

"I look pissed." I said.

"You looked like that a lot." She agreed. "You were miserable. And you were right. We shouldn't have been there; I should have listened to you from the beginning."

I got that from her. She admitted she had made my life hell and that she hadn't been happy, either. Despite igniting a new lust for my writing and publication, despite the healing we had achieved the last couple of years, she needed to move on, this time on her own.

She asked me to use some white shoe polish to make a peace symbol in her back window. She had the truck loaded to the point she couldn't see through anyway. She left in Spring of 1995.

She called me. She wrote and sent pictures of the late hour daylight. She was staying in Anchorage and enrolled at the University of Alaska toward a journalism degree. She started writing in the college newspaper, the Northern Light. Somewhere along the way, though, D followed her up to Alaska and they rekindled their romance.

CHAPTER 31

1995 – WINTER BREAK, ANCHORAGE, ALASKA

I hadn't flown in a couple years, not since coming home from Florida. My mom and D were settled in Anchorage, both working, and wanted to have me for the holiday break. I was excited to go to *Alaska*, even if it *was* winter. Maybe I would see the Aurora Borealis!

My route to Alaska in 1995 was Tulsa to SLC to Anchorage, at the age of sixteen. I was competent to travel on my own thanks to previous experience. There was an odd familiarity to the movements of air travel. Seeing that big mountain looming over Salt Lake City from the air was impressive.

Flying into Anchorage felt—steely. Nearly the top of the world in December, stark white snow streaking earth, stone, and concrete. The mountains in the distance were reminiscent of the Rockies, but bigger. These were ancient things slumbering on the horizon.

The exceptionally short days fucked with me and I slept a *lot*. I'm trying to remember my mom picking me up, because of course she did, but it was later in the afternoon, and I had been in the air almost all day, it was *late* according to my normal concept of time. Only a *touch* of jet lag.

I think I was shocked at all the incongruous information the place was giving me. Nighttime lasted too long. Icy conditions, cold in the air, but *not* the painful, stinging, and blowing cold of Oklahoma. Would I even need the parka my dad shelled out for?

Her place, a duplex west of Far North Bicentennial Park, was in a normal, suburban neighborhood. Albeit one whose small front window looked out toward a mountain. Its peak would become a little whiter and brighter as passing cloud structures dumped ice and snow at the upper elevations. The place had two bedrooms, a bathroom barely big enough for one person, and a front room that had the kitchen within it and your decision on what to section off for the living and dining area. It was small, but they had all they needed or wanted. D had lived in a tiny apartment in Tulsa. Minimalism isn't the worst.

I was visiting family for Christmas. I would see Anchorage through osmosis, not that there was much to see in a place when the sun didn't come up until 10am and went down after you'd be getting out of school at 3:45 p.m. She and D continued going to work until their natural days off for the holiday, a three-day weekend since it was a Monday.

One day my mom did take me to work with her, she was working at UPS. She had good rapport with anyone. That was a superpower of hers and I saw it still quite on display here.

We went to a Christmas party at someone's house, a nice house. I have no idea who they were, but this was one of those warm, golden hued, exposed timber homes you imagine seeing in an Alaskan narrative. We played Dirty Santa. I ended up with a Hershey's Kiss dispenser that was a giant plastic cartoon character version of a Kiss. I wasn't lactose intolerant at the time.

My mom took me to a Wal-Mart to get a couple of posters if I wanted to make "my" room more *my* room. I got a Spider-Man poster and one of Kermit the Frog dressed and posing as David Letterman. I also got a Mortal Kombat demo and controller to play on her newly purchased Gateway PC. She was attempting to make me feel at *home*. Maybe she wanted me to consider moving back in with her? I don't know, she never offered the option, not directly, not in any way I picked up on at the time.

I visited her school campus, too, and this reminded me of the times she dabbled in advancing her education previously. A class here and there through the years. She felt focused on journalism here. Alaska was far away and difficult, but it was the challenge she desired. They had a hockey team, but she wasn't able to score any tickets for us while I was there.

D had skis, and I was both excited and terrified to try that activity out, though it didn't come to pass. It costs to ski, it's a major activity to get into with zero experience. My mom did take me to a ski lodge for me to take in the sights, though. It was a large cabin people could chill out in with huge windows that looked out on a hillside. There were skiers about, we watched for a little while. I appreciated the snippet of time.

There was a day we were going to go take a walk through the neighborhood, but my steel-toed work-boots were not good on an icy path. I could not walk uphill, I could find no purchase, my mom and D made it to the top of a rise and watched me pitifully struggle. Who knows what they thought, but I was growing frustrated with my plight.

I looked up to them. "Go on, I can't walk up the hill, I keep sliding back. I'll go back to the house."

I love the outdoors, even if I hate the cold, but sometimes the outdoors does not love me back.

She did drive me out to a glacier site. I saw mountain goats clambering sheer cliff walls amidst low clouds. I saw grey, frozen sea water. I don't remember the name of the place we went to but seeing the blue-white jagged expanse crawling up into the mountains feeding a sheet of frozen water was impressive. What shocked me, however, was this place not behaving as expected. There was a huge crack in the sheet of ice. Here. In winter of 1995.

I was seeing climate change in action. I had no problem accepting that "inconvenient truth," I had already seen it. I crunched through the 1987 Christmas ice storm in Tulsa. I "flew" through the air on winds from Hurricane Andrew on the other side of Florida. Now Alaska melting in the winter? I've been living through climate change my entire life.

CHAPTER 32

D took me out for dinner one night, a guys night, to Hooters. Yeah, I was sixteen, probably the perfect age for that, but it got awkward quick.

"Can I start you guys off with a pitcher of beer?" our waitress, in a tank top and booty shorts in late December, asked, looking me dead in the face and not even questioning if I was old enough to make that offer to.

I was offended! "I'm only sixteen!" I yelped.

Did I look that old? Flashes of memory popped: I was served a Flaming Doctor Pepper when I was maybe twelve; noting how angry I looked in the old photo; a gray hair when I was only ten. Was I already an old man?

The waitress apologized, embarrassed, but D laughed, saying "You should have just said 'yes!'"

We all laughed it off. But something was still expressing itself to the world through me that was aging me. Sure, I was a lethargic teen struggling in an alien environment, for some reason though, her offering me a beer without question made me feel all the growing up I had had to do. It should be a funny memory. I don't remember dinner or conversation, I remember feeling old.

———

One thing I hoped to see was the Northern Lights. D drove the three of us in a direction for a while. We stood out in the cold looking up for a while, but I don't think we got far enough out. There was a streetlight within view, which I knew was ruining our night vision. It was cold and dark. Not dark enough, though. Not the right time, or location.

For how much nighttime there was, and how much I slept, there *was* one night I was up late and opened the little window in my bedroom. I intentionally *felt* the air, breathed it slowly, knowing I was someplace completely different from anywhere I had been. I *might* have seen a wisp of luminescent green on the horizon. I might have *wanted* to see it.

The time I spent alone, I spent reading or watching movies among mom and D's collection. I played Mortal Kombat and customized the screensavers she had on her PC. I read Shakespeare and Poe. Othello with Laurence Fishburne was in theaters, and I was hoping mom could take me to see it, but we didn't get to do that.

I did however experience my first earthquake while watching Star Wars on VHS by myself.

I was sitting in a rocking chair, when I noticed something on a bookshelf rocking as well. I knew I couldn't be rocking the chair that hard. I stopped and placed my feet firmly on the floor where I felt an *un*earthly sensation. If you've never been in an earthquake, and you live in a place where they rarely occur, the shaking floor simulators don't do it justice.

A roiling within the earth, like waves on the ocean. This wasn't major, and looking them up for that year, there wasn't anything much greater than 3.3 in the time I was there. I was by myself; do I get in the hallway? Go outside? Before I could recall anything remotely safe to do with my body in the event of an earthquake, it was over.

When my mom did have time to spend with me, there was a lot of driving around and chatting. She told me about how the native population is soft spoken if not downright silent. That people would pick up kids walking home from school, and they wouldn't say a thing. It terrified me that Alaskans offer rides to strangers and that these kids *took* them. I did watch Northern Exposure, though, and yeah, Elaine Miles' Marilyn Whirlwind was that way. It made me think people talk too much to fill up silence.

We stopped at a gas station where they had Jolt Cola. Impossible to find in Oklahoma and fabled to be a higher caffeinated soda. This was before energy drinks. I thought I was basically going to do cocaine! I burped a lot.

I learned the Edge was a national radio broadcast franchise and not only in Tulsa. For some reason Smashing Pumpkins' *Bullet with Butterfly Wings* sticks out in my mind as we rode around.

More music stuck out, though. Mom and I got into a philosophical musing together regarding facing God. Both *Counting Blue Cars* and *One of Us* were in heavy rotation on the airwaves in 1995. I asked her if she would look God in the face.

"No!"

I was surprised by her chagrin. "Why?"

"I don't think we're worthy to look on God, it would be disrespectful."

I was undecided on God. "I *would*. I would because I would want to know everything. Why? Why show up now? Why so much hurt in the world if He's so powerful?"

A black and white, adolescent condemnation, I know. I was sixteen.

There wasn't much argument to our different points of view. I don't think she thought I was brave or thought that *I* thought that I was brave for saying I would look a God who showed up in the face. I couldn't articulate quite yet that the concept of a god that can manifest itself and *prove* its powers surely then wouldn't be a god, but a marauder, a narcissist, a jerk terrifying a less advanced species with its parlor tricks. I *would* look a charlatan in the face. She believed a truly higher power should be revered, if not feared. That was *her* take at the time. I think we all have thoughts on God.

I had to start shaving every day beginning there. I've never been a particularly hairy beast and my beard comes in thin and patchy. Being in Alaska kickstarted something, though. My facial hair started growing faster, I noticed stubble within twenty-four hours of shaving. Mom said it was the ash in the air, Alaska being volcanic at times.

Maybe it was the environment? Maybe I hit a late growth spurt as I was there…there *was* all the sleeping.

Hormones, circadian rhythm, or early onset depression? All of the above?

One morning, baking an egg sandwich in the oven, I reached in bare-handed to grab the sandwich—yes, it was dumb and risky—and I burned the back of my left hand against the top heating element. I hit it right at the angle and it was quick, I don't know if I heard my skin sizzle or myself hiss, but I yanked my hand back and immediately put it under cold running water.

Does that work?

I would have a penis-shaped scar on the back of my hand for about a year afterward. It was a hilarious souvenir.

My mom wanted to introduce me to a writer friend of hers she was pen pals with. McD wrote sort of gonzo horror and dark fantasy. He had also been published in the Outer Darkness 'zine, and that was how they became acquainted. We quickly made friends through letters through the mail. One last influential man Irene would sprinkle into my life. I appreciated this one, though, he was a good friend and mentor while we were in touch.

I don't remember Christmas itself. What gifts did we exchange? I know she got me some hockey memorabilia, a hat and a banner for her university's team. I know I called my best friend at the time and made the two of them speak. I think I was trying to force her to remember that I felt at *home* back in Tulsa. I know she took me to a tourist shop to try and find something uniquely *Alaskan* to take back home. A decorative plate for my dad and some tchotchke for myself.

There was snow on the ground, and I saw fresh snow dust a mountain top from a distance as a cloud system passed over it. But during my trip, it was the first time in a decade Anchorage did not have a "White Christmas." As they defined it for Alaska, anyway, it did not snow on Christmas Eve or Christmas Day. I did not see snow fall on me during my trip.

CHAPTER 33

What I ended up coming home with, though, is the last heartfelt moments I had with my mother, before I would leave. I don't know where D was, maybe working late, I think they both worked odd hours, or maybe it was odd because of Alaska time. Regardless, we were alone. Music on and candles lit.

"Do you remember your girlfriend in kindergarten?" she asked me.

"Yeah?"

"Do you remember wanting to give her a ring?"

"Yeah."

There's a spark of memory, six-years-old maybe, my "girlfriend" in kindergarten, the girl I "like-liked," but it was the getting the ring itself. My dad took me to a mall, we visited one of those kiosks that sets up in the concourse between shops. Costume jewelry mostly, cheap trinkets, perfect for kids. Why was it important to give her a ring? I must have been impressed by my mom and dad's wedding. A ring was how you told someone you loved them and wanted to be with them forever.

"When your dad took you to buy that ring for her," she started, "he thought it was cute, so he bought a ring for me, too. I kept it because I thought it really represented *love*. Innocent, unconditional. I want you to have it. And I want you to give it to someone you *really* think is special."

Now, cue every girl I knew in high school going, "I know *that* ring." *I'm sorry.*

I was irresponsible with the gift my mother gave me. I interpreted it as an urgent matter I had to figure out, and quickly. I needed to have a high school sweetheart and get married and start a family by twenty! I wanted to live a perfect life despite all the childhood heartache I already knew I had gone through. I wanted someone who would love me back as much as I wanted to love someone. I was in love with the idea of being "in" love. That ring, my mother impressed an importance on it that I did not appreciate or respect at the time. I still have it, it's in my wife's possession.

My mom wanted me to keep love small, pure, and simple. I chased it up and down, after people I didn't have chances with, or did, and ran them off being too *much*. The moment, though, that she gave me the ring, I can sit myself back across from her. I know she's giving up something. She's held onto that ring, through her marriage to M and into her relationship with D and anyone else I didn't know about in between, she held onto this trinket because it reminded her that things could be simple. That I should be reminded that love and family can be simple.

———

Ted Stevens Anchorage International Airport. It all begins with this ending. I didn't—couldn't—know it. Were the walls blue or was it pale light? I was an ogre with my bags, I felt big. This had been a transformative trip, part of me didn't want to leave my mom, a bigger part wanted to go *home*. It was morning, a little red in the sky. We were talking when I noticed her intensely staring at me, beginning to tear up.

I knew the moment was filling with gravity. I didn't believe her then. Occasionally the memory would surface in the intervening years, and I would wonder with increasing conviction, "What if she's right?"

Because she would be.

"What?" I asked.

Her face contorted a bit, a threat of a sob rising in her throat. She said as quickly as she could, afraid she would start crying, "I feel like this is the last time I'm going to see you."

Was she granted a premonition in that dwindling window of time on our relationship? Or was it that crueler side of nature serving up coincidence? Either way, I feel personally attacked by the universe. Her words haunt me.

I could feel it, the weight of her emotion pressing down on her soul and radiating out to compress us all into a crystal we would never forget. When we saw each other next, I knew I would scoff, and we would laugh—*surely*. The weight of that emotion that shined brighter than any star hung for a beat. Then I was appalled, aghast, confused— then, caught in the moment I saw her begin to lose it, I felt an over- whelming urge to comfort.

"Don't say that." I said, probably robotically. I pulled her in for a hug. She let go a little, letting a sob loose against my chest. I felt too big, she was tiny in my arms. My panicked brain flashed my life before my eyes all the times I went to her for comfort in this exact same pose: crying into her chest for fear of that which I couldn't control. She talked about it that time in Florida. We had fled from and chased each other from one tip of the country to the other.

I think I offered some well-meaning platitudes, the moment of horrific scrying subsiding. The waves begin to form here, rippling off the edges of the crystal in time she willed into existence.

As I sat on the plane, immediately as we pulled from the gate, it began to snow. Snow blankets things, freezes it all in place, and covers it up. Snow didn't fall on my trip until I left. I've never known how to feel about it, especially in context. *Does* nature speak to us?

There was a delay in SLC *and* OKC that made me late arriving home. It was such a long trip home, too much time to think. This was before cellphones and the phones they had built into the back of airplane seats at the time required a credit card. I had to trust my dad was being kept informed by the airport. He told me as he *did* wait, some assholes started talking about plane crashes.

The flight from OKC to Tulsa was silly. There were maybe ten people on the plane and the flight itself was probably less time than the jockeying around on the tarmac. I went to the back and took a window seat. A flight attendant asked if that was where I wanted to be if I had the whole cabin to choose from.

Why she was judging my unspoken paranoid logic that if the plane crashes nose first I'll live the longest is beyond me.

It was colder than Alaska and blowing snow when I stepped out of Tulsa International Airport. I felt defeated. Alaska had *not* been as brutally cold and snowy as I had feared, but dear old *Oklahoma* was having white-out conditions for a welcome party.

My mother's face the last time I looked at her escapes me. Our last embrace wasn't enough. I struggled to freeze this moment in time, to remember *her*, versus wondering what she was thinking about. She had already used up all the magic.

Did both of us wonder about that moment as seconds turned into minutes turned into—forever? Was she worried I would meet some unexpected end? Was she worried about the plane? The flight delays *were* due to engine trouble, but not really. Your car's check engine light is on and you decide to have it looked at. You wait an hour and a half, it turns out the gas cap wasn't airtight. That kind of boring thing.

Was she clairvoyant or was there writing on the wall I was missing? I talk about hemming and hawing over how to feel about my mom, even at this time, her moving to Alaska felt like running away, even though I had had a good time visiting. Our relationship was about to get very rocky, and I already knew most of the stones. Could she see my reckoning coming before I did?

I cherish my last few days with her. They were good days. I'm glad that the last time I spent in physical space with her was *good*.

CHAPTER 34

1996-1998 – FINISHING HIGH SCHOOL

didn't *know* I was doing this, but the act of creativity was soothing hurts I had simmering up from deep within. I drew my own fighting game instruction guides with how to do all their moves. Only for myself, I didn't copy them to share with friends. After writing back and forth with McD I started writing short stories in earnest.

All the way back to my first short story, about the fleas, there has always been horror. I had grown up with it, afraid of it, unable to turn away, morbidly curious. But I also loved science fiction in my entertainment, the real world was full of awfulness and American news has always been obsessed with violence and debauchery. Writing crime fiction or literary, realistic fiction was never of interest; I had enough of the real world. I wanted to write weird and different tomorrows. The horror always came through in my science fiction, though.

I also realized if I wanted to write *good* science fiction I would have to at least be a little scientific while math, technology, and science are not my best suits. I tried to write stories from an average person's point of view in an otherworldly situation. I still love science, even if I don't always get it, and will always try to massage a little into what I'm working on.

In becoming more creative, I began identifying with new kids in school and my longtime childhood friend and I grew apart. We had gone to driver's education together, our dad's alternating dropping us off or picking us up. He got a car at some point and called asking if I wanted to go cruising. I didn't. Not with him anyway. It was a dual thing. I didn't want to hang out with him, but I didn't want to hang out with anyone else, either.

I would get into these phases of wanting and finding pleasure in being alone. I didn't nap. I listened to music, wrote, drew, played video games, read, or watched movies (or sometimes a combination). I was in a constant state of *doing* something, and doing those things by myself, not having to entertain anyone else or obligated to interact, was preferable.

I had some jock friends. I had some drama and band friends. I also hung out with the "bad" kids—drinkers and smokers. These were the friends I knew I could expect to see at the pool hall, and we would play pool, foosball, arcade games, or shoot the shit about life for sixteen to eighteen-year-olds. Then there was the group that was sort of them all rolled into one. I started hanging out, away from home, in public, with this group. Some of whom I still trust with my life to this day. Some I would hurt unforgivably.

I believe my nostalgia for the 1990's is not only the media I enjoyed or the friends I made and enjoyed those things with, but an explosion of *self*. I recognize upon reflection the flaws I was wrestling with, things that were hardwired, learned, and chosen; some of which could and would evolve. I was becoming *me*.

I had started going by J.D. the first year of high school. On the first day of school, the first roll call of the day, the teacher called out "Justin" and three of us raised our hands to say "here."

He laughed and said a last name, not mine. Once he read the next one, mine, I asked to be called "J.D." on the spot. That old nickname my mom had called me that I refuted. This was my name now. I was choosing who I was becoming and how I would be known.

"Justin" sounds weird to me now.

Going by initials isn't profound. I could have come by that naturally, or went wild and gone by "Dwayne," but who the hell would *that* guy have been? I chose "J.D." on the spot *because* of my mom's nickname that I had once been appalled by. I haven't ever put that in writing before, it's an internal fact. My mom named me twice. I go by a chosen moniker that I received from my mom, not simply letters.

My relationship with my dad began to alter in the way parents with kids growing up do, but we never had it rough with each other. I eventually stopped going to hockey games to either stay home or go hang out with friends. He never forbade any behavior—within reason. My curfew was I needed to be at school on time every day and to at least pass my classes.

We still went fishing when the weather permitted. I got tons of sunburns. There were movies. The bookstore. He didn't much care for Super Nintendo, even though he happily got me one and several games over the years, but when we got a PC to run Windows 3.1 ahead of Windows 95, PC gaming was relatively simple on any hardware. We competed in Asteroids for high scores, he eventually became good enough he could roll the scoreboard for however long he decided to sit there.

When we finally played DOOM, both of us were hooked. If one of us was already playing when the other wanted to, we would watch over each other's shoulders, backseat driving or copiloting puzzles. We admitted to each other that if we were playing it alone, it would sometimes creep us out, the sounds enemies would make from unseen areas. It was a fun kind of spooked we couldn't get enough of.

I also admitted in my *PUNCH/PANTS* collection that my short stories *Gate* and *Tower* were heavily influenced by DOOM. They were among my first published short stories. McD encouraged me to submit them to other 'zines around the country he was aware of, and taught me how to find more. Starting in late 1996, I was submitting short stories to magazines I found in The Writer's Market. I took a few big swings, Clarke's World and Asimov's, but I wasn't there. I found acceptance down in the same small market as Outer Darkness, alongside McD and my mom. It was a start.

Even though they were obviously printed at a franchise print shop, I showed them off with pride to my classmates. People knew that I was an author. Both of my parents were proud of me, even though all I had been paid was a free copy of the 'zine. They encouraged my writing; they knew it was making me happy and I was trying to make something of it.

I was still quietly working on that universe spanning epic, and as I began to ingest more horror on my own, in short story suggestions from McD, as well as movies and novels, I began to want to tell a darker fantasy, and added elements that would fill up more of the space within the infinite life of a universe. I began to craft the villain of the entire epic, and gave it many names, depending on the era it was in. One riffed on a name from Brian Lumely's Necroscope series, and would come to represent my online persona, "Kitradu."

This is another name choice that I made in high school. The villain of my epic is my perennial screen name. Anytime I needed to make a new screen name for a website I wanted to have a presence on, it was Kitradu. On a screen, that's who I was, that's how people on the other side of the screen knew me. I still carry it with me. It's my Twitch and YouTube handles. I would tell friends—online and off—if the world "ended" and we entered a Mad Max style rogue-world, I would go by Kitradu.

We all thought the world was ending soon, anyway. The year 2000 was fast approaching and we weren't even aware of the Millennium Bug yet. We thought it would be the Second Coming or World War III or another American Civil War.

Even though the '90's were great, and we had all this freedom of expression—and it indeed created magnificent art—we were sure everything was inches from hitting the fan.

I began to buy into doomsday fervor, having my own nightmares about apocalyptic scenarios. I worried and thrilled that I might be clairvoyant. I thought I was an "empath" like Deanna Troi from Star Trek: The Next Generation, but honestly, I feel empathy from already living a varied life. I recognize when someone else is not comfortable in their own skin. I wanted to be a mutant superhero with mind powers. I didn't want the world to end.

I hadn't been blind to the world I lived in and the ebb and flow of war. The Cold War still lingering over the '80's and our drills to get under our desks. The open warfare in Iraq in the early '90's. The unease in the area that has never settled. Was Russia our enemy or our friend this year?

I wasn't a telepath feeling everyone's unrest. I was exhausted with bad news from early on.

CHAPTER 35

t wasn't current affairs or paranoid entertainment that caused the greatest stress, though. I was informed, not maliciously—more, *unwittingly*—of an "alternative truth" to the story of my mother's departure from my biological father's family. I had had enough bad news. I was ready to explode.

My dad was combing through boxes full of documents in search of some this, that, or the other thing, when he found my *original* birth certificate, accidentally left behind in the divorce. He alerted me and showed it to me. On the form it said "Justin Dwayne (Birthname)."

"My name was *Mulroney* when you adopted me…?"

He was confused, too. He didn't remember the document itself and failed to remember it appeared that way in the adoption proceedings, but here it was. It led to a conversation that tweaked the story my mother had always told me about our flight from Mountain Home, Arkansas and that abusive family.

My biological grandparents had convinced my biological father that my mom had an affair and I was not his child. She was forced into a divorce and given a settlement on condition she signed away her rights to Jeremy. She was shunned, ran out of town on a lie, and forced to give up her first son in the process. She was only eighteen.

It wasn't the battle to save both her sons and having to sacrifice one to save me as she had convinced me of for years. She wouldn't have been savvy enough for that. She couldn't have been; not that she dissuaded me from such allusions. I don't know why she ever posed herself as the tragic hero in her own story, this choosing to give up one to save the other; maybe some sort of penance? She was a victim, coerced, bullied—*beaten*—because of a lie, and she in turn told a lie that was somehow worse than the truth.

I did feel sorry for her, but I was also angry with the deception. At the time there was an unfair, retroactive expectation that she should have fought harder for us and not taken a *settlement* and given up her rights. I had been offended. I interpreted it as she had *sold* Jeremy, and I reacted harshly.

The three of us were in email communication with each other at the time, and I told Jeremy everything. My initial side of the story and the truth I had now learned. He had had his own slight variations on our family's sad origin. I caused a storm with my mom and could never get a straight answer out of her about why she told a lie that made her look worse than the truth would have.

In her mind, the truth *was* worse. Admitting she made a poor decision under duress and having to concoct a story that saved her *some* dignity in a terrible outcome still had to have the same terrible outcome. I immediately detested my mom's logic, I felt betrayed. I felt betrayed on Jeremy's behalf, even though I'm sure he felt his own ways and didn't need my sympathy.

All this pent-up anger about a lie when I was a King of Lies. I never stopped to appreciate the irony. At the time, never extended any grace.

We kept in touch, though, and she moved around. She left D and Alaska, she moved around, New Mexico, Oregon, some places here and there I didn't even know about. I got over my anger and we talked more cordially. She and Jeremy began living together and/or near each other and bonded. I heard about it from afar. I never got to visit as she never seemed to be stable enough to host.

Where she lived and what she was doing was the job-hopping I could never keep up with all over again. It seemed she didn't sit still for more than a few months. I had no idea how she afforded it or survived the stress. At the time, please forgive the racial connotations and appropriation, she fancied herself a *gypsy*. She was willing to portray herself as a traveling mystic, going where fate willed her.

We are not Romani.

I don't know how many times she moved after she returned to the contiguous States. There are periods in there that even Jeremy was out of touch with her. They both had some tough times out there as I was finishing up high school. I'm aware of drug use and possible physical abuse.

That's the thing: my mom went off on her own sometimes. She would lose touch for days, weeks, months at a time. Where would she pop back up? What stories would she have? Once she claimed to have worked with Robert Redford on a movie set in New Mexico!

There was an evening my mom called late, 9:45 p.m. on a week-night my time, but she was in Oregon, two hours behind, not thinking about the time difference.

"Jeremy and I tried magic mushrooms and I want to try them with you!"

It was sort of an invitation to visit? I quickly became uncomfortable with the topic, scared of illicit drug use, *her* safety, Jeremy's, mine...yet, intrigued?

"No." I said over the phone. "I don't even like getting high."

It was true, then, smoking weed made me feel paranoid. At least, with whatever I was exposed to at the time.

They were dings. I was being judgmental. I wouldn't be as harsh, now, but something about how the last few years had played out made my mom seem far too erratic to be taken seriously. Internally, I was criticizing her for it.

Jeremy had met and married someone, and in March of 1997, my niece was born. Justice Destiny-Star, named after me and Comet Hale-Bopp discovered only a few years earlier. Our mom was there for Justice's birth.

I was excited to be an uncle. I knew I could be an asset for this new person born into the world. I saw things a little differently than her parents and surrounding family. I didn't think I was better than them, I knew that I was different, and if things ever became difficult, I wanted to be there for her. To do what? At seventeen?

She was born with a small hole in her heart and had to have surgery to correct it. We were all scared, but the doctors were experts and good at their job. She pulled through fine. My mom took the opportunity to warn the condition was congenital, that she thought Jeremy and I both may have murmurs in our hearts, as well. No doctor has ever corroborated this as a fact.

To be honest, I was jealous of my brother. I was lovesick. I hadn't had any romantic endeavors…a lot of pining. Jeremy was out there starting a family. That was the dream. To be with someone, to start living a family life that was better than anything we had lived through, to create a life worth living. I was also admittedly jealous of a daughter.

I had this rollercoaster of a relationship with my mom where sometimes I wanted off and nothing to do with her. If I had a daughter, could I get the relationship *right*? I was already seeking to relive my life vicariously through the relationship with my child—when I was seventeen and single. Maybe not for the right reasons at the time, I wanted to provide *better* than what I had got.

CHAPTER 36

I n my senior year of high school, I would start a relationship with a girl that would last a few years. We loved a lot of the same music, and she got me into playing electric bass. We were both visual artists, drawing and painting, photography, sculpture and mosaics. She was impressed that I was family-focused, she bought into the idea of having a family—one day. We were still in school with many more years ahead of us for all...*that*.

I painted murals around the school. I started a band with my best friend and a girl who was playing guitar with my girlfriend, but *we* were gonna be the real deal. We played Deftones riffs and never had a drummer or singer. Two guitars and a bass. It was fun.

For my creativity, my girlfriend became obsessed with original drawings I did of the Nerds candy cartoon characters. I would randomly draw my own versions, in costumes or performing activities in the margins of notebooks. She wanted individual drawings, on the blank sides of index cards. She started creating lists and complained if I didn't take her suggestions seriously. I grew to hate drawing Nerds, but not before enough of them existed that most of the school knew I was capable of imaginative interpretations of a candy cartoon. At some point, in a first real "test" of our relationship, I had to refuse to draw more Nerds. It might have been better if I had let go when we were giving ultimatums about Nerds.

How I had stacked my classes through the years, I had the opportunity to graduate at the winter break of 1997, if I wanted to. If I did that, I wouldn't be eligible to walk at the graduation ceremony in May. That was important to me, for at the time, I was one of only a handful of people in the Mulroney family to graduate high school, my mom claimed, anyway. *She* hadn't finished high school.

I stayed in school to graduate with the rest of my class and friends. I did my due diligence and asked my school counselor about scholarships and grants and what I could apply for. I was too middling of a student. Too average. Grades good enough to graduate, but nothing to excite a college as to my prospects. I knew I was going to be the youngest, most famous author anyway—who needs college?

That last half of the school year, early 1998, President Bill Clinton lied under oath about an affair with a young lady. The affair was bad, lying was bad, abusing the power of the office was bad, but he wasn't abusing his power for political or financial gain as some administrations have since. Not in that instance, anyway. Everyone was making fun of the victim in the situation, body-shaming her, slut-shaming her. We still aren't past that kind of petty shit, but I recognized it then. Women deserve better treatment from society, even if they are in the wrong.

Titanic hit theaters and I saw it probably ten times *in* the theater because my girlfriend was obsessed with it. I appreciated the music at least. I got pretty good at slipping in MST3K-style jokes. Along with a bunch of other folks with their significant others paying for repeat viewings, I contributed to that first ever billion dollar earning movie.

1998 had a lot of scientific discovery, too, that gave me, as a writer, a lot of ideas to work with. Evidence the universe was expanding at an accelerated rate. Polar ice in craters on the Moon is enough to sustain a human settlement. Europa might be hiding a whole ocean. That bogus report about vaccines causing autism was published that year. Steps forward, leaps back.

As graduation approached, and I started getting my senior paraphernalia, I got addresses of the Mulroney's that my mom had access to and started sending out graduation ceremony invitations. I did not expect a grand showing, I was hoping for that return gift of a check or cash in the mail. Some of this family I hadn't interacted with since that trip in 1991. A few did send nice congratulatory salutations, I think I got a few dollars, but the response to my upcoming graduation did not seem to impress many.

I had swollen with pride at my achievement. I wanted to see and share it with my brother, my mom, and my niece. My mom was the only one who started making plans to come visit.

Jeremy and his wife were breaking apart. There were times I communicated with both him and his wife, separately, who both asked me to talk to Irene on their behalf, to broker some sort of truce, or counseling. She didn't want to help. She literally didn't want to; Jeremy and his wife were adults who could make adult decisions on their own and she wasn't going to get into their business.

I suppose there's a stance to be respected there, but from my point of view, they valued her insight and guidance, and she was with-holding it. I can't even speculate on why. I did talk to her about it, trying to convince her *her* words carried power that people respected.

Ultimately, Jeremy and his wife split. Justice went with her mother.

Jeremy wasn't going to make it to my graduation. As I continued speaking with his now ex-wife for a little while, she made promises she and Justice would try to make it to my graduation. Maybe I could at least meet my niece. My mom still planned on coming for a week to visit around the ceremony.

Justice's mother would eventually back out of visiting and for a long time, I lost touch with them. When Jeremy and I would occasion-ally make contact, he would give sporadic updates on Justice's wellbeing.

Despite all this reaching out to family, communications fizzled. My sequestration in Oklahoma put me far from anyone (I thought). Even my mom had to revise her trip from a week to a few days, to maybe only a couple days, to "Sorry, I can't get off of work that week, but I *will* be there in spirit."

I was disappointed. I felt hurt. One thing I thought my mom was excited for on my behalf and thought she would want to share with me, despite months of lead-time to prepare, years, I was class of 1998. It wasn't a moving target anymore. I never failed or had to retake classes. I was proud and the people, the *person I* wanted the approval of, were unmoved.

As school wound down, I was taking three art classes and library science. I was fucking off all day at school to hang out with friends in their respective classes. I grew more cynical. Should I have been done with this already? Was I wasting my time? Was this all bullshit only *I* thought was important?

I had those musical experiences; I painted those murals. I spent a few more months being a kid with other kids. I wouldn't go back on that at all. When graduation passed, though, I felt empty and unsatisfied.

I graduated May 12th of 1998, at least in the top half of grade averages, but I had gamed that *slightly* with those unnecessary classes the last part of the school year. For the first time in my entire student career, I got straight A's on a report card and I didn't even go to half of those scheduled classes. It raised my GPA. Committing to the entire year of school inflated my numbers, on paper at least.

Sitting between my two best friends in my class at the ceremony, I said about high school, "It was like I got there, and I was, like, 'yeah!' Excited for it. Then I started running around in circles for what seemed like forever and then someone said I could stop, but there was nothing gained."

I didn't feel ready for the world. I *wasn't* ready for the world.

I related that detail to my mom.

These are the emails we exchanged:

5/13/1998 Irene: Well, I am glad that your graduation went well. It sounds like your high school experience was about par as things go, or as Paul Simon wrote, "when I think of all the crap I learned in high school, it's a wonder I can think at all." Ah, education.

But…you did it, and now can focus on new challenges, whatever you choose. It's wide open for you and what you put into it is what you get out of it, or so they say.

. . .

I don't know what to tell you about Jeremy and (his wife). I think (his wife) is hurt and probably would like to stay together, but I don't think that's part of Jeremy's plan. I really don't know what his plan is, or if he's even thinking along that line. I just don't know. But, you never know how things can change.

I guess I should tell you that I've been talking to (M) for a while now. I know that probably won't make you happy, but there is just something that can't be explained and no matter how much time or distance between us, we can't seem to let each other go completely. All I know is it's been almost five years since I left him and I still love him. Maybe since you have someone in your life you can understand that maybe, just maybe, there is one soul mate in your life, and nothing or no one else will do. I don't know what will happen, but I just thought I'd let you know. You don't have to agree with my life, just please try not to be too judgmental. Five years of living alone has been the hardest part of my life, on many levels, and I just don't want to live my life unloved and alone. I hope you can understand that.

I'll talk to you soon.

Love,
    Mom

5/13/98 J.D.: All I can say is this: (M) is the only man in this entire world that I could kill and not care about it. There are people I hate and could probably hurt...but he? I wish him eradicated. He manipulates and is evil to the core. I don't care how much you think you love him. Remember that you once thought you should have listened to me when I always dissed him...you knew for a few moments that I was right. I hope you realize that I'm right again. If you start seeing him again...even if it's just over the phone...I can never talk to you again. I hate him...

Justin.

5/13/98 Irene: What makes you hate him so much? What exactly did he ever do to you to generate such hatred?

5/14/98 J.D.:

1.) He tried to blame me for the downfall of your original relationship with him.

2.) He was an asshole to all of us. Even YOU.

3.) He barely only tolerated me...on more than one occasion he would get mad at me for one thing and commend (Four) and (Three) for doing that same thing.

4.) He was a drunk.

5.) He abused my psyche...once told me I was a "worthless shit."

Irene, I can go on and on about all the little nuances around him that made me hate him. But most of all it was just a genuine hatred upon first glance. A feeling. You understand what I'm saying I know you do...there are just times when you know something or one is just wrong.

Frankly it appalls me that you would try and play your emotion cards with me...bringing my relationship into comparison to yours. They are so completely different! You think that because I love someone now that all my animosity towards that animal is just going to wash away? NO! You are fucking crazy to even try again with him. You apparently are just so desperate to HAVE someone that you'll sleep with the enemy again. Sometimes humans get jacked and they have to deal with it.

And now the reason that I'm uneasy about yours and my relationship: You had two sons...and didn't even TRY to keep the both of us. If you really loved either one of us, you'd have been there our entire lives. But hell no. You had to chase your dreams and become independent. You wanted to live your own life. You saw that with us you were going to have to actually become vulnerable. You were going to have to become HUMAN. Oh, no, fuck that...I want to live "my" way. Did it ever occur to you...that maybe, just maybe...instead of an actual spousal "true love" you might have found it in your sons?

But I'm probably just prattling to deaf ears. You won't listen to me because you're stupid and jaded. You think that you have all you need, when what you really need, and really needs you, is crying in the corner, begging upon those same deaf ears I speak to now. Jeremy and I. You probably could have made a difference in his life recently, but you "don't like to get into that with people."

It's all about you. That's all it's ever been or will be. And now you're losing your son. I'm assuming that with your letter asking my hatred of him, that the two of you are working things out and that soon the two of you will be back together. I'm truly sorry to hear that. I hope that you figure it out and realize, yet again, that he is NOT your true love and that he is a vicious monster. And you can tell him my hatred. Hell, invite him to visit me. I will gladly beat his face into a bloody pulp to express my true feelings to him.

If you are ever going to listen to me please let it be now. Yes, it may hurt you, but in the long run, it is for the better. After all...whom do you love more? Someone who is petty and likes to play with peoples (sic) emotions, or your own son? Your own flesh in blood is at stake here. This is not an empty threat...in fact, it's not a threat it's a fact, a warning of what WILL happen. If you "work things out," I can no longer call you Mom or Mother...or even Irene. I can never even be associated with you. I will break ties from you. I will end our relationship.

You might think I'm being ridiculous about all of this...but for me to act this way...don't you think there's something to my warnings?

Justin Dwayne Buffington.

5/14/98 Irene: If all this ranting came from someone I thought cared about me it might make me feel bad.

You can blame all your rage and hate on (M), me, whoever you want. But you, 18 years old, never held a job, never paid a bill, my son or not, have no right to be so rude to me or to anyone else.

I'm sorry you feel like you do. Hating people like that is hardly an attribute of an intellectual. Live and let live, Justin, or you will wind up bitter and lost. Like you are now.

I didn't respond. I think we both lost the plot. I was too angry. She was too agog. I had graduated *and* her thirty-seventh birthday was only two days before.

Spoilers: she had withheld information from me during this exchange. They hadn't only been speaking. In 1998 she visited M, from Oregon to Florida. No one is positive of the dates, but they know she went, an Aunt and M himself verified it. Either way, if she visited before, during, or after my graduation, she made the effort for him over me. When I learned that at forty-one years old, over twenty years after the fact, I felt justified all over again. Yet, guilty for feeling justified.

At the time, I had broken up with my mom. I disowned my mother. I said enough was enough and I said it in a way that I feel embarrassed by. She was right, I could have been far more cogent and tactful. The hatred ruled my reactions to things that threatened my peace of mind. I let it. It was defense.

I got a postcard letting me know where she was, but shortly thereafter creditors were seeking her whereabouts and calling *me*. She put me at risk with her debt. I found it funny, funny in that way that lent confidence to my decision, that I was better off without her.

She tried to call one afternoon, sometime in October of 1999. We had caller-ID on our landline. I answered, "Hello, Irene."

"*Irene*, huh?" she laughed.

I briefly remembered her calling her father by his name when we visited from Ohio. This wasn't as jovial.

She continued talking as though nothing had occurred between us at all. It was to notify me of a relative's passing. Someone I had met at three years old. I unreliably remembered a floating face from a photograph, but I didn't *know* them. They committed suicide. It was shocking, but detached, and she didn't seem too emotionally busted up about it. She was delivering a fact, but it was a means to an end.

She finally acknowledged our falling out and asked how I had been doing. It had been more than a year. I had a choice to make, and at twenty-years-old now, it felt unfair all over again. It felt heartbreaking all over again. How she aimed creditors in my direction when she was being felonious? This out of the blue phone call already wrapped in sadness?

"Better without you." I mustered. "I don't mean to cause you any pain or to hurt your feelings, but since we stopped talking, life has been a lot easier for me and I've been happier."

I was.

In the year since graduating, I finally started working regularly—in bookstores! The fear I had felt in losing the structure of school was being replaced by the eternally more brutal boredom of the *daily grind*. I was still with my girlfriend, and we were doing well.

There was a long silence. She finally said that was fine and that she was happy to hear I had found a good life to live. She ended the conversation with, "I love you."

"I'm glad you do...bye."

I wasn't trying to be cool. I'm no Han Solo. I *was* glad she loved me, but I didn't feel it from her. I know I hurt her then. That's a guilt I live with. She lied to me a lot. She betrayed my confidence and withheld information. Learning later that she had indeed chosen M over me in 1998? The other things that would come up later? She and I simply didn't click. Not anymore. Not as I grew up. We weren't right for each other.

I know some kids don't get along with their parents. Some have active bouts of arguing and violence. A lot of people have severed ties from one or both of their parents. I have argued the positives of detaching yourself from toxic individuals. I still believe that some people do not belong in our lives, no matter how they're related to us.

I wish my mom hadn't been one of those people.

PART TWO
WITHOUT

CHAPTER 37

1998-2001 – STILL AT HOME, TULSA, OKLAHOMA

After severing ties with my mother, I would randomly run into people who knew me through her, or friends who remembered her fondly from childhood. A callus gets built by repeated pressure. I had built calluses on most of my fingers from playing bass. I built a callous against this question of, "How's your mom?"

Some people I would or *could* unload on. Most, I said to them, "We fell out."

As I calloused, the callousness grew. I hardened. I was disappointed, saddened, and still angry. Resentment made me wish I was truly done with her. I may have said at times that she was "dead" to me. That *is* callous. I regret those sentiments in hindsight, but no one can know the future. I was angry. I couldn't put it into words.

I am still an advocate for severing ties from toxic people, especially if they're your family, because how do you escape an abuser who is *raising* you? You never do. They're a part of you, genetically and empirically. Their worldview shaped yours until you entered the real world and learned how poorly they had treated you, and now that past resides in you.

In me.

Anger was my vigilance. My mantra became "don't take abusive shit from anyone," and I proselytized that point to anyone who sounded the slightest bit irritated with a relationship. I viewed my childhood as a series of my *mother's* adventures I was an accessory to. Especially in those stepfamily years. When I told her my *line* had been crossed and she responded with aspersions toward my life experience? I didn't feel loved. I felt livid. It was a volcano that didn't settle for years.

Not that my life was hard after severing that tie. Some of my fondest memories of my "youth," exist in those last couple of teen years and early twenties. They're quick in the loading succession—if my memories are similar to files on a hard drive. I've learned in recent years that trauma creates stronger, more vivid memories. If things start going wonky and I'm spacey, all over the place in the times after I had finally stopped talking to my mom? It's not that I was no longer in trauma-mode, I began spiraling.

I made a difficult, and *traumatic*, decision that not only affected me, but my mother as well. It would affect my friends through my change in behavior. I don't know what kind of ripples it had in her life, because she apparently kept it close to her chest. What little I would learn later in life of her side of things was that she wanted to give me my space.

Sometime in 1999 or 2000 I ran into D at the Borders bookstore I was working at in South Tulsa. It was good to see him, and a surprise. I hadn't seen him since Anchorage and didn't know he was back in Tulsa.

He asked, "How's your mom?"

He was among the few I told the truth. He was understanding and related a tale of *how* she had moved to Alaska in the first place.

My mom had been staying with a friend for a little while between living with D and moving away. At fifteen I didn't understand or think to question how she was financing her trip or what her plan was once she arrived. She was going to "make it work."

...with his credit card that she had applied for from his trash.

I was aghast. Identity theft and credit fraud? My mother was capable of federal offenses *and* got away with them?

When he had learned of the crime, instead of pressing charges, he chased her down. But in facing her, somehow, they started their relationship up again.

Was he *that* forgiving or was she that *manipulative*? It gave me something else to be upset about. Why would I want to have that kind of person in my life?

While I thought I was building a better life for myself in her absence, instead I started emulating her. I jumped from job to job and as soon as I had a credit card I bought what I *wanted*. I didn't wait or save up or budget. I collected random things—entertaining ephemera like toys and video games that I would often turn around and sell off. I did put a lot of money into my music, but it was proving more an expensive hobby than a career path.

I would meet Jonathan Davis of Korn in late 1998. He was in the same mall in Oklahoma City my friends and I were shopping in. We were there for the first Family Values tour. Someone noticed my Korn shirt and said they had seen him. There were three of us and we split up to find him—I found him first.

He was in a record store. I recognized him from halfway across the mall. I rushed up to him, spluttering an attempt at, "Hi, I'm a fan!"

He had a handful of CDs; I could see Slayer's Divine Intervention at the end. Some of what he was picking through, I wondered, *is he picking this up for the first time, or does he have the money he can buy the album he wants to hear tonight while he's on the road?*

I admitted, *blurted*, to him I was nervous to meet him and didn't know how to compose myself. I wanted to ask him serious questions, especially about being in a band. He was extremely gracious and let me follow him down the aisles and toward the check-out. We talked about how any art needs persistence, but with a band, *everyone* needs to be committed to that persistence. A band is a team effort.

"Practice," He said. "All the time. Even when you don't want to. Practice more."

Honestly, as soon as he said that to me, I knew I would never make it. Not in the band I was in. His words rang in my ears with the revolving door of bandmates I would play with. I knew other artists who could make it, and maybe the right *team* could have worked, but I was always on the wrong side of ready. My mother knew I had been practicing bass guitar, drawing, and writing when I was in high school, but I wouldn't be able to share any of my original music with her.

Of course, a lot of what I was writing was angry about my childhood and some of it aimed at her. The blessing of grunge, alternative, and nu-metal was this openness to talk about the reasons Generation X and on are so fucked up is because the previous generations, our parents and the economical/political systems they were building in the 1970's and '80's, weren't good for the planet, the country, or us. I was channeling a lot of hurt through basslines and lyrics.

I did try to devote time and energy to my musical craft. If I was being active, even if I was dwelling in negative emotions with that activity, I was keeping my mind occupied. Otherwise, I could easily sink into bouts of depression.

I slept *hard* these days. I was a night owl, staying up late with friends no matter what night it was. If I was alone, I would work on creating something or entertaining myself into the wee hours. But when I would finally go to sleep, it would be deep, and if I had no alarm clock set, long. I know I slept nearly twelve hours a few times. I'm not a napper in my adulthood. At night, it might take a while to shut my mind up, but I would sink into a depth of sleep where I would drool a puddle and wake up with useless muscles.

There was an evening where tornadic storms erupted. A dangerous cell traveling along the Arkansas River, only a few miles from home. I could hear the storm. I could hear my dad up and he had his TV on watching the news. He was worried. I was sleepy. The constant thunder and whipping wind outside my window did little to dissuade me from my slumber. I didn't *feel* that I was in danger, I didn't get up to panic with my dad about the weather.

Amidst the cacophony the phone began to ring. It was 2 a.m. Who could be calling?

I heard my dad's voice coming closer. "Maybe you can wake him up, he won't listen to me."

My half-asleep face scowled as he nudged me with the phone saying it was my girlfriend.

I took it and smooshed the thing against my face. "What?"

"You need to get up and be ready, there is a tornado right next to your house!"

I sighed and listened to the outside world. My bed sat next to some double windows with a magnolia tree outside. Thunder and wind. No *freight trains*.

"It's fine." I said. "I can feel these things, I'm not in danger. It's just a storm."

She may have talked to me more. I ended the call, put the phone on the floor, and went back to sleep among the din. I'm not a mutant superhero, I don't have clairvoyance or control of the elements. I didn't take the moment seriously and I let myself slumber in danger.

There *was* a tornado that touched down near the river, however miles away. Not that I *wasn't* in danger. Weather in Oklahoma is often unpredictable, hence weather people come here to learn. I was lucky. Where I may have thought I was clairvoyant, I often think that was one of the first signs of an apathetic attitude toward life forming. I'd gone misanthropic, I didn't care about my humanity.

CHAPTER 38

I ended up working for four of the well-known bookstore chains. One of my earliest jobs I held onto for only a few days was at B. Dalton in Woodland Hills Mall. I was too afraid of the register and counting money and quit. Later I would work at Waldenbooks in the Promenade Mall. I would cross the street to work at Barnes & Noble only to eventually end up at Borders in South Tulsa. Barnes & Noble, however, backed up to AMC Theaters.

Right out of high school, I worked in a couple of movie theaters. The "Movies 8" across from Woodland Hills, then the AMC across from the Promenade. I was an usher mostly and got to stay away from having to handle money. One or both of my best friends I would end up working with a few times through these theaters and bookstores. At AMC, it was both. We saw a lot of free movies, and one of those friends would continue working in theaters for years. I got to see some of the greatest '90's cinema for free, often in private screenings after hours when movies were still delivered on reels of film.

One experience broke my brain, though. I saw The Blair Witch Project in one of our private midnight viewings with maybe six to ten other people in the theater. I went and sat by myself, I wanted to be absorbed in this "found footage." I already knew it was fiction despite the advertising campaign's allusions otherwise. The constant tension and dread, everything that fits together by the end of the movie—and that final shot? I was horrified. I was actually frightened in the theater, breathless. As the credits rolled, I had to force myself up. I walked out and said goodnight to my friends, then drove home.

A raccoon in a storm drain, not something you see often, caused me to yelp as I drove. I cautiously crossed my starlit yard. Entering my murky house, I snuck to my unlit bedroom, past my night covered dad. The dark, however, proved too much that night and I tried to sleep with the light on.

The fear wore off, but ever since? Nothing has spooked me quite the same. All that fear from childhood and getting my hackles up at anything horror and worrying about nightmares? Suddenly desensitized. I wanted to write something that effective.

I did not respect or care for my managers at AMC, they could be oppressive, and applied at Waldenbooks on a lark. I clicked with the bookstore manager. He was a little bit older than me, we both loved gaming and genre stuff in the store, and he asked if I could start the next day. I got out of that interview five minutes late for my shift at AMC, I went over to the theater and resigned on the spot. The shift manager was shocked and said I *couldn't* do that.

"I just did." I said, quite proud. This was my "take this job and shove it" moment.

"I quit," I continued. "I'm not working tonight; I've taken another job. That's what's happening here."

I worked at Waldenbooks for a while and made friends with the staff, though they were only ever "work" friends. There was an Asian girl who always wanted to play the "penis-game," where you yell "penis" alternately at increasing volume, the intent to not be the one "caught." We could get up to yelling it for our entertainment, usually to giggles throughout the mall of employees closing shops. Until a security guard stopped us.

There was a gay guy and we opened up to each other while working together. Only ever at work. We had deep discussions about sexuality, that he had been married to a woman not too long ago, came out to his wife who suspected, and now he lived openly. He helped me to absorb a lesson I had gleaned from something my mother had told one of my stepbrothers.

He had been come onto by another boy at school, and my mom tried to change his perspective on the matter. Rather than be mad he had been "accused" of being *gay*, instead, find flattery in the other person's attraction. He didn't have to accept it, he could say "no," same as if to a girl he didn't see that way. I understood that sexuality was complicated but could be simple if you're accepting. It is a part of one's individual identity, not a choice, and to treat it as a choice is harmful.

I would hear a coworker much later in my life try the argument that homosexuality *was* a choice to another coworker. I interrupted their conversation, firmly, but trying to withhold any malice.

I asked him when he *chose* to fall in love with his fiancé.

He couldn't answer.

I tried to use that to illustrate to him that no one chooses who or what they're attracted to. Even *if* it was a choice, *why* would they choose a life of persecution under arguments he was making that didn't hold up to his own experience with love? I may not have changed his mind right then, but I couldn't abide nonsense.

I can bristle and be abrasive about topics I care about, and just letting people *be* is a big one.

Getting there took some time. I respected strangers. I let acquaintances open their hearts to me because I was a good listener. I never considered my own problems, though. I didn't open myself to my best friends or girlfriend about the suffering I didn't know I was going through. I allowed everyone to empty into me. I was the group's councilor and philosopher.

I was also a philanderer. After Waldenbooks, I crossed the street to work at Barnes & Noble. I got close to a coworker, this time making friends outside of work. A few parties where I met friends of friends, knew at least someone from work, and went to unfamiliar parts of town. Then one night I brought this coworker to hang out with *my* friends. She kissed me in the hall, in the dark.

We nearly spent the night together but didn't get past a pulled-up shirt. I had a subconscious out when I would not turn my pager off. A friend kept pinging me. I sabotaged my own self-sabotaging.

I didn't care about my friend trying to find out if I was coming back to his house or not. I didn't care that I had a girlfriend. I also didn't care about this woman's feelings when I called her "my mistress." She was much more mature than me and didn't take that kindly and our making-out days were over.

That was by the time I had jumped bookstores one more time and was finally at Borders. I had other romantic interests, but I took them more seriously and broke up with my girlfriend. She didn't know about the cheating, and I wasn't going to confess, we ended things "better off as friends." I was out working in the world, and she was still in high school while also having a part-time job. She had next to no free time, we drifted.

I had wanted the high school sweetheart to turn into a marriage and family. I wanted to grow old and have that perfect love story that would prove to my mom somebody could be stable and happy with one family forever. I was resembling my mom more than I cared to admit. I wasn't strong when it came to careers or staying honest or faithful.

I started dating a woman my same age in 1999 and while we worked together, we kept the romance out of the bookstore. Our bosses knew of our relationship, but we kept it professional at work. Not that we didn't tease each other or go take extra-long lunches at the same time.

We got serious and fast. When we kissed at the turn of midnight going into the year 2000, I honestly wanted to commit to that tradition.

I didn't stop talking to my high school girlfriend, though. Cold comfort called. The heat of passion somehow felt exhausting. I started to *fear* how much I loved my new girlfriend and how much she loved me. When I decided to break up because things were becoming too much for me to handle, she expressed she had wanted the same things I had talked about, that family, why didn't I want it with *her*?

I broke it off because I was lazy. The effort I realized I would have had to put into stepping up to be that family-man? It was difficult, but also frightening: what if she took it away? I blamed her for coming on too strong, even though I had invited it, the challenge and the acceptance. I threw it away for the familiar.

I didn't see the irony. I was breaking someone's heart because they wanted to love me while I chased security in the past. You know, the same behavior I was angry with my mom about putting me through?

Not that I treated my ex-now-current girlfriend any better this second time around. We took comfort in having each other to cling to in loneliness. I still had my eyes open for other opportunities. I didn't devote or commit myself, and that was never fair to her. As much as I cared about respecting *people*, I didn't respect individuals; myself or my loved ones.

I ended up leaving Borders feeling pushed out.

While I had worked there, I had tried to be an active and engaged employee. I worked well in the different departments, music, books, periodicals, children's—that section where you find all the tchotchke shit that's impossible to manage—I even did well enough as customer service both on the information desk and the register.

I was assisting the periodicals manager the most, a pregnant lady who was training me to "manage" the periodicals during her maternity leave. An internal plan had been developed between herself, a general store manager (there were three or four of these at a store to cover different shifts and areas evenly), and the inventory manager to have me run the periodicals as a way to build experience. Once the periodicals manager was back from maternity leave, I would take over inventory when that manager was going to leave. I had a fast-tracked career path laid out and I was on board for it.

Unfortunately, one of the other general managers started getting close to my still coworker ex-girlfriend. Alliances formed. People fell on one side of supporting my advancement or the other. One of my two best friends was on his own career path at Borders in the music department. He stayed neutral, because he was friends with that opposing manager and my ex, and I never asked him to choose me over them.

How it manifested was that nearly every time I was scheduled to work in the periodicals—newspapers, magazines, and by the end of the year, calendars—I would constantly be interrupted by a supervisor from another department. Demands to come and help during someone else's break or some other crises of staff shortage. It kept me from keeping the racks organized and filled.

Magazines and newspapers of all kinds were still in high demand. We didn't all carry the internet in our pockets yet. This section needed a constant set of eyes on it, enough work for one person for an entire shift. But that made it seem trivial to anyone not versed in knowing which magazines and papers needed to be traded out by specific dates or how demand might make running back and forth with carts full of heavy paper exhausting.

By keeping me from my duties, the section suffered and looked disheveled, then putting me on the hook for not managing my section. I was being sabotaged. Sadly, the coalition in support of my advancement were outnumbered.

I made a decision one morning, an ultimatum I had given myself, I was going to switch out all of last night's newspapers for this morning's. It was a major endeavor that needed to be done before the store opened in half an hour. I convinced myself that if I was interrupted during this process, then I was officially being harassed. It would not behoove the store to have day old national papers when we had regular customers who were in at opening to visit the café and purchase papers. If-then, I would quit.

I clocked-in and went straight to work. The new newspapers were in the back of the store's warehouse on the loading dock. I was cutting twine and stacking them on my cart to try to get to work. A supervisor whom I *had* been friendly with, even talked about playing music with, walked up to me with great purpose. He urged me that I needed to drop what I was doing for the moment, and began to move as if I would follow him. I stopped him.

"These have to go out first thing, before we open, and you *know* that. I'm expected to take care of this while my manager's out and y'all have been keeping me from that. I'm tired of it. So, I'm going to put these out—because they need to be—and then I quit. Okay?"

He was silent.

I was glaring at him.

I felt bad. I didn't *want* to quit; I liked the career path I had been set on. But the sense of being forced to fail urged me to leave before I was fired. I had once helped this guy by giving him a ride to pick up his daughter from daycare and taking them home when he had car troubles. We had been friendly. He was friendlier with the other guy.

"Okay." He finally said with a nod and then left me alone.

I finished with the newspapers and the store was opening. I went to the back and clocked out and told the managers what had happened, why I was quitting, that I was sorry I was leaving them short, but that I did feel forced out.

No one told me I *couldn't*. Frankly, no one seemed terribly surprised or put-out by my departure.

Life could have been different. I didn't have the guts to put in that effort. I wasn't ready. These were grown-up agendas and I felt incredibly out of depth. I was trying to start a band. I wanted to draw comics. I was still writing. I was at the movies every weekend. I bought the newest video games and collected Transformers for a while. I was selfish, and since I still lived at home, I didn't feel the pressure of financial responsibility.

That's not to say my dad let me be lazy, he *did* try to impose some responsibility on me. He wanted me to start paying half the utilities after I was finally holding down a job since I was still living at home. There was more I wasn't preparing myself for because I was stuck as an angry eighteen-year-old. I was in my own way, and I wrapped myself up in escapism and nostalgia.

CHAPTER 39

After Borders I bounced around different retail jobs. I worked at a Spencer's Gifts in Woodland Hills, I worked at the Toys-R-Us across from the mall, then Best Buy down the street. What I was learning working all this retail was that I didn't like the *public*. I got anxious and irritated. Sometimes I didn't restrain my disdain. I got a lot of criticism in my dealings with customers. It made me want to get out of the scene entirely.

I went to a temp agency hoping I could find an office job away from customers. I did work downtown for a week doing data entry for some company. Working downtown in one of those tall buildings seemed intimidating at first. I wanted the serious office job; I didn't feel serious enough for it.

The work was easy, but it didn't last. Once the project was done, the temps were no longer needed, and it was back to waiting for the next opportunity. I eventually landed a job working at an AT&T Cellular retail store. I sucked it up because this was specifically *sales*. I figured I would be dealing with people who came in for one thing, and most would be walking out with something. Easy enough, routine inter-actions.

I was dead wrong. Sales is worse than customer service, because it *is* customer service while also trying to convince someone to buy something they don't want or need. Not that I ever treated it that way. "No" was an acceptable answer for me. I never pushed or pivoted. I had every manager and supervisor in every sales position I would have criticize me for it while many *more* customers thanked me for it. Guess who I capitulated to? For the most part, I believe people appreciate honesty and transparency, even if it might upset them.

While working at AT&T, I began to work on a novel. I wrote the short story Suicide King there.

I also watched the 2000 Presidential Election Night coverage at work. There were no customers and we had pizza and soda. We joked about how ridiculous this was turning out to be. Oh, the horror that dragged on.

This was the first presidential election I got to participate in and the guy I voted for won the popular vote. My vote didn't count for Al Gore, though, because I live in Oklahoma, a winner takes all state, whose electoral votes went to Bush. I felt the sting of my will being silenced.

I would welcome and advocate for the dissolution of the electoral college for every voter's voice to be heard. Conservatives will complain that would hand the victory to New York and California, who are populous and liberal leaning. They are not the *entire* country. The winner takes all rules some states have silences minority voters who, in a bigger picture situation, would be contributing to their candidate's outcome. In more than two hundred years of American history, only five popular votes outweighed the electoral vote, and two of them happened in my lifetime to great disaster. I think a lot of what would come in the next twenty years would be different if the actual winners had won their respective elections. I watched it all start that night.

I was trying to make the band thing work. A longtime friend wanted to sing, and he and I hooked up with a guitarist and drummer who lived on some quiet property in Sapulpa. We ended up having two bassists, playing some weirdly tuned nu-metal fun music. We drank beer and played loud, late into the night.

In 2001, I started working at Saturn of Tulsa. I worked at AT&T

through the New Year holiday, but was let go a month or two in. A friend's girlfriend informed me that the cashier position was open at the dealership for the service and parts department. Still customer service, but, even more granularly focused. I would deal with the same type of customers daily who were told how much something was by someone else and I would process their payment. I didn't have to answer questions. Straight-forward.

I met with the sales and service manager. I would be the cashier, obviously, but I would also be responsible for balancing the drawer and taking the day's profits to the main office for deposit. Cataloging state inspection stickers. I could be asked to help port cars if the garage was short-staffed or busy. It wasn't an interview. I was handed the job.

Pending a drug test.

I hung out with potheads. My band openly smoked weed. I was still afraid of getting paranoid and didn't. However, I didn't care if they were high and smoking *around* me. I had grown up with it! Could secondhand smoke register in a piss test?

Thankfully it did not. I decorated my office in action figures, I was allowed to have a TV under my desk and my boss didn't care that I played a Playstation in my downtime. I beat a few video games at that job: Chrono Cross, Metal Gear Solid, Silent Hill…

I read several books, including Thomas Harris's Hannibal novels. I drew comics, including an attempt at a daily comic that I did for a few months called "In a Handbasket" inspired by the Far Side.

After hours, a lot of us would *stay* at work, lock up, and start drinking beer in the garage. I had a lot of great conversations, played yard games, threw a football, and played with broken car parts (you can send a football remarkably far if you set it up in front of an airbag that needs to be discharged).

I befriended everyone I worked with. We convinced one guy for a good long while that my name, J.D., stood for Jack Daniels, that my parents were alcoholics with a twisted sense of humor. When he started introducing me to other people as *Jack Daniels* we finally had to put a stop to it, but that was fun while it lasted.

I had camaraderie with these people. We only ever had a few women to hang out with us, one of the service techs was a lady, one of the receptionists partied with us, but it was mostly guys who did a lot of serious life discussion, among cars and the smell of oil and a lot of beer.

One of the mechanics was a musician and helped me fix a broken input jack on one of my basses. Another tech, a tall guy who looked forever middle-aged, claimed when he was younger he kept a youthful face for a long time and pulled some 21 Jump Street shit and sniffed out drug dealers in public schools.

He and I would get into this game where we would try to list off song titles all day, the rule being the next song title must be thematically similar, he would say Hey Nineteen by Steely Dan, I would retort Forty Six & 2 by Tool, Two Princes by the Spin Doctors, Princes of the Universe by Queen—you get it?

There were radios all over the garage. I became "lucky" with reaching the DJs on caller-ten blasts. I won CDs, movie tickets, DVDs, and small things with ease. Sometimes it would be a DJ who knew my voice when I said, "aw dang," when I wasn't the winner, then kept me on the line. Everything is always who you know. The biggest thing I won was a trip to Denver, Colorado to see Tool at Red Rocks, touring for Lateralus. I took my girlfriend.

Seeing Tool for the first time, in *this* setting, felt religious. A thunderstorm was off on the horizon, producing lightning alongside their performance of Reflection. Magic was real and it was nature. It was a moment for me. This was a combination of musical, visual, and natural art. A lesson in appreciating something you may never see again.

That was August of 2001.

CHAPTER 40

t rained on my twenty-second birthday. My girlfriend bought tickets to see the Crystal Method at the Brady Theater. We ate at Outback. I was in a foul mood, and even though I was genuinely thankful for the concert tickets, the rain and bluster on my birthday made me sour.

The morning of September 11th, I was already late getting ready for work. The Today Show was still on the TV in the living room. They announced a plane had hit one of the Twin Towers. They didn't have much information, it might be a small plane, but they couldn't tell if it was a terrorist attack.

The rhetoric at the time was tense enough that anything tragic could potentially be terrorist activity. Small planes had hit buildings on accident in New York City before. I was appalled that the anchor jumped to terrorists—then I saw the second plane hit and my world changed.

Our world.

That was real, not special effects from a movie, and people were definitely deceased, en masse.

I still went to work. I listened to the news all the way on the radio. That TV under my desk? News all day. Every TV in the building was on the news. We all watched in anguish and awe when the towers came down.

We all stepped outside after the flights had been grounded and noticed the eeriness of a completely empty sky. This lasted for three days. In denser populated areas, and Tulsa is an "international" hub, temperatures rose a few degrees with the clearing skies. No contrails lingering in the atmosphere allowed more solar energy to reach the ground. It was a strange way to see the daily impact humanity has on the planet.

A lot of thoughts went through my mind: should I join the military and help strike back at whoever did this? Should I be worried about family? Was I going to hear from my *mom*?

New York was her birthplace, we did have family there, and if ever there was a reason to seek out contact…should I look for *her*?

One of our newer bandmates, a second guitarist, announced he would be joining the army. I concluded I didn't have the guts. My left big toe was screwed up, even though I had had surgery to remove an ingrown toenail my senior year in high school. That was my excuse, anyway. I wasn't brave, but in the end, I'm glad I never took part in any of the fighting that would result.

I mean no offense to anyone who served in those campaigns, but when fearful discussions of drafting popped up, I was prepared to be a conscientious objector. I didn't want to serve in Bush's Army nearly as much as I feared serving in general. I had military family, my mom in the Reserve, two other aunts joined. On my adoptive family's side, two of my uncles served and came back from Vietnam. I have always been impressed by people who can step-up.

At some point that bandmate's girlfriend and our drummer started hooking up. They admitted this to me and, I guess, were looking for someone who wouldn't judge them for some friendly advice. I told them she needed to break-up with the other guy if this was what they wanted. Sometimes people move on, and quickly. They shouldn't string someone else on along the way.

I lumbered through the rest of the month, watching the news regularly as rescue and cleanup efforts continued around the clock in New

York. Investigations had begun, NATO had been triggered—but by whom or what still felt nebulous.

Al-Qaida.

Osama Bin Laden.

Terrorist cells in Afghanistan, but also Pakistan? Or supported by Iran, Iraq, or the UAE... Some Saudi nationals were allowed to fly despite the no-fly orders. The attackers themselves had trained here in the United States, even visiting aviation schools right here in Oklahoma. Meanwhile the FBI had been aware of it all and never moved on them. Things looked bad no matter which thread you picked up, victims or attackers.

September 26th was the premier date of Star Trek Enterprise on UPN. The world stopped for a few days around 9/11, some concerts were cancelled. Shows and movies and even albums with their cover art had to be redesigned, delayed. The world keeps moving even if you want it to slow down to let you breathe.

My dad and I were having homemade burritos. I had prepared my plate and was going to retreat to my room while my dad watched in the living room. We weren't on the outs or anything, we were comfortable sitting wherever at whatever time. I think I had barely sat down to eat, maybe taking a single bite, when the phone rang.

I didn't recognize the phone number or area code on the caller ID. I asked my dad and he shrugged.

"Hello?" I answered.

A woman's voice, timid at first, unsure if this was going to go as planned, asked, "Is Justin Buffington there?"

I was bewildered. I didn't know who it was by her voice. "This is."

I started walking back to my room.

It was one of my aunts, whom I hadn't spoken to since around the same time as falling out with my mom. We used to email each other, I shared my writing with her, but things had gone quiet. She sounded relieved and thankful she'd reached me, as though there had been some hunting going on. She explained she got our number from M. She was lucky we hadn't moved or changed our number in all those years.

"It's your mom—" She said.

Now, at this second in time I thought, *What now?*

Even though I had thought only a few weeks ago I might finally hear from her. Two weeks had passed with nothing. I may have even resented that fact. To end up hearing from my aunt instead?

"—she's been shot—"

There wasn't much time between this sentence and the next, but I had already thought, *She wants to see me in the hospital, she's got that "life is too short" feeling; but shot? Was she in bad with a drug dealer?*

When my aunt finished, "—and she died."

We talked. There was only a little to reveal right then. An investigation was ongoing. At that instant, though, no matter how fast my brain was ready to jump to conclusions in the previous few seconds, it halted. It was silence, an expanding numbness where a void formed.

For a moment, there was eternity in there.

A thought solidified, unflinchingly, *There will be no reconciliation.*

My mom was gone forever.

I didn't know how to feel. This was *foreign*. I mean, I knew people died. My dad's mom had passed away and I was afraid of the funeral. I knew it was devastating emotionally, but—I *wasn't* devastated by this. I was shocked and at a loss for how to react.

I know I walked back through the dining room, my aunt still in my ear. I said to my dad, "I'm not going to eat this." Presenting my plate as I took it back to the kitchen. "My mom is dead."

I know I shocked him, but I was in my head, and I didn't process anything around me.

Back in my bedroom, I told my aunt that I hadn't kept in touch with Irene since I had graduated high school three years ago. I hadn't spoken to anyone from the family since then.

She had died on September 15th. She was only forty years old. She was living somewhere in Alaska again.

I wondered if 9/11 had anything to do with it.

I didn't cry. I didn't lose composure. We talked.

I was *confused*. What am I supposed to do with this information? I thought I had been a happier person without her in my life, but now a hole inside of me was exposed that could literally never be filled. I wasn't angry enough that I wanted her *dead*. The thought about drug dealers came from concern. How are you *supposed* to feel about the death of someone you convinced yourself you were done with, but they're still intrinsically a part of you?

It's that quiet loss for how to react that I sympathize the most with when the media talk to family members of people who have been killed. Those people who should be emotional wrecks are somehow cool and able to speak coherently on camera to strangers. The emotions don't always hit the same day, or week, maybe ever in some cases. Losing someone suddenly, startlingly, there *isn't* a proper reaction, and people shouldn't be judged for how they react.

I don't know how long we talked, but I gave her permission to share my number. I would get calls from people I hadn't spoken to in decades over the next few days.

I called my girlfriend and told her. She came right over. She held me and expected me to be upset, but she was more upset than I was. I wasn't catatonic—I felt a rapid, twisting whirlwind of different emotions and none of them stuck around long enough to *feel*. I could only say *confused*, because I knew I should be upset, that maybe I should cry or rage, yet I didn't. I receded into myself.

I took that next day off from work, everyone understood. In speaking with family, I hadn't spoken to one in over *twenty* years: my mom's mother. I hadn't seen her since I was learning to walk and did not remember her.

I would only ever speak to her the once, and she didn't seem torn up by her daughter's sudden passing. I had lived under the impression my mom and her own mother had a terrible relationship and that was a significant part of my mom's distaste for Jehovah's Witnesses. I quickly understood as the stereotypical aspects of a conversation with a JW unfurled, the needling about familiarity with the bible, the sound in her voice as she tried to split concentration between talking to me and writing in her log how much she brought up religious points. I thought I was atheist at this time, but I didn't want to fight her. The "conversation" became more evasion than sharing sympathy. I wanted to know more about my mom's youth, my own—my grandmother had been there for part of it—she offered me nothing.

Speaking with Jeremy and my aunt who first called me the most, as they seemed to be the last closest family to her, I ended up giving the ultimate word on how I understood my mother's final wishes: to be cremated. I recalled conversations where she thought cemeteries were permanently littering, taking up a plot of land for the "rest of time." She didn't like staying in one place while she was alive. She wanted to be dust on the wind.

It was in this reconnecting I learned that when my mother joined the Army Reserve, she gave me to another aunt with the instruction to raise me as her own. My mother gave me up, when I was only two, to her sister. The aunt I felt inexplicably familiar and safe with in those old visits to New York and New Jersey. My mom was married again, to someone I don't remember—or maybe I do—it could have been that guy she argued with and broke the wall, it could be the man from the earliest memories, I'm not certain, but going into the Reserve and dealing with that marriage were enough to give me away.

During that time as a toddler, I developed separation anxiety. If my aunt wanted to go out, still young herself, maybe needing a break from a kid—whatever—if she needed to leave, I became upset. Other family would have to distract me to keep me calm.

When my mom returned from the Reserve, she took me back. She had a few bad relationships, some of which I might remember among those early life memories. I was told I had been, for all intents and purposes, kidnapped at one point. Or, at least, I was in a man's custody against my mom's will, and it was with an aunt's help they retrieved me.

It wasn't all bad history about myself, though. I learned truths about her youth, who was Irene before she was a mother. Even when I spoke to my mom about her childhood, it was vagaries, usually humorous. She and her sister sounded the same on the phone so they pranked each other's boyfriends. She did not talk about how her parents had separated. That there was infidelity and serial monogamy as her guides to relationships. She was dragged into the Jehovah's Witnesses by her mother, objectified by the church, and forced to drop out of high school and marry when she became pregnant at the age of 15 by the father's family who held a little power in the church and locally.

It made her despise her own mother, and learning these things, in conjunction with finally learning from one of my aunts that she was diagnosed bipolar, had a prescription for medication but was not filling it, it put a lot of our past into perspective. I began to realize even the worst of our history could probably be attributed to misunderstandings and poor judgement in a moment as the result of lived experience. We are all reactionary creatures and some of us continue to be the wounded beasts long after the scars have smoothed over.

It wasn't all tragedy. I learned a little about the time between when I had stopped talking to her and she ended up back in Alaska. That she had continued her relationship with Jeremy and they apparently had a mostly wonderful time together. Irene was still a rollercoaster, but as she moved west and north, she became a happier, more positive influence in people's lives.

I'm glad she had moments of happiness, reconnected with family, and had her adventures. At the time, I felt intentionally denied a decent relationship with my mom. I didn't hide it. Everyone I spoke to wanted to say how effervescent she was, how much fun she tried to have, and how she enriched the lives of those around her.

I knew a woman who could *do* those things, usually to get something she wanted. But she *wasn't* those things for me. I knew someone who was unfettered, coping with issues in unhealthy ways, and refused to face conflict unless she was the one making it. Yet, we were all talking about the same woman, and we were all right.

I went back to work the next day. *Everyone* took a minute to offer their condolences and say I didn't *have* to be there, that I could take some more time off if I needed to.

I didn't want that. I had been angry with her for such a long time, her death was confusing and disruptive. I couldn't pinpoint if I was sad, upset, or, with new facts about our lives emerging, angrier still. I was mad at her for dying. For being in a situation that facilitated her death and what it had done to our disconnected family. I could not express the sadness I felt that we would never come to terms with each other. Things had been quiet, even though I was in a spiral of self-destruction. That swarm of conflicting responses made being alone undesirable. My mind couldn't not think about waffling. I went to work.

I went to band practice that same night. I was the first to show up (who didn't already live there). My drummer said the same things. I didn't *need* to be there, if I wanted to hang out and drink, that was fine, but I wasn't required to play. I don't think he was trying to force me to talk about it, but I do think he was trying to offer some peace.

We stood in his kitchen making a couple of beers warm in our hands as I rambled about not wanting to ramble. I wanted to keep things normal. I didn't listen to anyone, how could they offer advice on my weird and unique situation? No one could relate to me, and I didn't feel relatable, or that I needed to be. I wanted to get back to work. If I was working—at work, on writing, music, art—I wasn't thinking about it, and assumed eventually I would get used to it, *over* it.

I didn't.

Things with the band unraveled as the affair came out and our drummer quit, ultimately also taking away our practice space. My singer, the other bassist, and I stuck together and started looking for another drummer. As I hung out at my singer's apartment more and started descending into a loneliness I couldn't put my finger on, my singer's girlfriend and I started flirting.

On a whim, I got both my eyebrows pierced. One hit a nerve and I couldn't move that eyebrow for months. The—*rush*? It made me feel cold and ill, "this is what dying feels like."

Afterward I was lying on my singer's floor while he and our other bassist went out for—stuff—probably weed. They were going to be gone for a little while. I was woozy from the adrenaline rush and my singer's girlfriend stayed behind with me.

This was all wrong, yet I wanted it, because I was feeling some-thing *different*—other than confused, other than lonely.

That night, lonely in a sea of potential support, she knew she could take advantage of me, and I didn't stop her. We had already been kiss-ing. Neither one of us cared we were in committed relationships, neither one of us cared about protection, we didn't care about disease or pregnancy (though, she would later claim she couldn't get pregnant due to health issues) or complications or repercussions. That same lethargy, even if it was from different places and reasons, that apathy and recklessness, was what we exercised with each other.

We kept it up for a little while, only stopping after nearly getting caught and barely able to cover it up.

I kept the band together into the next year. We found a drummer, the girl who had played guitar with me in high school wanted to take up the art and we built from the ground up. Our other bassist quit, but still hung out. We found a guitarist.

My singer's girlfriend and I buried our sins and moved on.

Before the end of the year, though, something would finally scare me worse than the Blair Witch Project. Final Fantasy X. I played it as soon as it came out on the PlayStation 2 and identified with Titus and his parental relationship and the fantastical representation of that strife. Even though there *are* Eldritch horrors in the game, it wasn't any horror element that frightened me. It was after a scene where the monster at the center of the plot, named Sin, decimates a military force on a beach. When you survive the encounter, you can explore the beach and there are observations on the carnage.

One text box said, "His eyes are open, but there is nothing there."

I left it on the screen for a long time. My thoughts on death prior to this moment had been that I didn't think about death. It was something that happened, but for the individual, they have no clue they're dead. You don't know you've been asleep until you wake up. Ergo, you can't know you're dead if *you're* dead. Now I was confronted with the concept of what happens to the self?

My reasoning still stood, but now I became afraid of the end of things, of oblivion. I don't want my *experience* to end. Even when I've been at my loneliest and lowest, I have never wanted my life to cease. I can't imagine growing tired of it, as I've heard some people claim they would. I don't think it's fair that there is an infinite universe with time forward and back in infinite directions and I am limited to mere decades in this primitive, edge of the galaxy star system with a rock that's "just right" for sustaining our understanding of life. I don't want to stop learning about the universe. I don't want to stop advancing as an individual. Five hundred years? Five million years? I want to *see* nature at an epochal scale, I want to witness dust become stars and worlds, I want to know what happens when a universe *ends*.

Now this video game reminded me, *alerted* me, to the fact that eternity is unattainable and effectively not real. Thereby, what happens to the concept of me should I die?

I became afraid of dying, losing my awareness and experience of "life."

The panic attacks even thinking about death that would result had me facing my mortality on too regular a basis. I developed this theory that maybe the self stays "on" inside the brain during the dying process, and the final, fading discharges of electricity—corpse spasms —is our screaming on the inside, imprisoned by our own bodies.

I felt a little insane.

It may have taken the game to trigger this fear, but it must have always been there. I had avoided my grandmother's funeral. I was refusing to process my mother's death. I dismissed thinking about death with anyone who brought it up with Shakespearean flourishes of "what dreams may come."

I wasn't okay. I *knew* I wasn't okay. I chose to ignore how un-okay I was.

CHAPTER 41

2002-2003 – AN APARTMENT IN SOUTH TULSA

I n 2002 I finally moved out. One of my coworker's was losing a roommate and I thought I was stable enough to take on living away from home. I made enough at Saturn, I thought I could handle it. It helped that he lived literally across the street from the dealership. I would save on fuel costs.

My dad was happy for me, though maybe a little melancholy.

At twenty-three I was "on my own."

There were still a lot of sleepless, anxious nights thinking about death. When I could sleep, there were a lot of nightmares then that I think a lot of people who have lost someone have: that my mom was still alive. The concepts were usually that she had faked her death, or didn't even know anyone thought she was dead, a case of mistaken identity. I would want to grab her and shake her, angry and thrilled by her presence, but it was always that viscous dream medium that keeps you from reaching whatever you want to hit or grab.

As time moved on, details finally began to emerge about my mom's final days and death. She had remarried and her husband may have shot her. The story went from she was shot, to she shot herself in the head. The word "suicide" was used, but it always seemed to have a question mark in parentheses.

The last time I had spoken to her she was telling me about a suicide in our family. I wasn't sure how to take it. I don't think I truly believed suicide was the coward's way out, I understood some people could be pushed too far. My thoughts went to 9/11 again. Or what kind of relationship she was in. Or, selfishly, how was she overall since I had pushed her out of my life? As soon as that detail emerged, I began to worry I might one day be suicidal, too.

I started having waking nightmares, especially in the evenings after showering. I might listen to music while showering, but I would be in my head. I started thinking—*knowing*—that when I opened my bathroom door, my mother's body would be standing there, her head-wound in gory relief.

One night the feeling became too much. If there *was* such a thing as spirits, ghosts, and hauntings, tonight was the night the horror would happen. I pressed my hand against the door and started to talk.

"I don't know why you were suffering." I said. "I don't know if you're suffering now—if there's a Hell... But if you're suffering because of *me*, please don't. I forgive you. I don't hate you and I don't want you to suffer because I was angry."

The dread faded. I opened the door, and there was the hallway. I was still wrapped up in my pseudo-grieving, I talked about this lonely exchange with a lot of my friends trying to find sympathy and guidance. I wanted to forgive my mom, but what I was failing to do at the time was to forgive myself. I was still putting my anger into her, as though she was spiteful toward me.

A good friend's mom explained being naked and wet is the ultimate vulnerability. Psychologically, alone with my thoughts, *wet and naked,* my darker thoughts ran roughshod. Could ghosts reach through that turmoil? Or was it my fears taking advantage of my loneliness?

My "affair" would be outed, by my singer, to my girlfriend. She didn't believe him. She had faith in me. I was at her house when the call came. Her parents had moved to Oklahoma City and she and her best friend were now living in her childhood home taking care of the utilities while her parents helped with maintenance. If my singer was making the accusation, then his girlfriend must have either confessed or been outed by one of her friends. I'm not sure how it got to him, but I had fucked up and it was finally time to be "honest."

I told my girlfriend the truth. Kind of. I would continue to lie about how intense or long it had lasted and how reckless we had been. I adhered to a lifestyle of lying to try and cover my ass to mitigate the repercussions I might face. If one layer of a lie faltered, I had another lie lined up to protect me from worse anger. I disappointed people by levels instead of all at once.

Of course, in hindsight, letting everything out would have been better. Talking to people about the confusion I lived inside of and the apathy that created should have been helpful, but instead I was met with annoyance, disbelief, and sometimes anger. Lying eventually became easier to interact with people through rather than difficult truths no one wanted or knew how to interpret.

Despite how nasty our breakup was, my girlfriend was still constantly in touch with me. Usually for one of two reasons: to demand more answers for the many transgressions and to rub it in my face that she was now fucking my singer, the guy whose girlfriend I had fucked. She reveled in telling me details and I listened as penance.

Sometimes, she would show that she still cared. She convinced me to see a psychiatrist for this next wave of lethargy I was descending into.

My first time seeing a psychiatrist, on my own, was different from the family therapist. I explained everything. A childhood where I felt let down and questionably loved, breaking up with my mom, her eventual death, and this last year of apathy—if I was alone, I did wonder if I was going catatonic. I wanted to be better and make-good and do right by my girlfriend. I still *enjoyed* my band and writing, and I didn't know if I wanted to even try medication because I felt I might lose my creativity (I was only at the beginning of learning about my mental health and unfortunately had biases against drugs the same way my mother probably did when she needed help).

He sat and listened to it all, but the one good point he made, I refused to listen to for a long time. He said, "I think you love your art and having that focus lets you function; but, do you *really* want to be with your girlfriend?"

I was offended at the time, but he saw in my description of my own life and situation that I was trying to be something to other people, rather than for myself. If I couldn't be happy with myself, how was I going to make anyone else happy? Why depend on other people's opinions of me to define that happiness?

He offered me a sample of Prozac, a two-week course, long enough to see what it would *do*. All I noticed were poorer quality bowel movements. I didn't go back to the psychiatrist or continue the anti-depressants. I wanted to focus on my music if that was good enough, not absorbing that I was relying on a coping mechanism.

In the fallout of friends with the breakup, at least I still had a band. I wrote a lot more thoughtful music about my relationships and feelings, wanting to play something beautifully complex but energetic, inspired by Tool, Type O Negative, and White Zombie.

I got a lot *more* time to write music when I was laid off from Saturn. The auto-industry had backslid through the last year, hitting the parts and service portions significantly, right where I worked. Each of the service technicians *could* do my job, and it would be a more fluid experience for the customer anyway. My boss held off letting me go, he fought to keep me on knowing what I was going through, but also genuinely liking me as a person and employee. The marching orders were given.

He invited me into his office and offered me a drink.

I said, "We're on the clock...?"

"You'll need it."

After he forced himself to let it out, my paranoia kicked in, and denial and negotiation tried to take over. Ultimately it came down to asking, "Is it something about *me* or..."

He waved me off. "No, it's all of *this*," he gestured at the empty air.

Trickle-down economics is real, but no one makes money from it. Quite the contrary. I'm a victim of it.

That gesticulation in the air toward the state of the world would become something all of us would adopt to express our ever-increasing despair.

I still worked at Saturn when the anniversary of 9/11 came, though. I cried hearing a rebroadcast of a radio program's minutes when they confirmed the terrorist attack. Later in September that emotional flood-gate would open again when I finally cried about my mom's death.

I was deeply affected by it now, worried *anyone* could vanish from my life now in an instant. When I couldn't reach my dad by phone the next day, I freaked out and hunted him down, playing pool at his usual place with his friend. Something they did every weekend. I shouldn't have panicked, but I had already worked myself up. I told him what was up, he felt for me, reassured me he was obviously fine.

I should have asked him for help when I lost my job. I should have moved back home when my unemployment dragged on for months. Instead, I used credit cards to pay insurance and car payments, because I didn't want to ask for help. I was out on my own now, and even though all signs pointed to my struggling, mentally and finan-cially, I opted for debt to maintain my independence.

My drummer worked as a night auditor at a hotel. I would visit her often, usually helping her perform some of her duties to pass the time. I started looking for the same position at other hotels to keep those night owl hours. I was lucky enough to land one. Since we kept the same hours, we spent a lot more time together.

She had maintained her friendship with my ex-girlfriend yet still cared about ours (as a friend, nothing ever happened between us). She wanted to see me move on and for her friend to let me go.

The girl I cheated with, it turned out, was pregnant and due soon. My ex called me to try and frighten me with this news. My drummer and I were in Texas (on my credit card) to see a band and friends. The call was on speakerphone. I told my ex she knew it wasn't mine unless that girl had been pregnant for a whole year. It was still a startling reminder that I *had* been careless. The attempt at public humiliation wasn't lost on me, I still felt penitent.

My drummer would get back at her on my behalf on another speakerphone call. She regaled her with how hot the stripper was that I hung out with the night before. Embarrassing though it was, I did appreciate my drummer aggressively being my *friend*. It felt how love should feel.

I couldn't quit trying to make amends—even though I was frequenting adult entertainment. I wasn't kidding anyone. I couldn't see how like my mom I was being, always keeping one foot in both worlds to make sure I was satisfying my desires. My ex would break up with my old singer and move to OKC to live with her parents. Distance makes the heart grow fonder? We talked a lot more while we were separated.

I was on shift and talking to my drummer on the phone when the second Iraq war started. I hated it. I thought it was a sham, even if Saddam Hussein was a bad actor, *this* wasn't the way. We were invading that oil rich country, *again*, under another president named Bush, and it all smacked of theater and legacy. People were going to die, and the global economy would get wrecked.

Eventually, a position opened at Saturn again and I took it despite the pay cut with the knowledge there was ample overtime opportunity. I would be back on days and back with a work family I knew and loved. They had never judged me for the shit I had gone through quite publicly. While I was there, I wanted to put in that effort that might get me a promotion or raise. It wasn't going to happen. The power structure started changing, like Borders a few years before, I rubbed people the wrong way.

I wasn't forced out, instead, I left when my drummer convinced me to join her and her aunt who were now working for a set of Cingular franchise stores. The base wage wasn't much more than what I was making, but there *were* commissions. It was sales. Sales and customer service. Again. I did have the AT&T experience, I could reap the financial benefits unlike with the temp agency, but I wasn't excited. I was just shifting jobs again.

Until I was good at it. My acceptance of "no" was often appreciated by my customers. They told their friends. I may not have been great at upselling, but I was signing people up. I was only there for a few months when, in an emergency, they had no one to cover their Owasso location. I was sent to run the store by myself. A newbie, with no one to turn to for questions on the spot. I excelled. Eventually that tiny little store would basically be mine.

I wasn't a manager and I didn't get a raise, but I was being trusted with property. I felt a little pride in that. I tried to do a good job. There were other employees, I didn't run the store from open to close, but I worked eight to ten-hour shifts either opening or closing the place, I was the primary fixture there.

There was a lot of down time. I installed a TV/VCR combo to watch movies in the supply closet. Checking inventory becomes redundant when no customers come in for the entire shift.

I started traveling to OKC more often to spend time with my ex who kept me in her life by teasing me with enough affection to keep me coming back. She knew how to manipulate my guilt and keep me promising to make amends. The further I got from it, though, the more disgusted I felt with myself, and recognized I had not been well, that I probably *wasn't* well, and I needed to do better. I wanted to gain my girlfriend's forgiveness.

Again, I was in a position where I needed to move on, *if only* I had moved on! I wasn't proving anything to anyone else. This obstinance wouldn't prove my mom wrong. I wasn't a better person driving myself deeper into debt and alienating my other friends for all the time I spent on the road. However, I had a *lot* of time to think in that hour between Tulsa and OKC, and I drove it way too many times.

CHAPTER 42

2003-2004 – APARTMENTS IN MIDTOWN, TULSA

had regained my ex-girlfriend's best friend's confidence and trust, which was regaining an old friend. She and I had been friends from before I had started going out with my girlfriend. We hung out a lot, often only us, watching movies at each other's houses or taking in something in the theater together. Nothing ever happened between us, even though I wanted to try.

I did ask about it. My "relationship" with my ex was too weird with the on-again/off-again bullshit. She also didn't want to compromise her friendship because *they* had been friends longer than *we* had. It was a soft "no" that didn't mean we had to stop being friends. I did my best to maintain that.

When Dan Brown's The Da Vinci Code was tearing up the charts and getting talked about across all media, I asked for it as a gift from… I guess everyone, because I got three copies. One from her, too.

I became increasingly fascinated by the concepts played with in the book, of sacred bloodlines, puzzles in plain sight, and my introduction to Gnosticism. This poorly hidden, archaic form of Christianity, its *existence*, made me interested in listening to what *all* the religions had to say, because I could see these intersections and divergences in a traceable family tree. I wanted to know more about what I didn't know.

My roommate and I moved out of our apartment together and each moved into our own solo living spaces. He stayed in the same complex, I moved further back into town, a little more centrally located. This was the first time I would have a place all to myself.

Between driving to OKC and back and living alone, I only had my own devices to be left to. I read more books on Gnosticism, and these sort of New Age views on Christianity. I started to back off again. Gnosticism has these super angels called Aeons and they lost me. New Age-anything reads as a caricature of stereotypical hippy culture to me. It becomes hard for me to take it seriously. However, it often looks cool and smells nice (unless patchouli, no thank you). These are my personal opinions.

It is *my* belief that everyone's belief is correct—for them. The exception being when you use that system of belief to cause harm. Then? I believe that you are hiding your own prejudices behind doctrine and divinity.

No one knows who's right. Clearly. Here we are in the Space Age and there are countless interpretations of multiple creeds and even more granular translations of their individual texts. Even science has its schools of thought and evidence that changes daily. The only certainty *is* uncertainty. If you believe in God, or Source, or Aeons, and you're making it through life and maybe making someone else's life a little better by existing the way you do? You're doing it right and your god smiles on you for it.

I strived to make this my belief: that belief was subjective, and therefore, a personal experience that no one can say is incorrect for someone else—barring that hurting other people bit. I developed a concept of God that I was comfortable with. In a broad stroke, I think God is akin to the Force from Star Wars.

God exists in everything, the atomic structure of the universe, and is experiencing life vicariously through our existence. Emotional struggles. Underwater volcanoes. What's on the "inside" of a black hole. Trees that sing to attract birds. It's out there somewhere, and it's a total shame that we are limited to these tiny swathes of existence, wasting our time on political and religious differences.

My hope for an afterlife, albeit I know I'm only hoping, is a quantum awareness, that our "self" continues to experience the universe at an unlimited level, made a part of the cosmic fabric and aware of the breadth of existence. God is in us, we are God.

I thought this through as I lay on a mattress on the floor, alone in a one-bedroom apartment.

I tried going to Southern Baptist church with my ex's friend a few times. Through cultural osmosis I had come to understand churches to be not much better than high school, full of cliques and in and out groups. I was not dissuaded from this belief, but there's always something to glean from an experience out of your comfort zone. People-watching can tell you all you need to know, and people should certainly be believed when they show you who they are.

She was embarrassed, and apologized profusely afterwards, but we watched a group of councilmembers defend their decision to oust a pastor that it seemed they didn't care for and found any tiny little thing to justify firing him. It was personal housekeeping business that needed to be done in front of the congregation because people were starting to divide and they wanted to show their decision was the right one, the church needed to unite behind it.

It seemed petty. It was amusing. This was exactly what I didn't want from church and here it was being served as the main course.

Maybe church wasn't for me. I still wanted to learn and, same as I believe God experiences the universe, "bad" experiences inform the whole. Hell is only ever our own making. Yet, I continued to irrationally fear death and cling to that old relationship hoping I could make *something* in my life "right" for all my own fuckups. I could never focus on me, only on what I perceived others as perceiving me, and what I could do about it if I thought I wasn't meeting their ideal, whatever *that* was.

Even though I had some growth occurring, I was refusing to learn and heed my own lessons. This is why I hate those years of my life. I know *hate* is a strong word, but, after 9/11, after my mom's passing, I became my worst self. I was on that path anyway, I wasn't being a good boyfriend before, I had my part in handling my relationship with my mom, but this was my lowest.

This was drinking every day. This was going to OKC on larks and concerts in Dallas and drinking heavily with internet friends. The band was my only positive focus, and even that was an excuse to drink with friends and growing stagnant as we couldn't find a singer with their own equipment.

I found a female vocalist who I clicked with, and my guitarist thought he was calling me out for it, saying he thought we were trying out singers, not new girlfriends for *me*. That hurt, but also stung with truth. I was lonely at home in Tulsa, but couldn't let go of my girlfriend who wasn't my girlfriend in OKC.

By now, she was going to college in Edmond, and had a one-bedroom apartment of her own. This is where I would come visit her most often, a few times in the middle of the night because *she* was lonely, and I couldn't tell her "no." By now, I had made her secure in the fact that I wouldn't quit trying to make things right with her no matter what the circumstances were. She started dating and telling me about her dates. It worked for a little while, trying to make us compete for her.

I never met the guy she hung out with the most, but there was a close call when we were all at the same mall at the same time about to see a movie. She kept the two of us far apart from each other, flitting back and forth between us to see who she wanted to hang out with. This was abuse. She was getting back at me now. We *weren't* a couple, but I had better stay available to her, because sometimes she acted as if we *were*.

I hate that I put up with it. Which, again, there's that word for this period of my life, *hate*. I let this happen to me. I perpetrated a lot of it onto myself. We can talk about a younger man's brain, in a time of not only global crisis, but a personal crisis as well. I was in a poor state with a track-record of poor decisions. Yet, I recognize pride.

I was certain of my ability to transcend my own transgressions that I would pay any price, financial and emotional. However, this was a new low and I struggled to justify subjecting myself to it.

By my reckoning, I had already proven I was willing to attempt her tests, and we had shared intimate moments in the time between and we kept coming back to each other, all despite what I had done. That could no longer be held over my head. I was past it. If she committed, I would commit. If she wanted to make me jealous and then guilt trip me into staying nearby with what I had done to her? I recognized she was taking advantage of me, and I wouldn't be a part of it anymore.

Was I in the right? Shouldn't I have broken it off instead? Why did I demand respect? Why was I continuing to be selfish? Would this be us forever? Constantly threatening to yank each other's emotional support from under the other with some emotional time bomb always getting reset...

I couldn't see how ironic I was being. I couldn't let go even when I knew I needed to because I was afraid of ever letting go of something again. I had created this ultimate fantasy of succeeding with the high school sweetheart and having an everlasting family in the face of my mother's flightiness and that old emotional hostage taking. Now I was both flighty (what else was dropping personal time between Tulsa and OKC and random trips down to Dallas for entertainment?) and emotionally manipulative—as was my girlfriend.

The trips became fewer, the intimacy faded. She made trips toward me instead, but it was more friendly hangouts with groups.

My drummer and I moved into a duplex together, though I basically lived by myself again. She had started a new relationship and wanted to move out of the band house where her ex still lived. We paid half of everything, but she mostly stayed with her boyfriend. It was my place that she paid to stash her stuff in. I was alone the first night.

I moved the last of my stuff in a rush, exhausted. I didn't even set up my bed properly, instead leaving the mattress haphazardly on the floor amongst the boxes and slept in clutter. Well—tried to sleep. We apparently lived across from a lively night community that by day was an empty strip mall. I could hear their distant music and the pitchy staccato of voices getting loud, laughing, or yelling. That, I could handle. Human white noise.

When the pops came, I wondered... When the low flying, circling police helicopters with spotlights giving residents little thought buzzed around for an hour, I was pretty sure. When my dad asked how my first night was the next day by phone, having heard of a murder across the street at the club scene on the news, I knew I had "heard" someone die. Nice first impression.

It wasn't fear for my personal safety alone that contributed to buyer's remorse, but a plumbing issue immediately upon moving in, too. Our place had three toilets, which was great if we were both home and maybe had friends over. A split bathroom connected the two bedrooms upstairs, and there was a toilet and sink downstairs in a closet underneath the stairs. My half of the bathroom had a toilet and sink opposite each other. I couldn't flush that toilet without it clogging.

This isn't some admission about unusual bowel movements. The toilet would randomly backup, no matter the contents. I called it in, the landlord would have a plumber out. Within a week, it was backing up again, to the point I quit using it.

It wouldn't let me ignore it, though. The pipes that led to that restroom were in the ceiling of the living room, and one day began leaking through onto my drummer's couch. I moved it, prioritizing cleaning her couch, thinking, *fuck this place's carpet.*

I called the landlord again, who said they would have someone out. They never cut out any ceiling or re-plastered. I continued to use the downstairs toilet for all my business. You would think being on the same floor and "system," the other side of the bathroom would have these problems, but her toilet and the bathtub never had a problem, only "my" toilet.

As we got settled in, there were times my drummer and her boyfriend had the place to themselves. They heard similar noises to what I was usually quick to explain away as those pipes. In all reality, questionable plumbing is probably the answer for everything. We both heard a rumbling, tumbling, rolling, sometimes *trampling* progression of noise from one side of the upstairs to the other.

If you were upstairs, it sounded as if it was coming from within the walls, especially in my room where it shared a wall with our neighbors who had three kids sharing the room next to mine. They were mostly good kids, but I would sometimes blame the "noise" on them.

Despite our independent and shared experiences with the noises and spooky vibes, it was our neighbor who seemed to confirm a general *something* was wrong with our place.

I came home, around dusk, but this was winter, not *late.* I got in the doorway and barely out of my coat as someone knocked on the door behind me.

I was more annoyed than startled, *who's been waiting for me to get home?*

When I opened the door, it was my neighbors, a husband and wife, looking stern and concerned.

"Hi?" I said.

"Is everything okay?" the husband asked.

"Uh," I was now confused. "I just got home, but yeah, I guess…"

"It sounded like there was a fight upstairs, a bad one." They said interchanging words and details with each other.

"I'm the only one here, and like I said, I *just* got home."

We all looked up the stairs directly behind me in the entryway.

I looked around the stairs through the living room and kitchen/dining room to see the backdoor looked closed.

"I think everything is fine, but thank you for checking in."

"Let us know if you need any help." The husband offered.

I thanked him.

After shutting the door, I turned on the stair light and pointed my ear upstairs. Nothing. The dark of my drummer's bedroom at the top was foreboding, though. I went and physically checked the backdoor— everything was in order. Now I had to go upstairs, by myself, and turn on lights and hopefully not find a murder scene.

I was greeted with nothing. At all. Nothing out of order, no accidentally toppled furniture, no vandalism from outside, no broken windows, not even my toilet backed up. That made my neighbors' alarm and concern more disturbing. *What* had they heard? They said a fight. Were there voices? I did not go back and bother them, instead swimming in my own anxiety about what-ifs.

I think I had another six-month lease on my hands. I didn't stay that long. My drummer was still paying her share, but moved her stuff out two months early. She and her boyfriend were moving along quickly. One of my best friends was house shopping and wanted to invite me as a roommate to help make the mortgage until he got settled. I was out of that place as soon as I could. Our last month was paid for.

Whatever was there, though, had to say goodbye.

The last thing I was moving from that apartment to my friend's house was my computer, which I had left plugged in and hooked up to the internet to pay the bills one last time for that place. I was literally there to do that, pack it up, and then stay over at my next residence.

Walking into the apartment it sounded as if someone was upstairs. I said "hello," though there was no response, and I didn't think anything of it. I went about my business at the computer downstairs in the dining room, thinking my drummer's boyfriend was upstairs. A thump here and there, something shifting, footsteps...

When I was done and had powered down my PC, I could see in the glass monitor my reflection, the back of my chair, the entire living room behind me, and someone standing behind me, midway between my chair and the lamp across the room.

"Ha, ha," I said, "I see you sneaking up—"

As I turned, the living room was empty.

I can tell you, in hindsight, with some maturity, with my ever-changing understanding of the world and our brains, I experienced pareidolia. Something in the convexity of the glass of the monitor, the angle of the light from the lamp on how I was sitting at that moment casting a shadow or blank spot in the reflection that my brain filled in with a man-shape.

The processing power our brains are capable of to fill in gaps in our perceptions with ghosts to keep us "ready" for threats is *amazing*. You can learn to recognize it, to dismiss the misperceptions as they happen.

At the time, however, I panicked.

I yelled out my drummer's boyfriend's name, I ran upstairs, checked everywhere; no one. I will note, as dismissive as I am of the supernatural, that place went *quiet* when you went looking for culprits. There was still nothing out of place, nothing new missing, no evidence I had missed him leaving without my notice.

I called my friend and begged him to come over after explaining my ghostly encounter. Some friend, though—he was too scared to face a ghost.

He told me to hurry up.

I did.

I let the property manager know about our eerie issues as we performed our final walkthrough. He didn't balk, instead relating his own creepy experiences at his grandmother's house. For once I didn't mind a conversation dragging on too long. I love "real" ghost stories.

This would be my last one, though.

Even though I don't believe my own senses from those memories anymore, I cherish the fact I lived in a "haunted" townhouse (verified by my roommate *and* neighbors!). It serves as a perfect segue point between two eras of my life. Haunted and knowing better; but, sometimes, both at once. Sometimes, one over the other.

CHAPTER 43

2005 – A HOUSE WITH MY BEST FRIEND, TULSA

2005 serves as a major turning point in my life. I was still clashing with my ex, our orbits growing further apart, but always fraught with emotional brutality when we came close. I would try to date someone ten years older than me and seriously considered if I could be a father figure to her kids. I was doing decent at work and making headway on handling my debt.

I still wanted to be a musician. I jammed and spoke with some other bands. Moving in with one of my best friends included another roommate, another high school friend who hung out off and on. The three of us lived in a four bedroom, two bath. The fourth room was kind of strange, built-in desks, in two folding closets side by side, a few inches of wall between them.

This would become a creative space for us. We gamed on our PCs, playing City of Heroes and Battlefield II with a group of internet friends from all over the country. Our roommate wrote synthesizer tracks there. My best friend and I wrote a movie script there. He had become friends with a local rapper who would come over and futz around on computers and musical equipment, too. There was a lot of creativity in the house, but not a lot of collaboration. Our artistic tastes were too different for us to see how it could come together. Electronica, prog-metal bass, and rap could totally work!

Living with friends was fun. We constantly had extra people in and out of the house. It wasn't parties all the time, and I knew most everyone who came by, I was being more social than I had in years, but it was effortless. People I knew. The New Year party I had gone to with my best friend and the rapper for 2004 into 2005 I knew *only* them. I felt completely out of place there.

I can look at this year as a last hurrah of exuberant youth. I don't lament that fact! Where I ended up was healthier. There, I was drinking heavily again. Socially. A lot. This was our frat house. We still took care of the place. We were respectful of living with neighbors and each other. We were all single and were gonna make sure we all had a good time under that roof. It wasn't all debauchery.

My own relationship problems became all encompassing, dragging friends in and out of things they wanted no part in. If I wasn't fighting with my ex, I was trying to be serious with a woman my new room-mate introduced me to who leaned on me for a lot of emotional support, but never let me more "in" than as a friend she would kiss sometimes. I couldn't force myself to commit to either of them, perhaps addicted to the emotional manipulation I subjected myself to.

The first half of the year was a constant back and forth between these two women, but I was also excited for Star Wars Episode III. I spent a lot of time online, both at home and at work, with friends from a Star Wars fan forum, and would still make trips down to Dallas to hang out. I wasn't trekking as often, but it would be Star Wars and a trip to Dallas with my ex along, that things would finally start to fall apart—permanently.

I think Revenge of the Sith is the best of the Prequel Trilogy. Having the complete trilogy does make Return of the Jedi have some extra emotional impact between Vader and Luke's interactions. Among our Star Wars friend group, that seemed to be the consensus, but that didn't prevent us from shredding it for our own amusement. There are no redeeming qualities to making the great James Earl Jones scream "No!" that way.

I took the day off to catch a matinee with the woman I was dating on opening day. I saw it a few days later with my dad. Then I planned to see it in Dallas at one of their theaters where they served dinner and drinks, something we didn't have in Oklahoma at the time.

My ex came with me, coming over to Tulsa to head down. I got top shelf drunk the first night with my friends, hitting two different bars and being given way too many drinks I didn't pay for. It was all in good fun, this was being social, right? I was having a good time and there was a lot of laughing and chatting and I *did* drink a lot of water alongside—but, I still had to get back to the hotel. I wasn't smart, I was lucky.

I felt fine on the drive, I wasn't blackout drunk—I never have been —but I think I pulled up all my anxious energy to keep me on target. It was only after I was back at the hotel and deeper into the night that I got sick. My ex was in the shower, and I was vomiting loudly into the toilet.

She looked out at me from behind the curtain, "Are you *okay?*"

I looked up, and for some reason, decided to say, "I'm fine."

I made that motion with my hand to express the enormity of "it all."

"This has nothing to do with you."

As I said it, there was my own voice inside my head asking, *one,* why did I say that, and *two,* did I mean it?

It was over. It took a little more time for us to admit it to ourselves, there were still some fights to be had. Shouting matches that never should have occurred. Neither of us should have been fighting this hard only to keep fighting each other.

Similar to 2002 after finally crying over the events of 9/11 and ultimately my mom, I felt a seismic shift inside. Maybe Revenge of the Sith made me reflect on all this desperately clinging onto things. I updated my glasses and shaved my head before seeing my ex again. I went to OKC to help her with some final moving from her college apartment to her parent's house. When she saw me, it finally struck her.

"It's really over, isn't it?" she asked, looking at my odd new appearance. "For real this time."

"Yeah, I think so." I said in a sort of relief.

There was no more intimacy, and only a little contact even left. Our mutual friends would remain our friends independently. They lived in Tulsa, anyway. They were eager to see us quit hurting each other and ourselves. The bullshit from both of us, all the time, was exhausting.

Towards the end of our long rollercoaster, she was diagnosed as having bipolar disorder. I don't say this as any admonition of her, I was reminded of my mother. It made a lot of the past emotional highs and lows make sense, but the damage was done and not all of it could be blamed on developing and/or undiagnosed psychological disorders. My own included.

When MySpace started getting popular, I was convinced to join by our rapper friend, as it was always a musically pivoted site. I loved being able to make custom homepages that could play music if you knew how to play with HTML in the early days. There were third party sites where you could design how your page would look and it would export the HTML for you to copy and paste into your settings. I puttered around with templates, customizing some of the scripts once pumped out.

For as fun as customizing basically a personal website that cost nothing to maintain and you could easily tell people how to find you, it was the beginning of social networking on the internet, and I found people and people found me. An old high school friend reached out asking if I remembered drawing her some cartoons of the Nerds candy characters.

That old specter.

We reconnected and by June, thanks to MySpace, I was on my first date with my wife-to-be.

I was properly single by then. My ex and I were rarely talking on the phone. The lady I was dating, who my best friend had set me up with in the first place, became a point of ire for some of my other friends. They viewed her as a negative influence on me, feeding into my depression, always wanting me around, but never letting me all the way in. It wasn't any healthier than my other relationship. I listened to my friends and probably broke that off less sensitively than I could have. I wasn't mean, but I was blunt. It is easier for me to be direct than to craft a sugar-coating. It is not always the best tact.

CHAPTER 44

At twenty-five, I would finally date someone my age, with a six-year-old daughter. Amber had a career in a local hospital, then working as a surgical technician. She took a lot of calls, and I was still working sales hours. We tried to meet when we had mutual free time.

Our relationship started off effortless, we picked up from our friendship in high school and an unspoken, shared attraction. Our politics and philosophies weren't eye to eye, but neither did we offend each other. In filling each other in on the last few years of our lives, we had seemingly been on an intercept course all along.

When I lived in South Tulsa across from the Saturn dealership, I grocery shopped at a particular Super Wal-Mart, typically late at night to avoid people. She did too, at the same store, for the same reason, around the same time. Strangely, she had seen a guy who resembled me working at the Wal-Mart closer to her house and she had wanted to approach him, disappointed when it turned out not to be me. I was working the overnight shift at the hotel around that time, which itself was near her house. Not that we would have run into each other there, but to think I was but a stone's throw from where she was, coincidentally when she was seeing my doppelgänger.

She had been divorced for a few years, maintaining her house and custody of her daughter solely. She was an inspiration as someone who took what life threw at her and handled it deftly. She had no credit debt, buying the house from her grandmother with cash payments. Her family owned and rented out a few properties, a practice they were actively getting out from under when I came into the picture. The entrepreneurial spirit was evident, and she benefitted not from nepotism, but her own industriousness.

Working her ass off a little too late into her pregnancy and before she should have gone back to work to support her new family, at times, on her own. One income supporting two adults and a baby who would eventually be diagnosed with Cystic Fibrosis. Amber was a soldier who did what she had to do to keep herself and her daughter safe and healthy. Her husband did not share in this work ethic and gave up his place in their lives.

It was a hard six years before we met and she was certain romance wasn't in her cards. The effortlessness we felt? That lack of judgement for differing views? Someone it felt safe to relax with?

She gave me a card once, being nice, "Every day with you is a little more Saturday-ish."

We were in love for a while before we ever said it out loud to each other. She said it first. I didn't want to mess anything up, I didn't pounce. We talked about it, and we wanted to take it seriously; I loved her, too. We didn't want to wear the word out, to cheapen the experience. We said it a million times to each other after getting giddy with the ability to finally admit it to ourselves, each other, and our friends and families.

Being in love with Amber came with accepting responsibilities and understanding boundaries as the "boyfriend" of a mom to a little girl. At the time, she was going by Nikki, and I loved her, too. All of us took some time adjusting to a new relationship dynamic. This could be a family. I was reminded of my own youth, only a little younger than Nikki, with a new guy who made things way different in my world.

Amber was a much more discerning and conservative woman and mother than mine was for me. Being able to step into a co-parenting role, to suddenly take on a child along with a love interest, *this* was a lifestyle choice. Falling in love with this dynamic was a massive commitment for all of us, one with a lot riding on it.

Fortunately, it worked and kept on working. I spent more time there than at the house with my friends.

My ex wanted to stay friends, but pushed too many buttons with me, she only ever wanted to have that last little bit of grasp over my attention, rather than moving forward. There came a time when I had to change my phone number, and once that relationship was finally severed, I began to shake off an old life and build a new one.

CHAPTER 45

2006-2009 – A HOUSE IN NORTH TULSA

L ife moves fast when you can feel yourself settling down. I had recognized the passage of time on numerous occasions, I had once remarked how apt the lyric about missing the last ten years in Pink Floyd's Time was. I feel it all the time. I'm not alone, a lot of us '90's kids *still* think the '90's were only ten years ago. Stability, a loving home environment, a family growing together, those things made life more fun and relaxed, and time slipped by.

There was no trauma to make every waking minute a memory I couldn't stop recalling. Rather, I was making happy memories with a woman I was in love with and her daughter. I moved from my friend's house to hers. We got a couple of American Staffordshire Terriers, a favorite breed of Amber's. Yes, a boy and a girl, but they never mated. Creole, brindle coated with white patches on her neck and feet, as though she wore a collar and gloves, thought Brody, blue and white, was her baby since she was already full-grown when we brought him home as a puppy.

We also adopted a tabby kitten from our vet and named him Devo Mega Man. Only I say the Mega Man part, but it *is* his name. Then we adopted Mr. Purrcival James Jenkins who was a distantly Maine Coon-ish, grey, old man who didn't sit on anyone's lap for a year, until I took a day off and was watching monster movies on some deep cable channel when he nestled between my hip and the arm of the couch. Eventually, some cuddly arrangements in various positions would become our norm, for watching shows, playing games, reading, writing. He was a constant companion.

Life still dealt blows, though. I lost my job at Cingular because I rubbed the owner the wrong way. I don't know, we didn't jibe. They imposed weird new guidelines in an effort to stress me out, specifically. This was dress code shit, and sales quotas on accessories that I never pushed on customers. I tried to meet every expectation anyway. I had others depending on me now.

They fired me after I "failed" a secret shopper encounter. These people would come in and expect you to list off every promotion and take them on a half-hour tour of plans and phones and accessories only to walk out without a sale and hold your job in the balance as they tried to remember if you mentioned this or that on their checklist in the car. They dinged me for a specific item about discussing the phone hardware. However, in their final, personal comments, they addressed how knowledgeable I was about the phones. I've always suspected they mistakenly checked one box over another. I was a good salesman, I was bending over backwards to meet my employer's demands, and it *was* stressing me out.

They moved me to another store—another slight as it was a longer drive—but I loved the new place! I had recruited my old roommate from Saturn and we got to work together. I had big plans on how to use the space… None of the effort counted. Failing a secret shop was a fireable offense, even if said offense contradicted itself.

I tried to file for unemployment, only to be denied, and the citation given included that same secret shopper document. My unemployment representative even found it strange and flimsy, but, by the letter of the law, they had to deny me. In Oklahoma, if you're fired for a "valid" reason, which the employer can make up, you are not eligible for unemployment benefits.

I didn't handle any of it well. Being fired, confronting my once friend and former boss about the denial of benefits. I was lashing out at a perceived personal attack. Even if it *was* one, what did it matter now?

I didn't have the job anymore. The income was gone, and I had better get to work finding work, especially with no support in the meantime.

Maybe I took it personally because I did have this family situation I was working on securing. I spiraled, though this time much more inwardly. Amber was there to help keep me steady and assured me *we* would figure it out. I *had* support.

Around the time our first anniversary came up, I found temp work at Hilti that would turn into a job that I would hold onto for a few years.

Hilti is an international construction power tool company and they are proud of their heritage, global reach, and achievements. Posters of facilities and Hilti sponsored events from all over the world filled the halls and offices of that massive complex. There were a lot of international travelers in the hallways. Eventually my boss would be a Hungarian woman who was married to a man from Sri Lanka and they had a beautiful baby together in the time I worked for her.

What I did at Hilti was call people and ask if the information we received from their application for credit was correct. Credit verification analyst. I made sure Hilti's salespeople got the right information before we performed a credit check. Oftentimes these salespeople would visit people on worksites, there was always room for mistakes and I was there to catch them before we denied a customer credit for some tools or materials they might be needing quickly.

Eventually I would get more into the credit side of that credit verification, but it was always calling customers, typically guys with some colorful language, especially the Western Canadians. I didn't have to sell them anything, I didn't beg them for more information, it was not the worst job I ever had.

I read a lot, either the newest Dune book by Brian Herbert and Kevin J Anderson, or old scifi, getting into Edgar Rice Burroughs and reading his John Carter of Mars and Pellucidar books. I learned that George Lucas and a lot of modern science fiction and adventure owe a major debt to Burroughs. I mean, Lucas lifted words and entire scenes from these books. It doesn't change my love of Star Wars, if anything, I love it more for brazenly wearing its inspirations on its sleeves—if you know what you're looking at.

I started writing more, a number of short stories that appear in my collection *PUNCH/PANTS* were written on my lunch breaks on a laptop I lugged around in a shoulder bag. I gave myself acute bursitis. I wrote a whole novel.

The grand project I've been working on forever I re-tackled and banged out over a hundred thousand words on. Not *In the House of In Between*. A book that I might release one day, I won't spoil it here, but I did it! I wrote a novel for the first time.

It turned out someone I worked nearby knew a published author, Richard Cox, who worked in another department. He introduced us and he read a little of the novel and some of my short stories. He was encouraging and supportive. We would email back and forth at work, talk when our departments encountered each other.

As I grew more comfortable writing again, *being* a writer, I let go of playing music altogether. I had been meeting my drummer every once and a while to jam. Having fun playing one night, enjoying nonsense noise, managing to sync, I thought about it as we played. I was done. This wasn't going to take off for me. I told her I wanted to focus on writing my fiction and she was supportive.

As you find life going your way, when the constant reach to fill voids is replaced with fullness, what's going on under the hood becomes more evident. Amber and I both faced accepting and learning about our mental health. There were times it got intense, and we had brushes with falling apart. We put in the work.

CHAPTER 46

As Facebook became more popular and I finally made the jump from MySpace to the more popular social media platform, back when you picked sides (it's never not been polarizing). I started re-reconnecting with the Mulroney family. It had been a few years again since talking to some of them, including my brother.

Having a family, having hardship, recognizing my own mental health, I had had some time to mature, or time had beaten me up, I don't know. I was able to have a conversation with both my brother and an aunt about why we let time slip away again: they didn't need the anger I seethed.

I understood. I was angry. I was still angry, but realized it came from having such a unique relationship with my mom compared to the relationships everyone else had with her. I sounded disrespectful. To me, however, they sounded delusional.

I was finally able to make the delineation that when I spoke to family about Irene, I was always talking about a woman they did not know, and vice versa. I wanted to know more about who she became, and who she had been. In starting that journey, I would only find more questions, some of which may always remain unanswered. Some of the research was too difficult to bring myself toward.

I relied on what I could find online for a long time, and the accepted answer of what had happened and what had led up to it was, it's *complicated*. I can tell you some of it will always be a mystery by the sheer nature of how it happened. I found an article from a local newspaper that gave a graphic account of the incident of my mother's death.

With permission from the editor at the Mat-Su Valley Frontiersman:

TALKEETNA MAN CHARGED WITH MURDER

By JO C. GOODE-Frontiersman reporter

Sep 21, 2001

TALKEETNA -- A suicide report turned into a homicide investigation last weekend, resulting in a Talkeetna man being charged with murder in the shooting death of his wife.

Rex B. Davenport, 32, was arrested early Sunday morning, just hours after he called troopers from a Talkeetna-area bar to report his wife, Irene Davenport, 40, had shot herself with a .357-caliber revolver at their lakeside cabin, according to Alaska State Troopers.

Davenport was arraigned on a first-degree murder charge Sunday in Palmer District Court and is being held at Mat-Su Pre-Trial Facility in Palmer in lieu of $250,000 cash-only bail and a court-approved, third-party custodian.

According to court records, Davenport called troopers at 7:12 p.m. Saturday from the H & H Lakeview Restaurant and Lodge, which is across from the Davenport cabin.

Trooper Skip Chadwell said he met Davenport at the Talkeetna-area lodge and told Davenport to stay there while he went to Davenport's home.

When the Talkeetna trooper arrived and saw the scene inside the cabin, Chadwell said he immediately called for help. Soon several other troopers arrived, charging documents stated.

Inside the cabin, the troopers saw a grisly tableau. A pool of blood surrounded Irene Davenport, who was lying motionless on the floor. More blood spattered the ceiling and walls.

The woman had suffered a head wound so massive that a portion of her skull was torn apart, according to court documents.

Investigator Randel McPheron said the bullet that caused the devastating damage to the woman's skull was a jacketed hollow-point bullet.

Davenport told Chadwell he and his wife had been drinking together at home earlier that evening when they began to argue about Davenport getting a new job, according to Chadwell's affidavit, which accompanied the charging documents. Davenport said their altercation was only a verbal one.

The Talkeetna man said he was about to leave the cabin with his shotgun to go target shooting, when he said his wife threatened to shoot herself if he left.

Irene Davenport grabbed the .357-caliber revolver out of a backpack, then, Davenport reportedly told troopers, put the gun to her head and shot herself. Davenport said he immediately left the cabin to report the shooting, according to court records.

Investigators were apparently suspicious of Davenport's story after they discovered what they said was evidence that a physical struggle occurred inside the cabin, according to court records.

An easy chair was lying on its back a few feet away from Irene Davenport's feet. An iron frying pan with its handle broken off was on the kitchen floor and slats from a pantry door were damaged, according to charging documents.

Investigators said in charging documents there were no apparent wounds on Irene Davenport's head consistent with a self-inflicted contact gunshot wound.

Troopers found the revolver on a long white skirt Irene Davenport was wearing. Investigators alleged that a swipe mark on the bloodied floor indicated the gun and skirt were moved after she hit the floor, according to court documents, and that there was blood on the revolver's grip, trigger, hammer, and cylinder, but not on the barrel.

A witness told troopers he was fishing in a canoe on the lake that night when he heard an altercation from inside Davenport's cabin, court records stated. Just a few hundred feet from the cabin, Glenn Turner said he strained to hear what the couple was arguing about.

According to charging documents, Turner said he heard a woman screaming, shouting several times, "Put it the f___ down." He said he then heard a loud bang he thought was a firecracker. A large man then walked out of the cabin and headed toward the highway, he said. The woman's screams stopped, Turner reported.

Sgt. Dallas Massie found a brown leather holster lying on the ground by a path about 30 yards away from the cabin, court records stated. Davenport could not tell troopers how the revolver holster ended up outside when the last time he had seen it was in his wife's hand, he told troopers.

Davenport told troopers he and his wife had married a little over a year ago, McPheron said. Davenport's cooking job had recently ended at the Mount McKinley Princess Wilderness Lodge, troopers said. Massie said he met Davenport when he was a cook at the Talkeetna Alaskan Lodge.

Massie said troopers had never received any complaints of domestic violence from the couple.

On Wednesday, troopers had received Irene Davenport's autopsy report. However, McPheron declined to comment on the results, citing the pending investigation.

Davenport was scheduled to appear Thursday at a pre-indictment hearing.

This is both not accurate, but not inaccurate. It took eking out tiny bits of information over years from different family members, to figure out how my mom had ended up back in Alaska, married, and dead from a questionable gunshot wound to the head, with the only witness being her husband who did not end up facing murder charges.

I tried to find out about Rex, to see if he was in prison, but his name is only present in connection to this case. Not that I was savvy at looking up people's incarceration status or criminal records. I didn't request the police report or my mother's death certificate for a long time, afraid of what I would find there.

It turned out Irene had been out of touch with a lot of family for long periods of time, and it took police a few days to even contact someone to inform them. Hence that slow crawl between September 15th and the end of the month when my aunt finally reached me, probably the last person to know and the one who hadn't spoken to her the longest.

That same aunt, along with my brother, had gone to Alaska to help settle affairs, including taking care of my mother's body. They met people who treated them as outsiders. But learned of Irene and Rex's place in the community. Irene grew on them. Rex not much at all. Their marriage was weird, they seemed to at least be in love, but did argue in public about his employment and drinking sometimes. My aunt met Rex after he had been released, the murder charge dropped when the medical examiner could not conclusively determine how my mother was shot in time to continue holding Rex.

She interviewed him for the police. He gave basically the same story as the article with little deviations here and there, but all effectively the same. They were arguing, a gun was produced and she threatened to kill herself with it, he called her bluff trying to leave, and she shot herself. The question lingers around the production of the gun: did he introduce it or did she? It's then a branching narrative from each possibility and the crime scene as it's presented.

I had wondered in the past *what* they had been arguing about. Could it have been her lamenting 9/11? Could *that* have been on her mind? I always feared the attack and the status of her mental health made her *suicidal*. There are accounts Rex gives where she says if she could kill herself, she would, and he gave her the gun to do it. In *that* situation, given their drinking, *is* that suicide?

The truth, as close as you can get to it, is that a gun ended up in her hand and her head was shot. My truth was that she wasn't in the right state of mind, and in a heated moment, with a gun introduced, she acted impulsively. My aunt agreed, believing Irene could have been angry enough to go, "Watch this, motherfucker!"

I would live with that nebulous understanding of my mother's death for too many years, afraid of one answer that might be gleaned if I dug any further: *was it* suicide?

That *that* could be swimming in my DNA terrified me. I've never been suicidal, but, there have been times where I wished the world would stop. I was too afraid of death to be suicidal. If it was *in* me, though? If that was a voice that might wake up one day? I didn't want to confirm it because I believed it was a possibility. I was in denial about something I had no proof of one way or the other and I didn't want to manifest it into existence with confirmation.

On the other hand, if it wasn't suicide, if he murdered her and got away with it because of shoddy police work? Could I handle that?

Or the third, lingering in the middle ground, option: she shot herself with a gun he gave to her, her decision-making skills clearly impaired, and since he was the only one there, he got to control enough of the information that he kept himself out of prison for her murder. Not negligent homicide, second-degree manslaughter, not even charged with providing a weapon to someone who was impaired. Nothing about her death would stick. He went to prison for two years on a weapons charge, he was an ex-felon in possession.

That was reality. Re-confirmed, now a little more solidly, backed up by media from the day, reconnection with family who had had time to process their own feelings. It was always going to be a mystery as to what truly happened in that cabin that night. Rex would have faced greater charges if anything more sinister had occurred.

That has always been a hard pill to swallow. A man who may not know I exist, is responsible for my mother's death. He may not have killed her with his own hands, but he provided every means to facilitate her death, then said he didn't do it. Because he was clean—the scene did not indicate he had cleaned himself, his saving grace—he got away with it. It didn't matter even if she was suicidal. It was his gun and his heartless carelessness that appeared objectively clear.

Why wallow in it further? It would only depress me more to read about how he got away with it and how her final actions might influence me in any way. More denial. Why *seek* new reasons to be angry? In truth, the fear was only a partial excuse. Anything definitive would be that—definitive. I don't think anyone in the family ordered the police report for similar reasons.

This led me to biannual fits of morbid curiosity. I would look up her name, or variations on her name, to see if anything new would pop up with the growth of the internet. If slivers of mystery remained, maybe I could keep my mom in my life longer. It was only the same article for a long time. Reading it again and again, different details hit in different ways at different times, the article saying something different each time.

There were one or two occasions where I did find something new. Sometimes something about Rex being the subject of a prisoner transfer, a follow-up article in the Frontiersman from early 2002. I would share it with family, though it was always old articles that had finally been uploaded to the internet in a newspaper's archives.

When the only time you reach out to family is once or twice a year outside of their birthday on Facebook to talk about your mom or their sister's death, you become something of a pill yourself. Not that I pushed family away again, but if I wasn't the black sheep, I certainly draped myself in black any time I interacted with them.

However, as I said, these would be fits around my mom's birthday and the anniversary of her death. Well, all of September became a month of mourning, which made having my birthday at the top a final week to enjoy summer before I dove into depression. It's a difficult month every year.

I wasn't exhibiting signs of bipolar disorder, I never felt that. I never had the highs, I had intermittently deeper lows. They kept getting *longer*.

I wasn't the only one slowly suffering, though. Nikki had a health scare that put her on steroids at a young age, threatening her with diabetes. Amber was having her own issues with work and the strain that put on her psyche. We had a hard 2007 and nearly fell apart in 2008. This was a family, now. I wasn't about to give it up. We did hard work couples and families do.

Becoming more conscious of my mother's plight, taking mental health—mine, and those around me—much more seriously and sensitively, I learned to accept things more graciously. I still had some growth and change to go through; don't we all approaching our thirties? Those years facing adult decisions as a child, was a cheat sheet now. I *had* to be much more patient and logical in my decision-making and reactions, especially in the face of other people's situations I had no say in or concept of.

Amber had started house-hunting in 2008, decided on a house that she wanted, talked to the bank, and bought the house completely on her own. There were times I felt I was being held at arm's length, but from her point of view, she was protecting herself and her daughter keeping things in her name, especially when I carried a lot of debt. I couldn't argue with the logic and considering my debt, I would probably make the situation more complicated. We weren't married, I was a live-in boyfriend, but I always did my best to pitch in half.

Moving in 2009 was a family affair and both of our families helped. We got a moving truck and moved in one weekend.

PART THREE
WITHIN

CHAPTER 47

2009-2020 – A NEW HOME, TULSA

'm home now. I have lived in this house longer than any other place I have ever lived. Of course, my dad stayed in my childhood home for thirty-seven years. Living in one place a little over a decade isn't a major achievement by the average person's measure, but for me this was around the twentieth time I had moved at only thirty-years-old.

I don't know how many times I've moved. My mom and I moved many times before I could hold onto the memories. There are those snippets of memory of different people and places, apartments and houses; how many and which of them were places I "lived?"

Having this one place, and living the life I have, stability became a luxury. I had to work to get here, and a lot of that work was in this house. It was also almost completely documented online. Nearly everyone was on Facebook, tagging friends, sharing their locations, posting photos and videos of their daily lives. We all became way more connected, and it was quickly apparent this could become toxic.

Loads of people shared only the happier, brightest moments of their lives, creating an illusion of perfection. Some of us were the opposite, posting how mad we were at the world. I existed in the middle, sharing *everything*. As much as I continued to shrink from wanting to hang out in groups or ever having to deal with *people*, I still had ambitions towards being a creative entertainer. I shared everything, hoping something would click with people.

Not three months after moving, I was informed my department at Hilti was being absorbed into another department. The job I was doing would still be done, but since it was with another department, the manager chose to force us to re-apply for our own jobs. We, and this was five of us, were given nintey days to find another job within the company if we weren't kept by the other department. None of us were. I applied for several other jobs within the company, checking the postings daily, and when the other department finally gave me the opportunity to interview—*for my own job*—I had grown a full beard, gained weight, and hadn't cut my hair in two months. I looked and felt disheveled. I no longer gave a fuck.

I chronicled the experience, showing the growth of my "severance beard," as I counted down my days at Hilti. If I found a job outside of the company, I was basically free to go. If I didn't find alternative employment by the end of the ninety days, I would be given the equivalent of six month's pay. I didn't technically meet the requirements to be eligible for a severance package, but they considered the year I had worked for them as a temp in their decision to compensate me for the awkward situation.

I watched a little of the World Cup during my next period of unemployment. I watched the entirety of the Heroes TV series with Nikki on her summer break.

I received unemployment benefits. I tried to get with some temp agencies. I applied directly for positions beyond and below my experience. The first place to offer me a position indicated the pay and I had to turn the job down because I was making more on unemployment. I even told them that. It was offensive and that was more than ten years ago. Pay hasn't gone up since, and unemployment benefits don't last forever. Eventually, I had to take any job if it was offered at some point.

I took another niche sales job selling rugs for a third-party vendor operating out of Mathis Brothers Furniture. I had worked as a cashier at Evan's in midtown after high school for a little while. It felt a little eerie being back in a furniture store, revisiting past employment experiences.

Leaning over a pile of 3' x 5' rugs, I read Robert W. Chamber's The King in Yellow on an iPhone 4. I read several more Edgar Rice Burroughs books. Classics with no presentational flair downloaded for free through the Apple bookstore. The influential throughlines that continue to inspire stories gave me new motivation to continue working on my own worlds.

I wrote the short story Eating Crow on my lunch breaks, imagining a larger world around it, but it got away from me and I kept it down to a short story. Instead, I started recontextualizing everything I had already written, what stories I had written, ideas I had swimming in my head, and future plans (writers think about things they don't feel the confidence to write just yet, don't they? Just my anxiety?), into three realities that can interact. Yes, I have a multiverse, and a little bit of it is out there to be teased out.

Having a new phone that was convenient to read and write on also gave me greater access to those social medias and communicating with family. Even family I didn't know I had.

My brother informed me that I had a paternal half-sister and that she wanted to contact me. I also have a half-brother whose name is also Justin. My biological father did not grieve his divorce from my mother for long, nor provide for his progeny.

I spoke to this half-sister on the phone a few times, sharing our life stories. Maybe it's me, maybe it's social media, we didn't stay in touch very long. I mostly interacted with her during my lunch breaks from work, which I took in a nearby cemetery.

Afraid of death? Eat with the dead. It was quiet and I could be alone.

The job wasn't terrible—at first. The manager revealed herself to be savagely micro, often lurking out of view, off hours, to make sure we were doing the job "right." She would confront us on the spot if she was particularly upset.

I saw how miserable she was making her employees, including myself when she threatened to take sales commissions from me when I didn't follow her order of operations. A customer I had helped in-store asked for a showing on one of my days off. The other sales reps assured me they hadn't complained, and her vindictiveness was unwarranted. I organized an effort to oust her. I wasn't going to idly take abuse on the job anymore.

I reported about that on my blog. I felt vindicated. I had protected fellow employees. We felt close-knit. Until the new boss. He laid me off when sales slumped—coincidentally a week after I ran into him and his wife at a job fair. I had never wanted to stay in customer service and was always looking. He assured me that *wasn't* the reason, I was the newest hire—besides himself.

It was all for the best, at that time, anyway. The next day I had already lined up an interview at a temp agency I was going to visit during my lunch break. Now I didn't have time constraints! It was a while yet, but eventually they hooked me up with Bank of Oklahoma where I would work for several years, do a lot of writing, find things out about myself, and eventually feel bullied at work again.

It's all online. I didn't have fear of missing out, I had fear of not reporting enough.

The things I didn't write about in those years, however, were deeply personal. Amber and I both struggled with our mental health and relationship. We teetered again and there were times I stayed with a friend or my dad as we worked on things. We *were* working. We both received diagnoses, therapy, and medications that helped balance a tumultuous home life.

I was diagnosed with treatment resistant Major Depressive Disorder, and Generalized Anxiety Disorder. I ended up taking a different medication every year or two, with the occasional bump in dosage or an additive or supplemental medication to try and calm whatever psychological symptoms were impeding me the most.

What symptoms? I was letting the grind of my life show. I was tired all the time. Not sleepy, again, I've never been a napping individual, but mentally tired, emotionally exhausted. I let it gnaw at me for years before attempting to treat it. It was a complacency in comfort that had come between me and Amber. I wasn't much more than a bump on a log and I didn't care. Apathy isn't pretty.

Meanwhile, my brain would randomly throw me into crisis for no discernable reason other than it could. I had a series of recurring night-mares, three or four of them over a few years. That may not seem often, but there were night terrors that I ended up sitting with in dreamtime for maddening amounts of time. I would finally wake up in the real world wondering if they were true and it would unsettle me for days.

In the dreams, I would suddenly remember murdering someone, sometimes in my youth, and realizing I had gotten away with it for years. I would freak out! Should I turn myself in? Why did I remember it? Were the authorities onto me now? Moreover, why the hell did I kill someone? It was a lot of repercussions my mind would jump through and the emotional impact to suddenly experience? Hovering between my mind being awake while my body is asleep, this dream reality would invade waking reality and cause a panic attack that would usually kick me awake. The lingering anxiety made me question reality and my sanity.

I realize now, not having had one of those nightmares in a long time (jinxing myself), they were born from a self-imposed guilt, feeling responsible in some part for my mom's passing. I know that's conceded. I know that she lived a life beyond me and parts of it were amazing for her. I knew it even then. Unrealized, unresolved grief, a sense of dread that hung over me all the time manifested itself in inescapable ways.

My anxiety is my body vibrating 100% of the time. I am in a constant state of *clenching*. It wreaked havoc on my spine and shoulders, which only contributed to the exhaustion. Panic attacks happened sometimes out of nowhere. It was my body betraying me through my bowels that caused the most trouble at work.

There is something about trying to do a time-sensitive task, especially if it involves physical activity, that urges me to retreat to the restroom. This gets gross: my body becomes a broken ice cream machine and, I don't have diarrhea or solid turds, I endlessly evacuate.

When your boss believes you spend too much time in the restroom, what are you supposed to say?

I got a letter from my psychiatrist explaining my diagnoses and how stress in the workplace can affect me. I involved the bank's HR, but they weren't helpful at all.

At the same time, though, I wrote another novel, *In the House of In Between*, put together my short story collection, *PUNCH/PANTS*, and wrote several short stories and the novella *Red Clouds*.

I landed an agent that I stayed with for about a year, but that fell apart as communication broke down and I saw no results. I knew being an artist wasn't going to be lucrative, I knew I couldn't expect fame overnight. When my agent refused to share with me who they were submitting my work to or what kind of responses they (and thereby *I*) were getting, I terminated our contract. Maybe I was impatient, maybe I had a bad experience, but I learned it is hard in this business with *and* without help.

When our daughter started high school, she wanted to change her name. She went from Nikki to her legal first name, Autumn, and asked we drop a childhood nickname. She had gone through a couple years of major change, switching schools three times in four years, moving, stress with us, she began to craft her own identity and I was excited to see her making decisions about her own life.

In 2015, coming up on our tenth anniversary, Amber asked me how I felt about finally getting married. Now, I had never pressured her about it, I had asked if she would want to, but respected that she was happy with what we had. When we decided on a date, I tried to arrange everything.

I misunderstood some of the requirements for acquiring our marriage license and date before the judge. It was two trips downtown and asking anyone from Facebook if they were free to be a witness in the next two hours, however, luck was on my side. I arranged for us to be married by a judge who had some free time the same afternoon as our chosen date.

Autumn and my dad were there, too, along with an old high school friend.

I helped finance a trip for a few days back down to South Padre Island, the same place my mom and M had taken their honeymoon. I had loved the place, and I wanted to start reclaiming parts of my past and make them happier with *my* family.

The best part of the trip was when Amber thanked me, in all honesty, for bringing them there. I'm glad I was able to make it special for us.

Shortly thereafter I would adopt Autumn. Some people are lucky enough to record their children's first-something—laughter, steps, riding a bike—I have a video of my daughter officially signing her new name for the first time in the courtroom. Her grandmother, my mother-in-law, is adopted. This wasn't a foreign concept for any of us and it was a happy and long-awaited occasion. I had thought of her as my own daughter for years, this was paperwork, but it's the effort. I told the government I wanted her to be my daughter. The judge asked her if she was okay with this, and she said she was.

I am thankful every day for the circumstances that directed me to be a dad to this young lady. I know that everything I impart, in my low moments, at my best, is all tiny reflections of a life I've lived and the choices I've made based on those personal perceptions. We have gotten along our entire relationship, and I am proud of the person she has become. I was then. I am.

CHAPTER 48

I can pinpoint a devastating series of events between the end of 2016 and beginning of 2017 as *breaking* me.

Brody's health deteriorated rapidly, and when we took him to the vet, it was a shock to learn his lungs were filled with cancerous nodules. I felt guilty, but the vet tried to assure me dogs often do not show distress until it is indeed too late. I *still* feel guilty.

Amber and I took our dog to the vet thinking he'd get an antibiotic or antiviral and take him home to try and let him heal up. We came home with his leash. It was September.

I cried.

Hard.

For days.

I hadn't cried this hard when I thought I was losing my family. His death made my death-anxiety roar back into my every waking thought. I was shit at work, I was a mess at home, I was suffering. Not alone, Amber and Autumn missed him, too. This was literally the first time I had to face death head-on.

My dad's mom passed away far away. I avoided the funeral and was scared to talk to my dad about his feelings. My mom had been out of my life for a few years when she died. I didn't know how to *deal* with death. I had experienced grief disconnected and at a distance. This was something *new*, and I was afraid of it.

We lost one of our cats, my video game buddy, Purrcy. One morning his back legs didn't work and taking him straight to the vet, they told us he was in full-renal failure. We saw him off as a family, but I came home different. Purrcy's death affected me the hardest. It was January. This was unbearable.

We adopted another cat after Purrcy's passing, a female black cat named Nora Jones. The new trio of Devo, Nora, and Creole were beginning to settle in when a fatty growth developed against Creole's bladder. She was clearly in distress needing to urinate.

We had it drained, the vet believing that should last a while. She was suffering again the next night. Death wasn't done with our family and took Creole from us less than two months after Purrcy. We had to let her go from her pain.

I worry about neglect, but we took care of our animals. Brody was a shock, Purrcy and Creole were elderly. I don't know if there was more we could have done, or if we could have afforded it. I feel responsible for each of the losses, I was their *dad* and I had to let them go amid suffering.

It's hard to deal with even these years later. We adopted two more dogs since. Honeybear, a yellow Labrador, and Raspy, a mostly chill chihuahua; they are loveable. They are extensions to our family, not replacements for those we've lost.

I still miss my lost companions daily.

I took a week off for Autumn's Spring Break, and when I went back to work, I couldn't clock-in. A couple of people higher up than my boss came to my desk and asked me to join them in a meeting room.

A co-worker saw me passing by and asked how my vacation was.

I said, "It's about to be longer, I think."

I wasn't wrong. Before I had left for the day before my vacation, I had sent myself an email from my work email with a folder full of text documents. Short stories, ideas, concepts, things I would write in downtime, but the folder had something else in it. At some point, for some reason, even though I kept a separate folder for *my* writing from anything related to work, I mistakenly saved a spreadsheet with some important data on it into that folder.

It appeared as if I was trying to steal information. It looked *bad*. The email never reached me because their security software caught it. It's great that they did! I wasn't trying to commit corporate espionage.

Instead of reprimanding me, they fired me. I wasn't the best employee with where my head and heart were. I was crumbling under the weight of grief *and* another set of bullies for bosses. There would be no rebel rally this time.

I indeed made a boneheaded mistake, but other coworkers were shocked I was fired. I fought for unemployment benefits, trying to prove I had been in an abusive work situation that created the opportunity for errors. All I proved to my judge was that it was a mistake and probably saved myself from any further legal action by the bank.

I had no income. We had lost three pets. I was on Amber's insurance since we had married, at least I could stay on my medications as I tried to reorient and find work. I felt exceptionally defeated. Not to mention Donald Trump was President.

I became desperate and took a position at a Target store. I worked two shifts before interviewing for a position with a heat transfer vinyl supplier's marketing department. I was on my third shift at Target when that other position was offered to me. I finished my shift for the evening and promptly told the shift manager I was quitting, I had another job opportunity and there was no point giving a two weeks' notice since I was still training. We parted ways amicably.

The marketing position remains my daytime job, but even it has changed over the years, and tested my patience at times.

Working there, though, I signed with an indie publisher to release *In the House of In Between* in March of 2018. It took nearly six years from writing first draft to publication, initially having written it as a National Novel Writing Month project in November of 2012. It grew and evolved through the years.

Writing it, however, cemented my belief that there is no such thing as ghosts.

I read Harry Houdini's "A Magician Among the Spirits" as research, both for his guest appearance in the novel and what he expected from frauds of the day. The man wanted there to be a connection. He wanted to *know* that there was an afterlife and that us mortals could reconnect with our dearly departed.

With his mother.

All he found were elaborate tricks and underhanded financial schemes. They preyed on the emotional for their money, while claiming they were giving the grieving a shot at closure. He was disgusted and teamed up with local police to bust up charlatans, using his experience with stagecraft to oust their tricks. He and Scientific American offered a radical cash prize to anyone who could prove their connection to the "other side."

The prize went unclaimed. I bring the prize up in the novel. I wanted to write an accurate Houdini, someone who's taking in a mystery he can't solve. Not because he's being duped, instead, I am giving him a natural phenomenon yet explained.

I wrote a haunted house tale about screaming through time. About grabbing the fabric of space and shaking it until everything is happening at once. Because if I can't connect to the other side, then can I reach back in time to reconnect?

Houdini's wife held seances to reach out to him, but he never reached back. If there was anyone desperate and resourceful enough to make contact, it was him. He would have worked as hard on the other side to make sure it worked.

There are no ghosts. There are gas leaks and overactive imaginations. There are night terrors. There are hallucinations, voluntarily invited and beyond our control. Our brains are wired to find patterns and recognizable shapes, often as a threat to ensure we maintain our personal safety. When we are stressed out, when we are emotionally drained, especially around sadness and loneliness, it is hard to deny what we want for what is real.

I'll still write ghost stories. I believe in the stories. I've experienced a little of it all, the night terrors, the pareidolia, the weirdness of a place's echoes—those things will tickle your brain and tell you that evil is afoot and to hightail it immediately.

There is a thrill in responding to fear. The kick of adrenaline for your survival, *just in case*. Not to say I'm an adrenaline junkie, the opposite in fact. I enjoy knowing the adrenaline is coming. I get sudden bursts, however, anxiety attacks. Horror, though, gives that sense of fear when you're in complete safety. Writing it, trying to crawl under someone else's skin with my words, I must consider, what terrifies *me*?

Loss.

When I gave a copy of the book to my dad, he was surprised at the size. "You wrote a *real* book!" he said.

He read and he enjoyed it. But more than talk about anything I wrote, he wanted to tell me, "Your mom would be proud of you."

"I know." I said. "Thank you."

"I hope you do. She really would."

The book would eventually get me in touch with a group of YouTube and podcast creators, Bad Movie Night. Two of the guys on the show enjoyed it enough to invite me onto a special episode here and there to get my author's take on the first season of Shudder's Creepshow revival. Then I joined as a co-host of their Creepshow review series in the second season.

It may not be the official Shudder after-show, but we love getting to talk about the program. They're filmmakers and I'm a writer, we have different takes on what we appreciate and how we critique episodes. Drug Traffic from the third season is objectively the best encapsulation of our fears about covid and the government response.

It is a travesty that we did not vote it the best story from that season.

CHAPTER 49

Approaching forty began to weigh heavily on me. The *world* weighed heavily on me. There was always something coming out of the Trump White House. Pick a scandal. I was on Twitter bitching about it. In 2019, after turning forty, I applied for my medical marijuana license in Oklahoma after it was surprisingly voted legal here.

It was smoking weed that set up writing all of this.

Orange Kush. A sativa dominant strain from the first samples I bought, not knowing what had made me paranoid back in the day. Wanting a moment's bliss from my unquiet mind, I was interested in exploring the options. This one wasn't it. It created an urge to urinate —bad. *Real* bad. I only smoked it a few times.

I was stuck on the toilet feeling the need to pee. Nothing's coming out, yet I don't want to piss myself. I "remembered" sitting on a toilet in a dark room and someone *scary* in the doorway, but another figure as well. Tension hung in the air. I was expected to make something happen there and now. There was either a streetlight outside, the moon, or a night light, but enough light for wide-open pupils to make out the shapes around me. A bathroom, somehow familiar...

My high, anxious, urination-false-alarming brain shows me another memory with a similar bathroom and figures.

"Do you want to eat *this*?" the voice echoes out of time.

My brain wasn't done yet!

One of my aunts mentioned a guy who was irrationally angry about my eating habits. Could I trace that bogeyman to an actual known individual? Could I finally explain this urgent retreat to the restroom when anxiety struck? Has it *always* been my response to sensing I'm in trouble? To run to the bathroom and then "produce?"

Does this lend credence to two toddlerhood stories my mother would tell me: that she took me to the doctor about my eating and that I basically trained myself to use the potty because "I hated to soil myself"?

First, the doctor said I was healthy, "He'll eat when he's hungry."

That didn't attempt to explain or address the pickiness. Somehow, I was getting the nutrients I needed from whatever I *would* eat. Picky, not dying.

The second, though, she told me a self-training story of knowing what the child-sized toilet receptacle was and jumping straight to using it. I was proud of little-me for understanding the concept early on. In this lightspeed revelation occurring at forty while high, though, it made more sense that I was terrified of that individual. I retreat to the bathroom to avoid wrath. However, to be in the bathroom not producing incurs wrath. It's not about respite, but an undeniable urge that removes me from and causes stress.

High-brain.

When I shared the weird connections with my aunt, she thought it was bad weed, but there *was* a guy that it all lined up with.

I'm not saying it's what happened, but the jumble of the early fragments of memory don't disagree with the tumultuous nature of the rest of my relationship with my mother. She was in a bad relationship with somebody out there who abused me—possibly severely. The memories were always there, the context of their impact on the rest of my life?

My body's demands to retreat to the bathroom in times of stress could be some deeply buried, learned response. Conversely, I could have easily jumped to conclusions regarding fragments of memory while I was—at forty—aware of my anxiety, and now reinterpreting fragments of memory.

Maybe I should reinterpret *everything*? I'm as old as my mother was at the time of her death at this point and every time the topic is raised, I answer with shrugs and "I don't know." That's not fair to my mother. Keeping her alive as a dangling mystery isn't immortality, it's barely martyrdom, and I'm doing nothing with it.

My family, their friends who also knew Irene, knew this different woman and were keeping her alive in their own ways; celebratory, mournful. I walked around with a gaping hole in my history and heart, writing on her birthday, the anniversary, or Mother's Day, some sentimental blogpost about how hard those things were. I've missed her for a long time, I've told her spirit I love and forgive her.

But…

My story, my version of Irene, wasn't the same one everyone else got. Who she was before she had two boys is snippets of family stories. And it's the same after we split.

I have four seasons with my mother. A winter I have only fragmentary memories of, when she would give me up to one of her sisters to hopefully leave the monster in our lives. She retained custody of me and by the time I was four, she married my dad.

Spring was the four years I had a family, when I grew, felt love. But spring is full of storms. I witnessed divorce and marriage again.

Then she dragged me through four years of psychological torment. A summer of moving over and over with people who loathed each other. An influential era on an impressionable youth, with so much of it filled with anger and feelings of betrayal.

Our final season lasted longer than four years, but fall is a strange season anyway. It can be wet and gloomy. But those weeks of wet can contribute to beautiful changes in the foliage as trees begin to hibernate for the next winter. Bright, crisp mornings, but lengthening nights. From the time we no longer lived together to my breaking things off was about five years.

Winter inevitably returned over the period we did not talk until she died. A winter I remember. A winter where I made every same mistake my mother did and then created a few of my own for good measure.

Life keeps changing. Maybe I do live in seasonal four-year periods. Maybe my year is a twenty-two-year cycle. I'm close to living as long on this Earth without my mom on it as to when she was.

Cycles can be predictive. They can be beneficial. They can become burdens. And if the cycle is one that has become vicious, it can be broken.

CHAPTER 50

Capping off 2019 was a Tool concert for their latest release, Fear Inoculum. It was an amazing show, and if it happens to be the last concert I ever see, it wasn't a bad one. In December the first reporting of a highly contagious novel coronavirus came out of China, and its spread was terrifying the country. Fear Inoculum's messages felt poignant and prescient.

I feared COVID-19 before it even reached the United States, mostly because of who was in the White House. I knew he would downplay it and respond poorly, and—history speaks for itself. I was afraid it would survive on surfaces and mail-carriers, parcel deliverers, truck drivers, would be unwittingly spreading the disease straight into all our homes. I was afraid in January of 2020 that it would be wildly contagious, inescapable, that we would *all* have it in a matter of weeks.

I began reading scientific news articles to stay ahead of the nightly news. It had arrived, it was contained—no it wasn't. It's spreading rapidly in nursing homes. We need to shut down. The toilet paper situation! We need to shut down! "My hair appointment!" WE NEED TO SHUT DOWN!

Friday, March 13th, 2020, Tulsa initiated its lockdown.

Amber works for a hospital, she still needed to do her job, she was considered "essential." Autumn continued her college courses online from home. I stayed home, too, logging into my work computer remotely to check email, because there was nothing I could *do* remotely. There was a lot of doom and depression early on. Autumn and I tried to keep positive and active together. I wrote a few short stories during lockdown while she worked on school. We created a little separation of "work" and "home" in our days, busying ourselves with our own business and not being all up in each other's.

I read a lot as well. If it was still early in the morning, though, I might fall back asleep in the recliner, Kindle fallen to my chest and coffee going cold to my side. I never deviated from my weekly sleep schedule, I still got up every morning with my alarm, I went through the motions. I fell back asleep sometimes.

Depression.

I didn't want to be in this world.

I didn't want to die! I never had any such ideation. Instead, I wanted existence to cease, as it does when you are asleep. Dreamless nothingness, not cold oblivion—*stopped*. Let me breathe a few minutes, give me a break from nothing but bad news.

Yet…it fueled a lot of introspection. The movement toward doing a memoir became more real. I would turn forty-one this year—if I continued to survive the pandemic. That was older than my mother had lived. I was *as* old as my mother had ever been, and I was dealing with some fucked up feelings in a fucked up world, and the sympathy I felt for her became more rich.

I still feel childish at times. I have multiple stages of arrested development. The toddler who didn't know where his mother was when she went into the Reserve. The nine-year-old who went from "happy" family to *unhappy*-stepfamily and living in more places than there were years. The angry blip at finding out a lie was worse than the truth when I learned I wasn't born a Mulroney. The angrier termination of our relationship not long after. The devastated twenty-two-year-old me I have struggled to grow up from.

My body tells me I'm older. I feel it. Those swells of anger and despair are all signs of my depression and anxiety. I can't diagnose myself here, but PTSD crosses my mind. If I could gather up my stunted aspects for a family meeting, give them each a voice, I could hopefully show who I *am*, who my mother *was*, and even though we had it bad, I can *thank* her for the life I've lived.

Summer of 2020, a pandemic in full, devastating swing, a president unhinged about the upcoming election, swearing it would be rigged before polls even started coming in, the Olympic games canceled, the economy, housing, employment, everything in shambles—I felt *fine*.

The world was on fire (literally, California had it bad in 2020), *everyone* was as worked up and anxious as I felt on the regular. The reality of existence rose to meet my anxiety, and with all the negative hubbub, was this a sense of normalcy? I knew that wasn't *healthy*. After repeated questions in therapy about "what if this is as good as it gets" regarding accepting levels I achieved with antidepressants, this was the inverse for my reality, "how bad can it get?"

All the way bad.

Never forget.

In emailing with my brother about what he remembered about our mom between 1998 and 2001, I had asked him if turning forty-one was tough for him. I could feel its encroaching weight. It became central to the concept of the memoir. He agreed it was eerie, but he was supportive in saying I would do fine.

CHAPTER 51

2021 – HELL IS A PLACE ON EARTH

There are a few tracks that run through the end of 2020 and going into 2021. I changed medications from Wellbutrin to Paxil to Imipramine. I had been on Remeron for sleep, but changed to Seroquel in November of 2020. This throwing spaghetti against the wall approach put my body and mind through the wringer.

Reading up on Seroquel, I should see full results within a month. While I slept well on it, and I seemed to be capable of maintaining my daily schedule, on the inside of my head, intrusive thoughts began swelling. I freaked myself out, these were uninvited, but thoughts in my "voice."

I can point toward valid excuses; the stress of the last year and the medication changes certainly could have affected me negatively. There is shame and embarrassment that *my* brain, *my* mind, this computer only *I* can use, behaved in a way I felt out of control. I never put anyone in danger, I kept it inside, except for one time when I let slip, out loud, to my wife, an inappropriate thought, the filter for what's okay to say out loud had dissolved.

I was shocked I even said it. Amber was alarmed, but it was unusual, she understood this wasn't normal. The only major change had been that change to Seroquel about a month ago. I still had plenty of Remeron left, quickly read about any withdrawal symptoms I might face, and stopped the Seroquel that night. The next day I contacted my psychiatrist, explaining how intrusive thoughts were beginning to threaten my confidence in myself. I believed it might compromise my relationships, and I had made the decision to switch back to try to get back to "normal."

Surprisingly, my psychiatrist was okay with this plan, and we would revisit the topic in our next scheduled appointment which was in a few weeks anyway. I had a lot more to face in the next few months. Being forty-one was going to be a challenge.

Stress didn't subside. We had the election, highly contested, unlawfully manipulated, and not by anyone trying to *steal* the election from Trump. Rather, by him, his family, and cronies breaking several laws. We knew this at the time. It was reported live.

The pandemic was not going away, the vaccine was still on the way, but we had reached a point in development that things had taken too long in public opinion. Realistically, it was an amazing display of science, medicine, and industry coming together to form a rapid process getting it approved. People were already refusing the vaccine's efficacy before it had been released.

This despite Trump himself had benefited from drugs and therapies no average American would have access to. He caught covid at a super-spreader event *he* hosted at the White House. Hopped up on whatever goofballs they gave him at the hospital, he made his despotic return to the White House.

The world was still on fire. We were headed into 2021! The pandemic surely couldn't last forever. For Christmas and New Year's, Amber, Autumn, and I tried to treat it as our entry into a new Roaring '20's. The original party decade emerged from its own pandemic and warring world. History *could* be repeating itself. Sad that we hadn't learned from our past. We, humanity, could try to reclaim our world, though.

I was trying to reclaim my own history.

We can all do this.

A major step in that came in the form of a Christmas gift from Amber. The package contained a plush Musk Ox and a printed card with Alaska imagery. I was confused at first, but I *got* it. My wife was offering to fly me to Alaska for the twentieth anniversary of my mother's passing. September was a while away yet, I could do a lot of planning between now and then, but this would be the perfect cap to my whole endeavor.

The photos of our New Year's Eve party—in our living room, the three of us with our cats and dogs—I was unhappy with how I looked in the photos. There was a firm decision to change my weight with the new year. No resolutions, I'm not good at those, I only say I want to "write and move more." Nothing unreasonable. The weight had crept up over the years, and as I got older, it most definitely became harder to shed. I cut out desserts, traded cookies in my lunch as a sweet snack for fruit, and tried to make myself move more. Losing was difficult. Yet it happened. I wasn't happy with my appearance, I made changes, they took time and effort.

Then January 6th rolled around. At work, I got a notification on my phone from CNN about the Capitol Building going on lockdown. It wasn't clear if there was someone sick, a shooter, a threat—for a little while. The photos and video started coming in. I sent Amber and Autumn a photo of that dipshit from the Loyal Order of Water Buffaloes playing Revolutionary in Congress. It wasn't a few idiots. It was potentially thousands. It was a riot that people *died* in. These were American citizens under the assumption *their* President encouraged them to sabotage the electoral process.

It was an insurrection. 9/11 all over again and the terrorists were calling from inside the house.

It made me consider how life was when my mom was forty, after a contentious election and terrorist attacks that threatened democracy. SARS wasn't far off, either. We haven't learned nearly enough from even a few days ago, much more *history.* Did she see her world in 2001 the same way I was seeing it here twenty years later? She had always leaned into a looming doomsday.

I've wondered if she had survived, if she made it to forty-one and beyond, if she had had the opportunity to enter her sixties today, *would* we have reconciled? When she worked for the college newspaper, she had an article published which could fit in today's zeitgeist.

In her own words, from October of 1995:

A View From Within the Belly of the Beast

Opinion

Irene Frances Mulroney

It seems to me that everywhere I go anymore I hear about people talking about God, Satan, and the fulfillment of divine prophecy. It's hard to ignore that these times, they are a changing. Everyone seems on the edge, and we all seem to be searching for an answer.

As for me, my search sometimes leads me in strange directions. Like the other day when a search for the correct spelling of a word led me to page 666 in my dictionary.

Odd you know, the things that make you go "Hmmm...." Page 666 of my 1980 version of the Oxford American Dictionary begins with stamina (which I have less and less of these days) and ends with standing (as in standing up for your principles).

But before getting to standing there are other words, like "stance." The second definition for stance comes complete with this sentence: "An attitude toward a specific issue, etc., a positive stance on civil liberties."

Civil liberty. It sounds so right, so important, so American. But the essence of our liberty as civilians seems threatened to me. Because, while taking a stance on a particular issue may be in vogue with some groups, it is becoming all too clear that too many committees, too many special interests, and too much political maneuvering is making for a very unhealthy society; one that is only as free as the chains that bind it together.

Those chains are weakening because there are so many factions pulling for the truest slice of the liberty pie. The problem is that we can't have it all ways. We can't have the best jobs, the best homes, the best schools and the cheapest things without someone paying the price.

If the stance you take is based on information you're receiving from the media, you may find out in the end that you've been duped. Mainstream media have no interest in what's best for this country. Form over content, and the content is pretty lame if you really boil down the information.

They're certainly not going to tackle issues or put their prima-donna butts on the line by taking a stance. They know what happens when you take a stance in America these days. You could find yourself fired, sued, surrounded by jack-booted militia thugs, or color-coded gang members, or, worse, by other suave but incur ably stupid media hunks and honeys asking who had sex with whom, when, where and how?

Then there's the word "stand." As in Stephen King's "The Stand" or a witness stand, or, "it stands to reason."

Three words ... horror, OJ and unreasonable. The scary part to me is that while King may write very good and extremely scary stories, pure fiction. Life is now becoming more scary than any novel. The whole country was forced to take a stand on behalf of the issues confronting one man.

It stands to reason that we should be much more in tune with tackling the issues of crime, growing unemployment and underemployment, and the child abuse that goes hand in hand with both those problems. It's not likely that we're ever going to make any kind of dent in our society's concerns as long as we keep swallowing the drama launched at us through the television.

This is one beast that is way out of control, standing alone as it does as the only source of information for a large, large portion of our population. A reasonable person would take one look at the whole OJ thing and ask, "What's up with that?" There are people murdered every day in this country.

We don't really care about those victims or the perpetrators. But the one who lacks reason falls for the game and plunges into the tempestuous waters that surround it as if that will solve the problems facing our country.

The Book of Revelations says that 666 is the mark of the beast that will bring about the end of the world. Or it could be a warning we need to be aware of. Personally, I find whenever I see the number I am the very least reminded of the evil that exists in our world. Maybe it's just a point of reference to keep us thinking. But the last word on page 666 is "standing," as in upright, as in corn not yet harvested.

All I know for sure, at least from my viewpoint, is that if we keep harvesting the fruits of frustration, pain, and lack of compassion there will be no one left standing.

The beast, real or imagined, will continue to grow. Because no one bothered to remember that three little numbers were supposed to remind us about taking a stand.

––––––

Reading this today, I worry my mom might have been on the wrong side of history. Distrust of the media? Projecting religious symbology on current world events? Or, would she have come around with time, if maybe she had family around her, and taken better care of her mental health?

Unknowable.

A fool's errand to even try and consider. The weight of our current world events is a lot for anyone. I can't try imagining my mother into this existence to think about how *she* would think about the world. It's projecting *and* mind-reading.

The year continued to test me. My daughter got her first job, a part-time gig at a retail shop in a fancy shopping center. A safe place to work, honestly. However, this triggered me, tripped a wire in my brain. My emotions spiraled out of control—*again*.

I compressed every possible future-telling scenario my anxiety could cook up packed into her first shift. I obsessed myself with the possibility any of them could come true; a customer or coworker hitting on her, and worse, while culminating in her ultimately leaving us forever. I tried hard to keep her safe from my own thoughts, because even I knew they were absurd. I needed help.

I had been attempting to practice meditation for a few months now, but the intrusive and maladaptive thoughts had reemerged and made practice difficult. I reached out for help through one of the new talk/text-therapy apps. I figured if I could talk to a licensed therapist on a near daily basis for a month, I could work my way through this clear spike in anxiety.

It wasn't easy. I wanted someone to *talk* to—well, rather, I wanted someone I could text with, I didn't want to literally *talk*—but I was paired with people who didn't seem to read what I was saying, asking questions I had already answered through my introduction. There was a random progress test that indicated I *was* suffering some PTSD (not a diagnosis). I tried to address it with the current therapist and things went silent. I switched therapists. Then had to *again* under similar circumstances.

Maybe the third time was the charm. Maybe this time I had someone who at least responded to *me* conversationally, rather than thrusting questions I had already answered and policy terms at me. I stuck it out for the rest of my time with the app. I only signed up for the introductory rate month, hopeful some medical changes—going from Paxil to Imipramine—would help as well. Though each therapist expressed personal objections to chemical treatment, which felt dismissive.

Then, I started experiencing harassment from my boss at work.

The universe squeezed hard in the Spring of 2021 as stressful situations converged.

Amidst everything, even writing this, I started writing something that felt fun to write. It was the project I dipped into to get away from this, from the news, from the world. It wasn't until I started sharing it with other people to make sure I was being appropriately sensitive with the subject matter that, even though I wasn't writing about me and my mom, I was writing about a mother.

My favorite Ray Harryhausen film is 1981's Clash of the Titans. As a kid, Medusa was somehow alluring and terrifying. A cosmic monster that was revolting and beautiful, and to see her was to be turned to stone. She was a forbidden object no one should behold.

I would quickly learn Medusa's entire myth, which consists of being created only to be executed, was a brutalization of a single woman simply for existing. There are two ways to read the origin—though she is specifically mentioned as being beautiful in both—one is that she had an affair with Poseidon in a temple dedicated to Athena; the other being that Medusa was an Athena devotee that Poseidon rapes in Athena's temple. Both end with Poseidon facing no consequences and Athena cursing the woman to her monstrous form for defiling her temple with sex. They're both terrible for Medusa.

Given the nature of the gods, I believe the rape a more likely story. However, I considered, what if Athena didn't *curse* Medusa, but granted her a power that would prevent anyone from ever attacking her again? If someone meant her harm, Medusa's gaze would turn that person to stone. In the ancient Mediterranean, what entitled man didn't mean a common woman harm? It would still be a curse.

I wanted to give Medusa agency, to change her monster's den to a place of safety. She was abused, she gives sanctuary to the abused. A safe place protected by a legendary "monster."

Then there's Perseus, sent to kill Medusa by a mad king with help from the gods because it's supposed to be an impossible task. I wrote about a more observant young man who recognizes charity, since he grew up benefiting from it himself. Their "fight" is a discussion. He's taking on the impossible task to save his mother. I made Medusa a matriarch, but a recluse.

Again, as I had done with In the House of In Between, I was dealing with my existential issues through my fiction. Write what you know, right?

CHAPTER 52

Reaching out to my mom's siblings was proving mostly silent. Not everyone wanted to respond. Not everyone had the patience to deal with *me*, the one-off, away from the family. I have always been keenly aware I was sequestered from my mother's family. I've wondered why. My brother and aunt that lived in Oregon, the two who had been closest to her near the end, gave me new pieces of information I had never known.

I never knew my mother had tried heroin. She had a rough patch between my brother staying in New Mexico to start his new romance and them all living in Oregon sometime later. There may have been violence. There may have been rape. Some of those things may always be unknown. My mother buried the negative.

An uncle who lived with my mother and brother in Oregon dealt with some anger and betrayal with my mom as well. The three of them got a house, but my mom fell behind and stopped contributing her share. It caused lasting trust issues for my uncle—her own brother.

Between my uncle and brother's descriptions of their time with her, she became reclusive. This would have been her late thirties. Jeremy said it took effort to get her out of the house, but she *would* have fun if she went out. I identified with that, but wondered what she was going through, and why she would have gone back to Alaska?

Jeremy shared that she was obsessed with Chris McCandless and Into the Wild. That she had been all the way back when she *first* moved to Alaska. Supposedly she wanted to follow McCandless's path, to have an adventure into the wild frontier, to be that nomad she wanted to be, even though she called herself a gypsy. I only ever saw her as restless and seeking challenge. She didn't disillusion me of that, even through their stories.

That made me want to reach out to D to talk about what he could remember of his relationship and that time in Alaska, especially how he had gone from being stolen from to living with her. He gave me a touching tale of genuinely loving my mom, and that he was willing to extend forgiveness and travel basically from one end of the Earth to the other for her.

They had broken up after she had lost her job at the NBC affiliate and moved to Alaska (on his dime), and he had traveled down to Mexico. Sitting on a beach, he *missed* her. He decided to find a job in Alaska, find her, let go of the financial betrayal, and try to make things work. He had only recently moved in when I had come to visit. She thought it was fate and it was meant to be. A hopeful romantic with the man she had robbed.

Things wouldn't continue working, though, and he left by May the following year. He spoke to her on the phone a few more times but fell out of touch. He wouldn't hear about her again until he was notified by my brother when she died.

Of course, I wish things had worked out for *my* family, that Irene would have stayed with *my* dad, but D was a good guy and adventurous, too. Jeremy and I both appreciated him. I think we both probably wish she could have stuck it out with him.

Finally, he shared a few photos he still had of her preparing a Thanksgiving dinner they shared with each other. She's wearing the ring she gave me when I visited. It was a wonderful little surprise to see that maybe she honestly loved the ring and meant every word she had told me that night.

There was another man who had been part of our story, too, and I learned something new from one of my aunts that made me feel compelled to address M for the first time in nearly thirty years. I hadn't corresponded with him since a couple of handwritten letters back and forth after I officially "moved out" by the end of 1993's summer break. I had seen his name pop up on Facebook, friends with an aunt. He was still alive, though as I understood it, a Trump supporter.

Best to narrow the conversation.

The reason I wanted to contact him wasn't to give him a voice in this narration, but to confirm something I hadn't previously been aware of: had my mom visited him in 1998?

My aunt said she went to Florida in '98, though she wasn't sure when, to try and patch things up with M. This lined up with what angered me in the first place, and the shrinking amount of time she was promising to visit, down to not coming at all—was that because she had already used up her vacation time to visit M, or had she committed to visit M later? Either way, did it matter? The decision was evident, she chose M over me that year.

I did not pick a fight with him. I gave him the briefest of synopses of my life over the last three decades, that I was writing a memoir, and asked him if he could give me his impressions of how he saw my mother in their time together. I also asked if they had gotten back together around that time. He was "old" when I knew him. I was asking him to dig into a past he probably hadn't thought of in the same twenty years it's been for all of us.

He effused compliments about Irene, her writing and creativity, and her impulsivity, which was fun sometimes, but also got her in trouble. He loved her, too, and much as I did not care for *him*, I can see at least that was true. He insisted if he had known she was in trouble, he would have seen to getting her help. They had stayed in contact even after 1998, which he confirmed that he had flown her down to talk about their "relationship." But when was it? Lost to memory.

He said he took her to a beach where they sat and talked. For them, I'm sure it was touching. For an eighteen-year-old me? I would have exploded with rage. Yet I would do the same in the following years. Go back. Try to rekindle the past.

In closing out the conversation, I asked him if he could recall if she was diagnosed as having bipolar disorder while we lived in Florida. He did remember her going to counseling, but she may not have talked about it enough, *that* he was hazy on, but it was familiar to him.

Here was a wholly new piece to a puzzle that made 1998 make more sense and hurt all over again. It also reaffirmed that I made the right decision for myself, though I still regret how I said it. Feeling that you're no longer a priority in someone's life whom you love, and feeling them double-down when you bring it up? You *must* let that person go. They are hurting you. Even family. Sometimes, *especially* family.

In the first week off Paxil and completely on Imipramine, things felt decent. In the last few weeks, I had had fits and bouts with panic and tears that I hid from coworkers. Anything sensitive set me to crying at home, it made watching dramatic shows almost difficult. These feelings were out of control, and revelations about my past were making things even more complex, but Imipramine, by itself, no longer on Paxil or Remeron, I was getting better, even sleeping through the night! I had found a good drug for me.

Going off Paxil brought withdrawal symptoms that I dealt with for —well, soon I wouldn't even be able to tell for how long. About four weeks on Imipramine, I developed a rash along my scalp, which spread down my spine. It was insanely itchy and no antihistamine or topical touched it. I investigated side-effects of Imipramine. This seemed unusual, but it was the *only* difference in my daily life.

I saw my nurse practitioner *and* doctor about it, separate bouts with severity of the rash, both agreeing it must be the new drug. They ordered me to cut off using the Imipramine, and basically wished me good luck with the withdrawal I was about to experience as I went on two rounds of prednisone.

I was now on a steroid going through antidepressant withdrawal from two drugs *and a self-imposed* emotional rollercoaster. It lasted a long time.

As I was going through all of this, I thought I kept up a decent front. I never complained to coworkers, I didn't take many sick days. Taking a sick day in the time of covid made people instantly weary.

We had a new employee, whom I tried to be cordial with, but

where we work, sarcasm flies. There was a day she asked for a particular type of sample that we normally don't provide, I told her "Too bad!" in a cartoonishly mean voice.

I then proceeded to help her find the stuff she was looking for anyway with another coworker. Someone in a different room overheard the exchange and took offense on the new employee's behalf. It went to their manager, who reported to mine.

My manager then sent me an email accusing me of being abrasive with the new employee but offering no context or specificity. I was caught off guard, I was literally confused, but she wouldn't elaborate and only told me to be "gentler," ending the exchange with a smiley face. That bit of sarcasm earlier was the only thing I could think of.

Though, that wasn't the end of it. She decided to bring me a laundry list of complaints about my behavior, including regarding my time in the restroom, and now using the word "rude" for my supposed treatment of the new employee. I had to stop her, to tell her I was going through some shit that I did not want to talk about with her, and that I show up to work and do my job, "…please *let* me."

The seriousness must have been conveyed because she backed away, offering that *if* I wanted to talk to her about *anything*, her "door was open." I *know* I shot a glare at that. To come to me with complaints about me personally and then try to offer a friendly open-door policy?

I talked about it with the therapist through the app, with friends and family, I didn't want to lose my job for my *attitude—again*. Amber told me to take the next day off, which brought its own ire from my boss when she needed a *reason* I was calling-in. I wasn't lying when I said I was having stomach issues.

When I went back to work, I had a long discussion with the general manager of the place. Upon investigation, it was that "he said/she said" hearsay I suspected, for which, the GM and the manager who had contacted my manager both apologized. I was asked if I wanted an apology from my boss, but I knew it would ring hollow. I was fine to let it fade away and keep on working.

Not that I exactly kept it to myself. I bitched on Twitter. I bitched to my podcast friends. I kept trying to focus on my meditation. I needed some sort of peace in my daily life.

It took a lot of work. The rash began to subside. The dark thoughts began to quiet. My control over my own emotions came back. Strangely? I felt fine. I was still taking Klonopin, for sleep and anxiety, but I was more than a month off antidepressants. When the allergic reaction cleared, my psych asked if I wanted to start something new.

I didn't.

That old question from the therapists before, "What if this is as good as it gets?"

I was *off* antidepressants. I felt no different than at my "best" while on them. It was *always* only ever as good as it was going to get. The question following that is: am I okay with that? Will I deal with it or change the things I need to?

I wouldn't say I was happy. That's a fleeting feeling, but content, and not in cold comfort; content with myself. This is me. I am nervous and small. A lot of us are. I contain universes that make me happy and I want to share them.

As I came up out of the haze of withdrawal and re-familiarizing myself with my natural chemical composition, a lot of re-contextualization was occurring. I am filled with a creative spirit that was delicately sewn into me by a woman who was a creative who also hurt and tried to find the best she could strive for as well. I *am* my mother's son.

Then my niece happened to be nearby visiting her family and friends between Missouri and Arkansas. She was driving with her fiancé's stepmother, both were vaccinated and asymptomatic. I asked both her and my family if we could swing a visit.

Justice was keen, but not sure on timing, she had places to be by times. We talked for a few days and found a window where she could stop by for a few hours as a break on her way back west.

At forty-one, looking a little modeled from the subsided rash, but otherwise healthy, I met my niece, now twenty-four, for the first time. We connected immediately. There was no discomfort, no awkward or uncomfortable silences, we engaged about family and pop culture (her fiancé's stepmom was also a Dune fan and the 2021 film was coming soon). Amber and Autumn enjoyed meeting her, too. I rarely have blood-relations nearby.

She had a couple pieces of knowledge about my mom I had never known, and it was yet another shock. I knew my mom had been in touch with my biological father at times. I knew he called her apartment when Jeremy was living there. Justice had a connection with that family because Jeremy is closer to them. I did not know my mom maintained that connection as well.

It came with a weird anecdote that she had told my biological father that she was thinking of leaving Rex and Alaska. They or someone in the house was doing meth and my mom dumped their stash into the lake they lived on. She maybe even talked about trying to come back to Arkansas.

This made me think about what if she successfully made it out? Would she have gone back to M? Or my biological father? If either of those turned out to be the case, how would I have handled it if she had ever reached out to me again?

It made me miss family. At the same time, I know I wouldn't get along with a lot of them. Maybe my mom saw that in me as I grew up. Maybe that's why I was left sequestered.

They're all little pieces of *my* genetic pie and being close to one of them crackles with energy and emotion. Maybe because all of us are spread out. Whatever connection family has, if it's in the feeling of a familiar body shape, a scent, a recognition of relation to that face... I missed Justice before she was even gone.

When she was leaving, standing in my kitchen, I hugged her for the tenth time, but *this* hug... I was back in Alaska, in the airport with my mom, and this hug felt physically the same, but without the sadness. This was a reemergence, a reconnection to something lost. My mom lives on not only in our memories, but in Justice. She's a little piece of her, and my mom got to see her when she was born. Another ephemeral, though sentimental, connection. Now this hug that felt the same as something I hadn't felt in twenty-six years, at some level, was a bridge back to that moment. Indeed, that reverberation back through history where I can tell my mom I love her, but also carry forward healthier relationships with families of blood and my own making. With Justice, we are 100% related, but we *chose* each other that day, and I think, I *hope*, it would make my mother proud.

I strengthened my family resolve at home, too. I had gotten into a conversation with my therapist regarding titles and parents, and I realized I was missing something at home. Not that Autumn calls out for us much, but my name was always "J.D.," even after adopting her. I was "dad" to anyone I was referenced to, I was "daddy" when she spoke for the animals. I asked if she would be willing to call me "Dad," if I could *be* Dad? Amber was a part of the conversation, as well. Autumn admitted she wasn't sure why she didn't anyway, but "yes" was the answer.

I was earning something. Now I was getting the recognition for the work I had done, I had earned the right to *be* someone's dad. I don't need to put my seed out there, I *have* a beautiful daughter I love. I have a wonderful wife that has let me be that for her daughter. Our family were the puzzle pieces we needed for each other.

CHAPTER 53

Continuing with practicing meditation, I ran into an exercise that brought up a concept I had never heard of: *existential loneliness*. A loneliness where "what" is being missed isn't always clear, and a symptom it can cause is the constant sensation that you cannot fully inhale. This was something I had mentioned to my therapist in a session before the pandemic struck. With everything that was going on? Writing this memoir, talking to family, learning new things even at forty-one-years-old about my youth, medication changes, and a looming trip to Alaska in September for the twentieth anniversary of my mother's death? I was struggling with existential loneliness before I understood the concept.

That hole in me can never be filled. It is a severed thing that only eats. There are aspects of people and situations that will trigger it, and I have ruined potential relationships with it, trying to fill a bottomless pit as quickly as possible. What am I offering to anyone when I only need and take *from* them?

Usually, it's silly things, needing validation and acceptance. The agent and the indie? Was I desperate for attention? Was I too impatient with the therapists on the app because I didn't feel seen?

Did that loneliness exist even before? Even as a baby, the being handed off to an aunt, told to raise me as their own while she handled a relationship and went into the military. Was I *always* missing my mom?

I had requested both my mother's military discharge papers and the police report as research for this book. Jeremy had also, independently, requested the discharge papers and received them before I did. It's a simple document. She joined the Army Reserve in February of 1982 and went through a six-month training course which put her on an obligation of five years, terminating in November of 1987. She got some recognition in marksmanship and photography, but those six months appeared to be the extent of her "active" service.

Six months is a long time for a two-year-old. That's a quarter of a lifetime! I understand why I was terrified of being out of sight of my aunt, afraid I would be abandoned over and over. It makes the fear of abandonment I've faced in relationships sharper in contrast.

As summer progressed, our political dumpster fire and the continuing pandemic were all that was on the news. If you're reading this and it is *still* pandemic-times? You know exactly how 2020 to…*whenever*, is hard to track. Is it summer? Is fall almost here? Should I put up the pool this year? When did I see that movie?

Oh yeah, Autumn and I saw Black Widow and Shang-Chi in the theater, vaccinated, with our masks. We're MCU fans, they're amusement park rides and a nice escape from the real world.

My dad moved out of my childhood home in the summer of 2021. He could afford the rent and expenses he was paying on it and had remained on his own since divorcing my mom. The landlord wanted to sell off their rental properties and my dad opted to bail. He moved closer to me, I can literally drive down the street to his house, which isn't terrible. This whole idea that at forty-one I have found some inner peace as I have shed negativity about myself, it also came with this severance from a crucial piece of my past.

All this time, in times of need, I had my home to go to. Except, when I'm forty-one, I'm a grown-ass adult and my dad needs to move. My grip on the past must be wrenched free.

I helped him move, of course, and that included taking some things off his hands he would have otherwise probably trashed. Including a box of photos full of vacation, family, and wedding photos of our family from 1984-1988. I scanned them to a group my brother made on Facebook to celebrate the memory of my mom. If you Google her name, those photos are among the top listings.

I can still see *my* old childhood home from the highway when I pass. It's hard not to look.

I kept in touch with Justice almost daily after she left, and she wanted to go to Alaska, too. She had always wanted to go, to see Alaska, but to get a little closer to her Grandma Irene, too. I had asked Jeremy if he wanted to go with me to mark the twentieth anniversary, but with the pandemic and his old feelings about the place from dealing with our mom's final affairs in 2001, he declined. I didn't push him. When she asked to come along, I told her I was going for somber reasons and I could be a wreck, but I would do my best to take care of her.

We talked through text a lot about our individual family experiences, much more willing to talk openly about deeper thoughts and concerns after meeting each other, rather than kind warmth over Facebook on birthdays. We learned about our own family from each other. She shared with me a letter my mother had written to her mother about the second move to Alaska, dated April 15th, 2000.

I tried to remember what I was doing in the spring of 2000—was I still at Borders Bookstore? Had I broken up with one girlfriend who was good for me to go back to another girlfriend who *wasn't* good for me, because—I know—I found comfort in the past, same as my mom. Was that where I was when my mom was finding what she referred to as her Heaven? A place that made her feel God, that made her believe prayers were answered through action.

It's dramatic, romantic, and some of it reads as a wannabe Hallmark Christmas Special. I found myself reading it thinking all the while, "You absolute loon!" Not mad, not surprised, not entirely sure I believed a word of it. It's fantastical, a glossed over version of what was surely an incredibly difficult journey to make northward in spring. Snow and ice feature prominently in her tale. Something I would see as a potentially lethal impediment she saw as beautiful and awesome.

She learned of a place she could rent and of a place to seek out a job at the first gas station she asked.

It's weird; she explained a "real Alaskan" as a Germanic white dude because he was rugged and a musher. She said his whole name in the letter. She stayed with him, but he was getting married, she explicitly claimed nothing happened between them. She could stay as long as she helped feed his animals and did the dishes. Yeah… It's weird. I worried while I read it. She recounted sledding with him and his dog team, and how she fell off the sled a lot and she had the bruises to prove it.

Mom? Did he hurt you? Are you writing a coded story in case anyone finds you?

Is that my distrust because she lied to me about elements of both of our lives? The only notes of truth come in her recounting moving a cat on this multi-day, cross-country journey and how upset the poor thing is, and she's all, "she'll get over it."

I felt bad for the cat.

She found a dirt-cheap cabin in the middle of nowhere with an outhouse and without running water. She was in love with it. This was magical to her. She wanted to save up to purchase a plane ticket for Justice to come and visit her the next summer. Justice would have been four.

I don't know what she was thinking. Maybe she intended for Justice's mom to accompany her? Late summer 2001 was a long time away and a lot would happen in the meantime.

I thought about how much she must have gone through in that year. What *I* went through in that year. A race we didn't know we were in. A race we are all in in someone else's memoir.

There's still a few more lines of letter left after that odd suggestion-more-than-question to fly a toddler to another state. "And tell her Grandpa I made it—I'm OK…"

I asked Justice if that meant her maternal or paternal "Grandpa?"

"Definitely (paternal)."

My mom had indeed maintained or reconnected with my biological father beyond Jeremy staying with her. Was she forgiving or stubborn?

Did she think she could dig back through her past relationships and find someplace comfortable to curl up again? *Was* bad easier?

It makes me think the darkest thought all over again, "Was I a burden that ruined her original family?"

She lost Jeremy and her marriage while pregnant with me.

I can't keep going down that road. That's not *my* fault, no matter how much any of this makes me *feel*, that's trying to reason with the unreasonable and impossible to control. Another space and time where I had no agency. I keep trying to write myself into corners, make my whole life, all my sadness, *my own fault*, as if even if she *did* resent me, why should I feel bad? That would be *her* problem.

A lot of this is half-assed attempts at journaling as if they're chapters, but this one I shared with Justice, because I realized she probably read the story as positive and adventurous. Why not? My mother *was* a storyteller.

Here I am having these familiar gut reactions of fear at my mother's seeming recklessness. Questioning our entire relationship and if mental health was the singular, abysmal reason that our relationship had such tumultuous ups and downs? The letter made me think and feel young and scared for my mother's safety all over again. That's what makes the resentment rise in my mind. That I can easily be transported back to that young brain, unable to handle the complexities of her misunderstood mind.

Justice was quick to comfort and validate that my experience was my own and she didn't begrudge me that. That her own relationship with my biological father as her "Grandpa" and that side of the family was different than anything I could have known. That she knows how her grandparents and great-grandparents mistreated Irene and me. We all have family who were once bad, or are currently objectionable that we still grit our teeth to bear in hopes something less topical saturates the conversation.

She also said that she believed Irene—maybe naively—did think she was protecting my well-being through some of her questionable decisions. My aunt said the same thing when these ugly self-defeating thoughts presented upon seeing my mother's discharge papers from her Reserve training. "She loved you, everything she did was to protect you."

It's hard to internalize that. Everything I talk about in this thing, it's a lot of negative memories because I feel constantly set up for failure by my mother. That's my problem. I have made it this far, not despite the life I've lived, but precisely because of it.

At some point I do need to accept the droplets of love Irene sprinkled for all the maelstrom because it is all I will ever have. There is love. I *do* love my mom! What I loved wasn't adventures, though we had them, it was being quiet at home. Quiet reflection, conversation, music, a blue haze in the air.

Sometimes I especially miss her. The existential loneliness kicking in. That unfillable void.

I can't know how my mother felt about me towards the end, why she didn't try, even though I told her I had had enough? I didn't need the Hallmark story, that would have upset me then. Maybe more post-cards with where she was living? I might have kept them.

When 9/11 happened...

I don't know, I'm daydreaming about the past in the middle of trying to write my reflections of hearing-in on a private conversation out of time and how my niece, the person who supplied it, both understands the pain, but also promises the love. And I keep resisting.

"Will you still think that after I've written everything down? There's a decade none of you know the truth about, but I was there. It was *my* childhood. And—I don't know."

Then I feel guilty. Yeah, I'm walking you through my emotions in real time. I recognize in my youthful behavior, especially in the step-family years, I was going the route of bad seed. I was angry all the time —why shouldn't I be? It was chaos! I stayed angry at her for that family and to learn, from her own script, she entertained contact with the original villain of our story? The guilt quavers under that. I wouldn't have been able to handle who she was being, and she didn't have the patience for my temper to try to work with me.

The letter honestly reminds me we weren't a good fit for each other. We loved each other in an attachment way. We had been through some shit together. That love grew toxic and harmful at times. Forty-one-year-old-me wants to help thirty-eight-year-old-Irene—and—that's not happening. No amount of weed or wine will take me back or wipe the feelings away.

I don't know what to feel most strongly about in the letter. The incredible and serendipitous luck? The wild adventure? The meanings behind the stories—their actual, drawn-out truths? I know it's my comfort and privilege showing, but deigning to questionable living conditions? My mother loved the outdoors, we went camping, but I never imagined her living in a cabin on the outskirts of civilization. There's wanting to impress a toddler granddaughter. There's staying in contact with someone she had always vilified.

Listen, this isn't a matter of time heals old wounds or forgiveness, this individual who happens to be the progenitor of my birth, was busted on meth distribution charges in 2021. He's not a good dude. Jeremy had a poor relationship with him growing up. He beat my mother while pregnant with me under the idea I wasn't even his. The crimes were committed and that's not someone I need in my life because they didn't want to be in it to begin with.

Seeing that my mother was in touch with him in some way wasn't a glimpse into some moving *growth* of character, but a display of continued questionable *judgement* of character.

In my opinion. Except, I feel logically correct in the assumption. Maybe I can be a Vulcan after all.

The *rollercoaster*. Not even a fun one at Six Flags. It's the twenty-foot-tall county fair monstrosity you can hear straining under its own weight and you're pretty sure it's the one those kids died on last year. Yet I keep finding myself on it. I buckle in and dig into the corners, looking for a little more to fill in the edges of the hole.

In talking with Amber one night, I brought up how the new information about my mom seeing M still hurt, but didn't change that I had come to forgive her. None of this new information has changed my forgiveness. It still hurts, I will always be the kid, and I still have things I don't know, and *won't* know. She asked if I would *want* to, because it might be more hurtful information again.

She's not missing any of her family history. Nothing has been lost to time, distance, or death for her, meanwhile I have a few years of my mother's history I will never know because of how she lived her life. If I *could* learn more, even if it was bad news, I would want it, to complete the picture of her, to fill that void with truth, rather than aching question marks.

I would still maintain my forgiveness.

My mom suffered, I believe, a lot more than she ever let on. A lot more than her brain put her through. It was more than bipolar disorder. It was a childhood of abuse from someone who was supposed to love her unconditionally. It was sexualization at a young age by *church* elders. It was getting pregnant twice as a teen and ran out of town for something she didn't do. It was having only her mother, her own abuser, as a role-model for relationships, marriage after marriage seeking security but always falling in love. I was dragged along, unaware of those first few years, of the damage she was rendering onto us both. Unaware *she* was unaware. Though she was older than me, she was still a kid, too.

She had a hard life that I could not appreciate because I thought my mom was brilliant and that brilliance meant wisdom and logic. I only gained perspective after her death and only because of things she never shared with me. I had made her life hard, too. The feeling that I was a burden isn't fair to either of us, but as I grew into my own opinions, I'm sure I was as burdensome to her as I thought she was to me.

CHAPTER 54

It is September 4th, 2021. Saturday. It's been a few weeks of eager anticipation. Today I scheduled to have my hair colored—brightly —red, with black roots. I met an old high school friend who owns a salon and survived this far through the pandemic. Brilliant and tenacious and a fierce mom, she made it work as drama of her own mounted *in addition to* the pandemic. Many of us did. Do. As she trimmed and styled, we fast-forwarded through idle chit chat to get to the good stuff.

"So why Alaska?" she asked excitedly.

Everyone thinks it's exciting. Alaska is basically another country, even though it is one of our fifty United States. Then I drop the bomb that I'm observing the twentieth anniversary of my mother's passing and that usually drives conversations to a halt.

Not with her. We talked at length about difficult parental relationships. How our mental health issues manifested, how early, what were the signs, "you might have noticed me shift in high school..." "Yeah, it was easier for us broken people to come together." All the while, she deftly styled and manipulated my hair, set bleach, washed, dyed—and we talked.

My hair came out wonderful, she was excited with her own work, and I love the look. A darker jewel-toned red for most of it, and black at the roots, it's not a clown wig glaring against my scalp.

We dared a hug, we're both vaccinated, and I was off as her next client stepped in. Serendipitous that we got that freedom to talk openly with each other for exactly the right amount of time. Or she's that good at doing her job. Maybe therapists and hairstylists should combine…

I'm turning forty-two tomorrow. I'll have made it through probably one of the most difficult years in my life since the end of 2001 and the rest of 2002. A similar trial of fire, on a twenty-year cycle? What will sixty-one bring?

I dyed my hair for a new look at forty-two. The pandemic rages, some people won't take it seriously, but medicine is trying its damnedest to catch up with stupidity. I'm starting forty-two off by going to Alaska to mourn and mark the passing of a mother I did not have a good relationship with. I'm going there vibrant. I will be a torch in a dark place. I will see *myself in* the mirror in that far from home place. I want people to see *me* in the stranger in town.

Then? I will be ready for when joy comes around the corner. Be that a new Roaring '20's or being happier with myself, in my own skin.

It has been a hard last year and a half, and I know shoes drop. In this moment, despite my positive feelings toward my personal wellbeing, I am indeed terrified of our state governments basically forcing kids back into school and then *prohibiting* schools from issuing mask-mandates. At this time, it's being contested and investigated, but every day that goes by, more kids get sick.

Despite holding a majority in the Senate, Democrats *still* can't pass anything because "Democrats" such as Joe Manchin aren't there to promote a forward and preparative agenda. He's a Confederate in sheep's clothing. He's a Southern Democrat, which is what the current Republican party was born from. The party ideals swapped around FDR's New Deal, liberal Republicans (think: Abraham Lincoln) became liberal Democrats and vice versa. Except for those fence-riding holdovers from the Civil War.

The Republicans want to clinch their fists around power even tighter. Active efforts to make it more difficult to vote. Seeking to over-turn Roe v Wade with a Supreme Court *We the People* had no say in who was on. Most of the justices were installed by presidents who didn't win the popular vote. They're the party of *limited* government? Everything they do is somehow stealing from someone, grabbing power from the weak and poor to keep the gears of capitalism grinding away. The Confederates want their cheap labor force back in order.

The people voting them into power don't want to wear a mask or get vaccinated because "my body, my choice!" No realization of the irony, no consideration beyond the end of their noses.

My nation is in trouble. The global pandemic is still active. Nature is lashing out with force we freely gave it. It might be the end of the world as we know it. I feel fine.

I also look fabulous.

CHAPTER 55

SEPTEMBER 14-16, 2021 – TALKEETNA, ALASKA

t had been an exceptionally long day. Up at my normal time to feed the pets. I stepped outside to see the sunrise, took a picture of it through the trees. Airports, planes. Lots of photos of the changing landscape. All the while, chasing the sun west *and* north to a later sunset than I was used to at this time of year.

I finally read the Breathing Method from Stephen King's Different Seasons. There was a sense of closure in that brief glimpse of King's weird horror predilections. I think it may be the story my mom wanted me to read the most.

There was a sense of closure, and irony, in finally finishing the book, the book from my earliest memories. Always rattling behind the door. It's about a mother going beyond the call of duty and mortality to ensure her child's safe entry into the world. Meanwhile, here I was, survivor in a world without a mom these twenty years, cherishing that long buried treasure at last.

I paused often to take photos from my window seat and to assure myself I was gliding through the ocean of our atmosphere in a metal tube, fighting that old motion sickness. There were clouds, plains, mountains, glaciers, and humanity scattered in between. We started to descend in a late afternoon Anchorage. I snapped a photo of a rainbow upon landing.

Justice would see and snap the same rainbow from her vantage at a nearby park, having already arrived. I picked her up and we booked it north. The sun went down on us at 8:45 p.m. their time—11:45 p.m. my time—after seeing the sun rise shortly after 7:00 a.m. in Tulsa that morning. Nearly seventeen hours of daylight for me, ending in Alaska —this side of Fall. Twilight lingered through our drive through Wasilla, Houston, Willow... The stars were out as we arrived in Talkeetna.

We stayed south of downtown Talkeetna, around the corner from the H&H Bar & Restaurant—close to where my mom lived. Fortunately, there was a cabin rental in the same area. The name of the road we stayed on also happened to be the name of a Buffington cousin who had said some kind things about my mom before my trip when she texted me a safe journey.

A lot of extra sunshine to charge me up for a heavy day ahead? A rainbow upon touchdown? My cousin's name as a reminder that it's more than me and Justice who cared about Irene. I believe mounting coincidences are the mind *seeking* patterns. I don't believe in signs. I believe in probability and chance. Shit happens and we are lucky as hell to witness it. I was *lucky on this* trip.

Justice and I smoked a joint and stared at the stars for probably an hour. We could see the faint blue haze of the Milky Way with our naked eyes. Neither of our phones, nor my new camera could catch it. We were both tired after a long day of flights and drives. I stepped out one last time as Justice began to bed down. I smoked and looked at the stars. Clouds were beginning to roll in and slightly obscure the view. Then, under the Big Dipper, against the tree line, flashes of green!

I made sure I wasn't imagining things, then burst back into the cabin. "Justice, get up—get your coat."

She was quick, and when she stepped out, clouds were threatening to obscure the Big Dipper, but I told her where to watch. Wisps of light flickered from the tree line and off into the void. Bigger, higher in the atmosphere, a light from a much larger source than a bolt of lightning. We marveled and giggled. Then went to bed.

In my first few hours of being in Alaska, I was seeing things I had hoped to see, but did not expect. I understood the aurora would be obscured by the rain system in the area right over our trip (a bit of irony to go along with all the luck). There was no guarantee I would see the aurora, even if we made a midnight trip to Denali, which I was not prepared for. Yet, there it was, only the edge, a shimmer, a wink of its existence.

When you live in the city your entire life, seeing a sky full of stars is a rare occasion. Astronauts talk about a new feeling toward humanity and their world when they see the Earth, I imagine a lot of people would feel a lot more humility if they saw raw nature and unhidden stars. I did.

In the morning we went for breakfast at a drive-thru joint at the junction where Talkeetna Spur Road continues to Talkeetna and forks off to I-A4. The H&H sits on the Parks Highway between two small bodies of water with houses on their shores. I pulled into the same paved expanse that contained a few small commercial buildings, a gas station, and the H&H at the end.

We ate behind a Subway sandwich shop and talked about food habits. Mostly: I have bad ones. She was a cook with business ambitions! My mom, my brother, and my niece love food, and here I sit with my embarrassing pickiness and anxiety.

We listened to Tool's 10,000 Days, because it's the love letter to my mom I wish I could have written. Maynard's artistic representation of his relationship with his own mother mirrored how I felt about mine. A Perfect Circle's Mer de Noms is angry, Tool's 10,000 Days is accepting. Same relationship, changed with time and perspective. Well written music can be as effective as drugs and therapy.

Pulling up the map of the area on my phone again, I related the tale of the article that described my mother's death and the events around it. There are only a few houses that fit the description given. We pulled up to a house that fit the narrative.

You might ask, "You *don't* know?"

As of this writing? I do not. I have asked family. I requested her death certificate and a police report. Family have declined to point on a map. The death certificate lists an address that does not exist, leading me to believe that in the day, it may have been a 911-address. The report is pending. Regardless, there was a driveway that seemed to lead back to one of the bodies of water "across the highway" from the H&H. It fits the description in a twenty-year-old newspaper article, that's the only reason we picked it.

There were "No Trespassing" and "Area Under Surveillance" signs. We debated, hemmed, and hawed about whether to defy personal property boundaries. I had parked in a leafy turnabout, and we took some photos of the trees and foliage.

I stared at the signs, at the house at the top of the hill, looking empty—if not dilapidated. I said, "This might be it. It looks about right for the description. Should we go up anyway? We can always explain ourselves honestly and apologize…"

Then we heard something overhead; a raven flying through the clearing of the driveway. It was massive, its weight cleaving the air with soft thunder. It flew up and into the trees beyond the No Trespassing signs, toward the house. More probability and chance.

I said something to the effect of, "I mean, I guess if ever there was an invitation…"

We walked up the drive, keeping an eye out for any signs of occupants. It turned out what I had seen from the bottom of the slope was only a covered shed. The cabin behind it was nice, but sparse. There were no cars and no one came to greet us. I continued to take photos of the surrounding area, but not of the house. I was suspicious whether this was *the* house, but it fit the narrative and it was fortuitously vacant—as if inviting us to look around. There was a walking trail that led to the "lake" on the other side of the property.

Alaska is marshy and filled with these oversized ponds from the millennia of glacial melting. We carefully descended as close to the waterline as the steadier earth would allow. I took photos. We talked. I talked out loud. I told my mom I had a home that was steady with a family whom I love and love me and I am okay despite—everything.

Justice said she felt Irene was there with us. Then we both noticed three ducks in the water. I took more photos. Was it the "three" of us being represented in these waterfowl?

I brought a small rock from our garden to chuck into the lake. I wanted to share a piece of my home with my mom's chosen home.

I flubbed it, though, the stone catching on my sleeve and barely going five feet into the muck. *Typical*. We laughed. The intention was still there, a stone from my home, to share with the place she lived. The ducks took off, seemingly as we had concluded our moment with the place.

I stole a pebble from the drive to take back home with me. These beautifully dark gray stones, almost black when they're wet, absolutely fill the landscape there, worn smooth from countless years rolling under ice. Hopefully the owner of the property will grant me the taking of a stone.

I turned at the No Trespassing sign, unsure if there was any surveillance truly taking place. I apologized for trespassing. I said that we wanted to see the lake and did nothing to their property (minus a few rocks).

We drove back to our cabin to put away our leftovers from breakfast and rested a while, both of us probably still out of sorts from the time difference and traveling. I know that each of my two mornings waking up, I would be sleepy and comfy enough to lay there, but I came awake around five in the morning regardless of the light (which *was* indeed beginning to filter in through the window). We talked about the experience, we talked about the rest of our day.

We drove up to downtown Talkeetna with its historical avenue of old houses converted into gift and food shops. We both bought touristy shit. We ate fish and chips, Alaskan Cod with sweet potato wedges, at the Denali Brew Pub. I had a nice ale, Justice had a whiskey sour.

There's an outcropping against the Talkeetna River that we hung out at a few times in hopes of catching views of far-off Denali. The river itself was clear, but flowing rapidly giving it a blue-gray depth that *looked* cold. It was, descending from melting mountain snow and meeting the Susitna River.

Denali peeked out a few times, but we probably had more fun following unmarked trails and trying to catch pictures of magpies. One was interested in us traipsing through saplings and river grass, jumping between branches, making it difficult to catch him on film. He was beautiful, a little bigger than a crow, nowhere near as big as the raven we saw earlier.

We bought some weed from the *only* cannabis dispensary in a good long distance. The shop itself was gorgeous and filled with mountain climbing antiques. We got a few pre-rolls, then went back to the park and sat in a dry riverbed. We talked about socio-political issues, the ways we could move forward if everyone would get on the same page, but agreed that would probably never happen because no one is reading the same book.

My ass began to freeze and tried to trigger a paranoid panic attack off a sativa-dominant joint. Even getting the shakes, I was recognizing that I was able to appreciate some of the coincidences and irony Alaska was offering. I would say later, it felt *typical*. Frustrating. Cold and wet. Still yet, somehow *fantastical*.

I said, "I hope she appreciated this. All of *this*. I know she *saw* it—" I looked at Justice, "You know? The difference between just seeing something and actually appreciating it? I know she thought it was beautiful, but I hope she *really* took this place in while she was here."

We walked up and hit that brew pub to shake off the weed. I overheard a group of old guys listening to one of their friends tell a story of going to a strip club and finding out some or all of the strippers were trans. He had been having a good time, completely unawares, until someone informed him by pointing out the "ladies" had "Adam's Apples." He joined in and let his buddies be playground children and "eww" at it all. I know that's everywhere. Didn't make it any less shocking to hear in a clearly colorful and character-driven little town.

We went back to our cabin for another rest-break (basically, a restroom we knew was clean and comfortable). We talked more, and after my musing that I truly hoped Irene appreciated this place while she lived here and since we had had such a beautifully eerie experience at "the house" and the little lake, it didn't feel necessary to go back right at the same time as Irene died to hold our moment of silence.

I started writing *this*. Justice was sorting school stuff, and an alarm I had set to mark the moment was upon us. We hugged and held each other for a few minutes to observe some silence and respect. We talked more. Where Irene lived itself was indeed serene, but it's a view you could find anyplace that has ponds or lakes. However, twenty minutes in any direction and you're surrounded by mountains, rivers, and lakes all readily visible from the road (weather permitting). I truly hope she appreciated that place. For a long time, I was mad at her for being here, I was mad at the State, and felt it might have killed her.

That evening, we wanted to tempt fate and head even further north than Talkeetna to try and get a view of Denali late at night to hopefully catch more aurora. This was when I found out Talkeetna is a dead-end if you don't know where you're going and my Google Maps app wasn't cooperating.

I said, "Is this the *end* of the world? There is no way out of town!"

We ended up heading back out to the *main* highway that leads to Denali, Highway 3, Parks Highway. It was raining, but I wanted to drive north for a "while." We would also have to get back for a decent night's sleep before we took off for our respective homes the next evening. Justice didn't think it would let up. Neither did I, this was going to be a bust, but, *fuck it*! We're someplace strange, let's explore in the raining dark. We drove up the side of a large hill off of the highway, near the East-West Express Trail which had a lot of no trespassing signs and a closed gate to anything that might have been a viewpoint. Back down to the highway.

We finally found something that sounded far more promising, Denali Viewpoint South; basically, a public, twenty-four-hour parking lot for RVs. There was a trail that climbed up to a viewing platform. We were high up; it was a climb to get there, a miniature hike. In the cold and dark. It was too dark and rainy to get any photos of the distance, but our eyes had adjusted enough that we knew what we were looking at.

Massive flood plains filled with rivers and creeks making lakes all coming from the base of this rising earth that, despite being hidden by clouds, we could still see its hulking form. Denali.

I caught something in my flashlight, though—snow. Now, we're in Alaska. I had driven nearly an hour *further* north from how far north Talkeetna is from Anchorage, getting closer to Denali National Park of course goes *up*. North—elevation—doesn't matter—getting closer to the top of the world no matter how you split the hairs. We saw snow.

It didn't snow for me in 1995 until I was leaving. Now it smattered some snowflakes in with the rain, barely visible. Some pictures are only for the mind. Some moments can only be held in the heart. That's what I hoped for my mom. That she had those, that there was happiness and peace somewhere in her time here.

We made our way back to the cabin. I showered, crawled into bed, thought for a while, fell asleep.

Before we packed and cleaned up our messes, Justice and I talked more; she had been nothing but grace and kindness when she knew I knew a different woman than her other family had told her about as she grew up. She never judged or argued. Instead, she related and saw similarities to her own life, past and present, to Irene, to my relationship with her grandma, and hardships she's faced with her own parents.

Every single person needs to make decisions in their lives to make sure that they can continue to *live* their lives. Some of those decisions involve letting go of relationships and people, or, at least, stepping away to evaluate and audit the situation. Sometimes we must determine if it's what we want or need, and much harder to answer, what we deserve, and what we *feel* we deserve. Self-worth is a hard thing to define, and it can be hard to build it when you don't feel valued by others in your life.

I told her, even *if* a parental relationship needs a break, don't let it go too long. I keep seeing more and more reasons why severing my relationship with my mother was the best decision for me. There is still the undeniable, inescapable guilt that comes with feeling *I* was the one who put the nail in the coffin. Irene didn't try to fix anything, either. I must accept that as well. We share that lapse in responsibility. Who was responsible for whom? Which answer is fair? Is there an answer at all? If there's an opportunity to at least keep in touch, maintain it. Know where they live. Acknowledge each other once a year. Anyone can change with time.

Before coming on this trip, after my birthday, my family finished watching the Clarice television show based on characters from Silence of the Lambs. The last half of the show is way better than the beginning, Rebecca Breeds who plays Clarice is good, but the supporting cast are what I enjoyed watching. Until—Clarice starts recalling different ways to interpret her own memories, and the fallout of how that changed other definitions in her life. One, her own mother sending her away, making Clarice feel unloved and discarded. She starts to wonder if maybe her mother had decided to give Clarice the *chance* of a better life when her mother couldn't provide. She was *protecting* her, even if the protection presented itself as abandonment.

That hit home. Hard. My aunts—and Justice who never knew Irene —have all said that about Irene and me.

Why the Army Reserve after I had been born? Why ask one aunt to raise me as her own? Why then take me back only to put me in literally dangerous situations for *years*. Why then let me go when I was tired, angry, and frustrated? The question I have wanted to ask Irene, "If you were trying that hard to protect me, why didn't you fight as hard to protect *us*?"

I tried to make that point when I was so angry in my high school graduation emails. But like Clarice, it would only come with time, and my own changes, that I would understand no one can answer that. Even if Irene were here today, she couldn't answer that. Why do any of us do the weird things that make us question each other? Illness? Culture of abuse? Immaturity? The absence of a stable, compassionate presence?

It's *all* true.

Driving back to Anchorage, in the daylight, was splendid. Mountains showed themselves much more readily. Huge expanses of wilderness stretched on as far as the eye could see. We found a clearing for power lines and took photos of the face of one mountain, only to turn around and see mountains in the distance. They're *everywhere*.

I drove us to the neighborhood I had stayed in 1995 and I walked that path that I couldn't climb before. It turned out to be a wooded walkway connecting two sections of the neighborhood. I got some good photos and we met a friendly tortie cat who let us pet her for a while.

We then visited Point Woronzof, a park that leads down to a section

of beach full of stones, suggested to Justice by a friend of hers origi-
nally from Alaska. We took several photos and I put my feet into the
Pacific. It was cold and the water had a slick sensation to it. Justice
took a *lot* of rocks, comically weighing her coat down. Usually, I would
try to collect more natural souvenirs myself, but I was worried about
what the TSA might think of a bunch of rocks (apparently: nothing—
they didn't hassle Justice at all).

I had wanted to get a tattoo, a stylized version of the ring my mom
had given me when I visited. I had tried to make appointments with
several artists beforehand, but wasn't ever able to solidify any plans.
We called one tattoo shop, only for an answering machine to say they
only work by appointment. There was another place down the street,
only to be denied as they were working by appointment, too. How the
gentleman phrased it was a warning that *everyone* works by appointment only. You know what? It's a pandemic, that's fair. I did try to
make an appointment for more than a month before heading to Alaska.
Perchance another sign? Was it necessary?

Justice asked me while we visited a park in Anchorage and finished
off our weed, "Did you get anything out of doing this?"

That's when I described the frustrated feeling amidst beauty. "It's
all around, it's not always visible. There are good moments, there are
things worth holding onto and cherishing. A lot of it is just overcast
and cold. I *was* angry. I've accepted that, there's nothing I can do
about it."

We tried to think of someplace to eat and I was looking at cozy
restaurants that might *feel* Alaskan. Those were all tiny-portion-serving
gourmet places that didn't even list their prices. I had joked about
wanting to eat at Taco Bell while in Alaska, to start a new tradition of
going to amazing places and wasting a meal on fast food. Olive
Garden popped up as I was searching and Justice said she had *never*
eaten at one before. A step up from Taco Bell...barely.

Before getting there, though, we saw a *nice*-looking Alaskan souvenir
shop. That meant that everything was expensive, but there were a lot of
real fur garments and accessories and a bunch of wooly mammoth fossils
for sale. We both found small trinkets to bring home to our families.

Olive Garden was too busy, or we took too long in the gift shop, but there was a Chili's right next door that seated us immediately and then didn't serve us our drinks for 10 minutes. The service wasn't great, but it didn't upset my tummy and we were able to eat and get to the airport on time.

TSA was relatively painless, but when you have a tablet and a camera packed away, you basically must unpack for them only to later hold up the line for people who have a backpack and that's it. Not anxiety inducing *at all*.

I went through the scanner, and the lady said, "You can deal with him," to a male colleague.

WTF?

He said I had an "alarm" along my left side.

"My left side?" I didn't reach for anything but patted myself curiously.

The agent stepped forward, ran his hand down my left side, and said I was fine and let me go. Maybe one of the rivets in my Levi's? I was through, whatever.

Justice made it through first and was waiting on me. She accompanied me to my gate. Remember that? Remember when you could do that with your friends and family? She had a flight, but no associated gate yet. Her flight would be a little under two hours after mine, she had time to figure things out while sticking with me until the last minute. We can't do that anymore in airports—see our loved ones off *at* the gate. This was undeniably a blessing.

When my group was finally called to cue up, she stuck with me, and brought back up what I said at the park.

"You don't have to hold onto that anger, it'll just eat you up."

"Oh, I'm not angry *now*," I tried to explain. "I just recognize that I *was*, that it was *justified*, and I'm getting to accepting that those are things I can't help or fix, they just were."

We talked about how our past decisions, as youths, those old ones when you had no agency in the world and maybe were coerced, forced, or afraid to say anything that would cause any *more* drama. The stuff us anxious people fret over forty-five minutes after laying down for bed. A lot of mine is with my mom. That's where my anger with her laid. Why didn't she protect *us*?

The decisions I regret in life aren't even mine, I was a kid who thought he could protect his mom and I picked up a lot of baggage for the effort. I was the one trying hard to protect us, I only have my own evidence to show for it. That's not my fault. Decisions I've made as an adult knowing I wielded the power, have been both the best I could make *and* the worst. This is life, I can't be mad at myself for something I couldn't control. Holding onto old anger to continue feeling justified in my decisions is only making me sour. I *was* angry, that was okay, and it is okay. That anger is in the past.

Justice and I were together, in Alaska, having life enriching experiences. Sure, the weather was kinda shitty. I could and should have taken more photos and videos. I wouldn't be there, with Justice, without that tragedy in our past. Even twenty years gone, Irene was able to draw people together. She still has that power.

That's the silver-lining to be gleaned from Irene's death: that a lot of our family reconnected and stayed in touch in the wake of her passing. That Justice, who has a romantic notion of Irene (a sentiment I am glad of), finds kinship in me—the one who has vocally lamented Irene's faults? That we desire maintaining our family and friendly connections? This experience wouldn't be possible without how things unfolded for either of us. Darkness makes the light even more brilliant.

Alaska is big. It's full of life. Even in Anchorage when you think you can't see anything for the urbanization, mountains stare down from miles away when you wait at the stop light. The mountains are huge. The trees stretch tall enough, there's only foliage and sky. Fungus and ground flora continue to flourish in the impending cold of fall and freeze of winter.

Two tiny humans met up to honor another tiny human whose impact on our family was, *is*, as big as Alaska. Threatening. Dangerous. Sometimes cold and dark. Sometimes *only* filled with light. A marvel. Beautiful and challenging.

Justice was enamored and seriously considered if she could live there. I reminded her of how winter can be, but only because I know I couldn't handle Alaska, specifically because of that. I saw, and appreciated, what I came to see. I'm glad Justice was with me. I don't know if I would have taken anything in, otherwise, I might have only *seen*.

I *was* angry, and there will be times I will remember something from a certain point of view or learn some new piece of information that will only further confirm those decisions I told Justice not to take lightly in her own life. Because confirmation bias isn't fun when you want to forgive and love the good memories. I've lived as a bottle of emotions waiting to pop every time I get rattled and I can't help but look at the young life I lived.

If Irene tried to protect me, she also thrust me into danger. She was and is in my memory, a chaotic dichotomy. I love her. I had to let her go. I had to get my life going. Time to keep on going.

I made it, Mom. I lived. I survived, despite *and* because of you. Others have survived their own lives that you touched, good and bad. Your memory is still quite alive, twenty years later, and maybe even in Alaska. If there are signs, we saw plenty of them. If I appreciated my trip, my niece with me, if I appreciate my family, my dad, and being forty-two—then I must appreciate that someone brought me into this world. She gave me the set of tools I have to deal with it, even if she didn't know she was doing it, or how to use them herself.

I'm sorry it ended badly, but it needed to end when it did. What I'm sorry for the most, though I have no control and cannot blame myself for entirely, is we didn't have that chance to reconnect.

Irene, I love you. I do still miss you. Thank you for making it an adventure to honor you. Justice and I won't forget, and you won't be forgotten.

CHAPTER 56

SEPTEMBER 15TH, 2001 – TALKEETNA, ALASKA

The police report came a few weeks after I made it home from Alaska. It's a devastating and gruesome read. I expected that. Some things popped up within the details that corroborated other stories. There was mention of friends at the house with meth and my mother dumping it, confirmation of the tale related to Justice by my biological father, but also a sign of the stress in Irene's relationship, though it was an unrelated event. From what I can ascertain and read between the different accounts, this is how my mother's life ended:

Irene had been living in Alaska for about a year and a half. She met a man named Rex Davenport, eight years her younger. They barely knew each other but agreed to get married. I do not know why, but I suspect it was a scheme—maybe to help each other up along life's ladder. She was living without running water, that cabin she had thought was magical maybe had a different feel when spring, summer, and bugs came along. They came to live in a house together near the fork in the road where the Parks Highway splits toward downtown Talkeetna.

He was an alcoholic who drifted between jobs, contracts expiring or getting fired from them due to his drinking. When he wasn't working, he bothered my mom for money wherever she worked—at one point taking her tips and using her paycheck to drink while she worked as a waitress.

Rex wasn't a good man. But short of the waitressing incident, they didn't seem to be abusive toward each other, according to people who knew them. He partied harder, he was younger, she was ashamed of him. However, they seemed to only have each other. He was a known drunk, and even though people enjoyed Irene, they didn't know much about her. She stayed quiet about her past, and had her eyes on the future.

There's a singular detail that's mentioned in passing that gave me a massive pause, amid reading a true-crime murder mystery straight from the detective's notes, someone said *she* had said she had "*a* son." I knew reading it she was referencing Jeremy. I'm not jealous of that, but it's hard to hear from your mom, from beyond time and death, that she took you at your word.

I cannot put thoughts into her head, I can't be that time-traveling psychic. It was probably easier to talk about the son she had a relationship with rather than bringing up such a painful relationship anytime she talked about her own kids. I had made it central to my character for years; she hadn't.

I admit that it hurt. Even if it was a stranger my mother barely knew. Why should I expect her to get personal and share *those* details? I will never be adequately free of this guilt, no matter how many examples I have that we weren't right for each other.

One night, they got into a heated argument. According to Rex—and Rex alone, but the contents of which are *kinda/sorta* supported by some associates of theirs—they got into it about his taking a new job because his current one was coming to an end. She was working seven days a week and he was drinking her paycheck.

They had been drinking all that day together. My mom drank, but typically at home. He had invited some—not even friends, people he knew from work—*acquaintances* over when he recognized them at a nearby gas station. He boasted about their house on a lake, and they were curious to see what this punk was pulling. They didn't see any rumblings of an argument or animosity between the couple. If anything, they seemed happy and affectionate and beaming with pride about their little slice of heaven.

After they left, towards 7:00pm, under a sunny sky and pleasant conditions, Rex and Irene erupted into another argument. He wanted to leave, to take his shotgun and target shoot. He wanted to bail on the argument. Somewhere between arguing and attempting to walk out, a frying pan got thrown and a pantry door had slats knocked out. She was probably cooking, the stove had to be turned off later. She was trying to do something she loved, and this happened.

A fisherman reported yelling loud enough to be heard across the lake.

According to Rex, my mom said something to the effect that she wanted to die. If he was going target shooting, "why not shoot me instead?" Or that she wished she could kill herself. Or that she was already dead.

She said *something* that urged him to produce a handgun that he reportedly carried on his person in a holster. He says he pulled it from a backpack and gave it to her. Or that he set it on the table. Or that he put the backpack on the table and let her get the gun herself. He always produces the gun.

A goddamned gun. That thing I didn't like as a kid—still don't— that my mother told me I had been threatened with. A device prevalent in America, no matter the state, and surprising in who has one while you don't even know. No amount of legislation would have prevented my mother's death. And nothing done today will help today. It will take time, wisdom, and attrition. Guns are devices intended for killing, and American culture is obsessed with retribution and death.

It was a six-shot revolver, loaded with hollow-point bullets. This was a gun he carried on his person posing as a biker according to one of the two work associates that had visited them that afternoon. Rex fancied himself a badass, but other than having the gun, wasn't convincing anyone in their small community. He had even tried to trade the gun for a car when he was having trouble with his own ride. Imagine if they had taken him up…

Either being directly handed the gun or after picking it up from the table, or backpack—regardless of how he delivered the gun to her—

she put it to her head and pulled the trigger. Irene's death certificate still reads that she was "shot by other" as the cause of her death; however, mention of the coroner's report within the police report deduced that the wound was self-inflicted.

It was physically devastating. The bullet fragmented on entry and destroyed the entire top of her head. Hair and blood found on her arm and the gun, sadly, were consistent with her aiming it at the right side of her head with her right hand. No evidence of her blood was found on Rex or his clothing, nor did any subsequent searches of the premises indicate he had changed or washed up after an altercation.

According to Rex—because he was the only one there—she died at 7:12pm. The holster mentioned, was found on the ground outside of the house. Rex insisted he didn't not know how it got there. It's glaring. The holster is on the ground outside of the house.

He walked from their house to the H&H bar down the street and called 911. Witnesses at the bar told police they thought Rex was more concerned with *himself* than that his wife was dead. He didn't initially want to call 911 because he immediately thought the cops would suspect him. He had to be *convinced* to call.

Unaware he was being recorded while on hold, he told people various versions of the same story, changing up details on the fly. A thing he frustratingly does throughout the entire police investigation into his involvement in her death. It's always the same: they argued, he wanted to leave, she wanted to die, he gave her a gun, she killed herself.

Remember they had been drinking? My mother was heavily intoxicated, livid with her louse of a husband about one of the all-time stressors—money—while letting her mental health go untreated. She had talked to coworkers about wanting to settle down and shed her nomad lifestyle. She had been interested in taking up new crafting hobbies. In a recent journal-entry the police had read, she described her heartbreak over the 9/11 attacks, but the entry did not seem to indicate any suicidal ideation.

Right then, she was angry, and sometimes when my mom got angry, she reacted. The bipolar disorder? Poor anger management skills? That one bad day?

I don't think my mother committed suicide. I recognize that she shot herself—under duress, given means when she should have had none, by the man she was married to. I believe Rex is responsible for my mother's death. By having that gun. By giving it to her, drunk himself. By being a bad person.

Over the next few months, character witnesses would attest he was only concerned with himself, showing little sadness or remorse for his wife's passing. Any chance he got to talk about what happened he gave those varying versions that all said the same thing: he gave her the gun, but *she* did it.

He also told anyone that would listen that he was getting out of town. He was going to stay with family in the contiguous and he freely gave contact information.

Guy's wife is dead. *My* mother. And all he could think of was to get away as soon as possible.

The police had a hard time contacting next of kin, did they know each other at all? He was eager to convince people she did it, he's "not guilty," he doesn't need to stay there anymore.

He shows no remorse, shame, or sadness. He sounds guilty.

Eerily, it was the "real Alaskan" she mentioned in the letter to Justice's mom who ended up helping the police the most. He had a copy of her resume on an old computer. It led to contacting my aunt, who had to hunt through my mother's past in turn to try and find *me*.

Rex did skip town. The police managed to find some charges that would stick. They hauled his ass back to Alaska, and the great wearing down of the seriousness of his crime began. The law is tricky and given the circumstances, that the only witness was the guy responsible, and he routinely changed his story? He's an unreliable *and* an uncooperative witness. How do you solve a crime the criminal controls the narrative of?

The only thing he served time for was being an ex-felon illegally owning the handgun.

He served two years.

Before they met, he was passing bogus checks. After her death and his sentence, he continues to run the same scheme. My mom's death is the only violent offense on his record. Though he never faced manslaughter charges, he will always be a part of what took place that evening.

I don't know if Irene wanted to settle down or why she would put up with such conditions. I do know she is dead *because* of him, whether he shot her or not.

In the end, she sounded tired, hopeful, and angry. A swirl of emotions and temperaments. I think a lot of us were at the time. A lot of us are now. I will never have a handle on everything, I will always be this similar swirl of emotions, but I can hold fast in the storms. I am not my mother, but she is central to my mast.

EPILOGUE

I n an article published early in 2022, picked up by reputable news
sources (I read about it from the Smithsonian Magazine), a
medical paper reported on an elderly epilepsy patient being
checked into a hospital after going comatose following a seizure. His
condition deteriorated and as they were monitoring his brain activity
with an electroencephalography machine, an EEG, he suffered a
cardiac arrest and died, having a condition to not resuscitate on file.
Being monitored, they could read exactly what his brain did in the
minute around his heart stopping.

Thirty seconds before and thirty seconds after, his brain flooded
with activity associated with memory recall, meditation, and dream-
ing. It seemed to indicate that a dying brain did indeed create an experience of life "flashing before your eyes." This kind of thing isn't
something you can plan for, and the patient was a special case with his
epilepsy. Did that contribute to the occurrence?

Except, it matches what we've seen in lab rats—not that *we're* rats.
Not that it's a guarantee that every death is the same. Clearly there are
countless ways to die. This old man, however, drifting away from his
mortal coil, had a dreamy meditation on his life as he expired.

Reading about this gave me a whole new anxiety regarding death.

Not about my own or any of my loved ones' future expirations, should I outlast them, but about my mom. Her heinous and violent death. It was gruesome and instantaneous. If there is a "natural" process to death, she was denied that experience.

Part of me became upset by this. If life flashes before our eyes to remind us of achievements, highlights, or something to ease us into the darkness, I wasn't even there for her in memory at the end. She didn't get to see me again before she shuffled off. Or Jeremy, or any of her siblings...

It also means she didn't have to suffer that early part of life all over again. The abuse from her own family and that of the father of her children. The loss, the torment, the wild ups and downs.

I hope the id is real. I hope that whatever it is that makes us, *us*— even if it's a brain's weird configuration of electrical connections—I hope it continues along the quantum medium throughout the cosmos. Reality, our space, this meat we're stuck in... I hope we're stuck in it and it's not all we are.

Hope.

Yet, the world moves on anyway, regardless of my fears. Regardless of what happened back then; what happens in my future that might contribute to other experiences. If anything, it means I need to actively appreciate moments as they're happening. It means I *do* need to reflect and hold onto memories. We're only ever a breath away from going away forever, and we might only see it once.

I will appreciate and share. I will make sure to keep my mom in my memory, and share her with the world, too. That way, she can live again and again in the rest of the world's memories.

For my mom, Irene Frances Mulroney, I love you. I miss you. You left, but you are always with me. I remain. I survived.

ACKNOWLEDGEMENTS

L ooking back on one's life, year by year, digging through photos and looking up what was happening at the time, is a daunting exercise. I have probably "changed" in the course of writing this book. I learned details about my own life I hadn't known until this writing. The world also changed around me while I was writing. I turned 41 during the global and lethal COVID-19 pandemic. I watched the President of the United States attempt a coup on live television. Even more dire global situations continue to unfold. Through it all, my wife and daughter have been by my side, and that stability and trust have been essential and life-affirming. The world is harsh, my life was already harsh, and they face hardships all their own. I love my family, and I know they love me.

ABOUT THE AUTHOR

J.D. Buffington lives in Tulsa, Oklahoma with his wife, daughter, two capricious cats and two devious dogs. He seamlessly weaves vivid nightmares and haunting anxiety together to immerse readers into a state of fright and wonder. A member of the Horror Writers Association, he can be found in many corners of the internet: https://linktr. ee/JD.Buffington.

www.ingramcontent.com/pod-product-compliance
Lightning Source LLC
Chambersburg PA
CBHW071143130626
46553CB00004B/1500